CHURCHES, JAILS, AND GOLD MINES...

MEGA-DEALS FROM A REAL ESTATE MAVERICK

STEVEN L. GOOD

Dearborn™
Trade Publishing
A **Kaplan Professional** Company

Vice President and Publisher: Cynthia A. Zigmund
Acquisitions Editors: Louise Benzer and Mary B. Good
Senior Managing Editor: Jack Kiburz
Interior Design: Lucy Jenkins
Cover Design: Design Solutions
Typesetting: the dotted i

Published by Dearborn Trade Publishing
A Kaplan Professional Company

Printed in the United States of America

03 04 05 10 9 8 7 6 5 4 3 2 1

Library of Congress Cataloging-in-Publication Data

Good, Steven L.
    Churches, jails, and gold mines : mega-deals from a real estate maverick / Steven L. Good.
      p.   cm.
    Includes index.
    ISBN 0-7931-7748-0 (6x9 hardcover)
    1. Sheldon Good and Company—History.   2. Sheldon Good and Company—Anecdotes.   3. Real estate business—United States—Anecdotes. 4. Auctions—Anecdotes.   5. Real estate agents—United States—Anecdotes.   6. Good, Steven L.   I. Title.
HD278.G66 2003
333.33′3′0973—dc21

                                       2003011802

DEDICATION

To my wife, Jami, and our kids, Scott, Logan, and David, for giving me time off to share my adventures with the world.

To my partners and associates for sharing the adventures together.

C ontents

One scene in the movie *The Wizard of Oz* gives me goose bumps. Dorothy is busy living her life on a small farm in Kansas, and everything is shown in black and white. All of a sudden, a storm kicks up and she (as well as her house and everything else) is sucked up by a tornado and crashes in a strange place. Once things settle down, Dorothy opens the door to her house and as the door opens . . . Poof! Technicolor.

I've had, and continue to have, a similar experience—except when the door opened in my case, all sorts of cool deals came my way from all over.

It sure is fun living in Technicolor, traveling down the yellow brick road, making all sorts of unique friendships, and, best of all, defeating the wicked witches of the world and converting their castles into condominiums.

1

HOW IT ALL STARTED

Our auction company is to the real estate business what Sotheby's or Christie's is to the fine art and collectibles business. *We use auctions as an alternative marketing technique and have built the largest company in the United States specializing in this technique.* We use our brokerage company as an augmentation to our general business plan, and although the companies are similar in some respects, we run them independently of one another.

We began our business in 1965 and since then have sold more than 40,000 properties valued in excess of $8 billion. Our geographic territory includes Hawaii to the west, the entire Caribbean to the east, Canada to the north, and Mexico to the south. We also do spot jobs in Latin America and western Europe.

When I started in our firm in 1978, we had about 20 people. Today, including independent contractors, we employ between 300 and 500 people. We have a number of companies, the two most prominent of which specialize in real estate auction and commercial real estate brokerage.

Four major themes have been pivotal in our success. First and foremost, *relationships* must be formed, nurtured, and protected. This is done in a number of ways but irrespective of their genesis, relationships, wherever possible, must carry the day. Second, even though relationships are critical, execution of the task or jobs at hand must be consistent, as a reputation is built on *consistency of execution;* anyone can talk of good execution, but few can execute jobs consistently. Third, capturing the attention of the media through interesting stories, relationships, and good and consistent execution allowed a broadening of our company's appeal, its people, the sale of our clients' properties, and our programming—all a big part of our company's success. Finally, using all three of the above themes to build our brand made our company the leader and industry standard in our industry. Our company handles more than 70 different classes of real estate. They include:

- Houses
- Townhouses
- Mansions
- Estates
- Condominiums
- Co-ops
- Time-shares
- Interval ownership homes
- Homesites
- Subdivisions
- Development land
- Raw land
- Large acreages
- Farmland
- Ranches
- Hotels
- Motels
- Resorts
- Marinas
- Golf courses
- Hunting retreats
- Fishing lodges
- Private islands
- Dock-o-miniums
- Ski resorts
- Mountains
- Gold mines
- Mineral rights
- Office buildings
- Apartment buildings
- Commercial buildings
- Strip shopping centers
- Regional shopping centers
- Freezer cooler buildings
- Special purpose properties
- Trucking terminals
- Airports
- Movie theatres
- Bowling alleys
- Private clubs
- Restaurants
- Bars
- Nightclubs
- Industrial warehouse buildings
- Industrial manufacturing buildings
- Industrial and office parks
- Ground leases
- Retail buildings
- Libraries
- Elementary schools
- High schools
- College campuses
- Corporate retreats

- Churches
- Synagogues
- Jails
- Police stations
- Fire stations
- Sanitary improvement districts
- City halls
- Exotic game farms

- Performing, subperforming, and nonperforming loans
- Leases
- Subleases
- Parks
- Private lakes
- Timberland
- Developable air rights
- Summer and specialty camps

I could probably find some other categories, but what's the point?

Each one of these categories represents a different business and has subclasses as well. For example, within the "Houses" class, we handle new houses, used houses, foreclosed houses, trophy houses, track subdivision houses, custom-built houses, houses in huge metropolises, houses in the middle of nowhere, and houses priced under $100,000 or over $10 million.

I am a regular source for the news media and always get a kick out of it when someone asks, "How's the real estate market?" I always reply, "Which market?" Do they mean residential? Perhaps commercial? Maybe retail? Or industrial? Or . . . ? The point is that there are a lot of different types of properties, geographies, local and regional economies, and other factors that go into answering a seemingly simple question.

Our client base is likewise amazingly varied. We represent, or have represented, virtually every type of real estate owner that exists: private individuals, small businesses, banks, investment bankers, partnerships, publicly and privately held corporations, insurance companies, branches of the federal government, school boards, churches, nonprofits, cities, towns, boards of commissioners, and on and on.

We built the business by constantly promoting several things, many times simultaneously. First, we promoted the nature of the client base that was retaining us. We felt that because many of our clients were household name companies, public association with them would accomplish two things: It would elevate the reputation of our company through the association, and it would also prompt potential clients of similar types to seek us out, particularly if they found themselves in a situation analogous to the one we were handling for their competition.

Second, we avidly publicized the variety and caliber of the properties that we were engaged to handle, specifically focusing on the message that we specialized in handling quality properties for quality companies. As the variety of the types of properties that we handled grew, we also focused on promoting our specialty service capabilities for the particular asset class as well.

Finally, we took steps to present our company and ourselves as down-to-earth, approachable types and made ourselves highly visible to our potential clients via endorsements, sponsorships, and participation in a myriad of trade associations and affinity groups. As part of this effort to grow the business, we successfully secured exclusive endorsements or sponsorships of our events by groups that included the U.S. League of Savings Institutions and all of its successive organizations (now America's Community Bankers—at one time 3,600 savings and loans across America); NACORE (the International Association of Corporate Real Estate Executives—now CORENET); and FIABCI (the International Real Estate Federation). We even sponsored two international real estate auctions with the National Association of REALTORS® (NAR), the Urban Land Institute, the *Wall Street Journal,* and some 37 other prestigious real estate trade organizations.

All in all, our concept of growing our brand name through the aggressive promotion of our client base and successful programming paid big dividends in expanding the sphere and scope of our company.

IT WASN'T ALWAYS LIKE THIS: HOW WE DEVELOPED THE BUSINESS

When I joined our firm, we were a local commercial conventional brokerage company that auctioned real estate from time to time. Our vision for the industry was very limited, as most people thought that auctions made sense for only bad properties in marginal locations where owners just wanted to dump them. The auction alternative was thought of as a last resort and used only when all else had failed.

Always Seeking to Expand our Platform Was a Key

The most important common denominators were the neverending quest to expand our platform—*our standing in the business community that draws potential clients to us*—and to differentiate ourselves from our competitors. There are several realities to running a service-oriented business that people commonly overlook. First, to the extent that everyone in our industry is seen to be the same—they are. Consequently, to the extent that you are seen to be a commodity, the ability to control market share, margin, and employee base goes right out the window. Second, niche marketing in disorganized markets is the right place to be—less competition, good margins, and institutionalization potential is easily gained and maintained. Third, service organizations that seek to lead must attract and *retain* top talent, perhaps the most difficult task *because bright stars burn the hottest, and consequently creation of a stable, albeit growing, corporate self-identity is very important.* I made it a point to run our company as a team, which was, and continues to be, the greatest challenge because people, markets, and the industry continue to change and evolve. The only way we can grow is by attracting talent that will be committed to our firm and its industry, and through that commitment our associates must be given the opportunity to earn great livings and ultimately acquire wealth through partial ownership of the firm.

Perception Was Not Reality

The first thing that became apparent to me was that most real estate is *not* easily valued. Add economic turbulence, uncertainty, and market volatility to the mix, and all of a sudden real estate owners in need of disposition services are looking for a solution better than selling their properties in traditional ways. It was our task, then, to demonstrate that our programming worked, and worked well, for clients that chose us because they *wanted* to, *not* because they *had* to.

Identifying and then promoting this concept opened the door for us to call on anyone who owned real estate that fit the "not easily valued" profile. Not only that, but many owners within a relatively short period of time became further dissatisfied with conventional marketing programs once they learned a better alternative existed, and they sought new applications of our evolving solution.

The next step was to demonstrate that our programming worked and preferably for a client that had a high profile, which would enable us to tell our story with integrity and believability. Here we caught a terrific break.

As a result of having a real estate auction specialty, we were called by a major publicly traded U.S. homebuilder to develop auction programming that would help it expedite its selling of new homes. At the time, this proposition was quite new and was opposed by some of our senior associates on the theory that developing auction programming was outside the scope of our core traditional brokerage business. One of our more progressive-thinking associates asked to develop this opportunity and, for no other reason than that I thought it would be fun, I asked to participate in helping to develop the program. Ultimately we developed a four-phase program for residential homebuilders that allowed them to compress an 18-month traditional sales program into 10 weeks, thereby helping them to avoid the enormous carrying costs associated with holding vacant homes during a slow sales period.

The first residential auction was for eight houses in a developing midwestern suburb. The result? Over 1,600 people attended the auction; the client did so well that over the next several years they returned to have us conduct similar events for the company in some 13 states.

A valuable by-product of this opportunity was that because of the client's profile all of its competitors stood up and took notice of our alternative programming. Skeptical at first but given an irrefutable track record and unprecedented results, the homebuilding industry seriously adopted our programming as a viable alternative whenever it had properties that were not easily valued. The key during this time was for us to constantly call on the industry, which was done through a variety of media.

We, like many other service businesses, have always been big on solicitation of potential clients. We don't wait for the phone to ring—we make it ring. In this regard, we adhere to a couple of truisms that we have, for all intents and purposes, institutionalized. They include the following:

- Why do people do business with you?
  First because they know you.
  Then because they like you.
  Finally (a distant third), because they believe you are competent.
- Who gets the account?
  The guy who asked for it last.
- Are deals important?
  Deals come and go. Relationships carry the day.

- When is the customer *your* customer?
  When he or she says so.
- What's the key to customer loyalty?
  Good executions—you're only as good as your last deal.
- Why do the media cover your events and company so closely?
  Because we only solicit them when *we* think we have something
  relevant, and then we are good at telling our story.

For several years our residential auction programs met with such acceptance that we sold thousands of new homes principally for residential
developers and homebuilders. We were able to proliferate the demand
for our services by following a variety of strategies, which were followed
in no particular order but were followed nevertheless. The strategies we
followed to proliferate demand are described in the following sections.

Get the word out. Where we had a good story or client or where
what we were doing showed a market trend, we shared it. We shared it
with the media, potential clients of a similar type, the homebuying public, and the institutions that provided financing and legal services for
our clients. It was because we were selling terrific brand-new, nonflawed
housing for some of the best names in the residential homebuilding industry that we were able to move away from being associated with poor-
quality, distressed properties.

Broaden the scope. Another interesting phenomenon followed:
Owners of nonresidential properties began flocking to us on the theory
that if the who's who in the residential business used our services, our
services would work for high-quality nonresidential real estate as well.
Consequently, hundreds of financial institutions including commercial
banks, savings and loans, and insurance companies turned to our programming. With each success, other potential clients of the same type
watched and, after becoming comfortable, jumped into the game.

Protect the vision. All the while we continued to broaden our platform and branding. More important, we were building them in our
vision—not someone else's. We were very careful with whom we did business and with the nature of clients' engagements, and we always, *always*
sought to be as straightforward as we could be. We found that accuracy

solves a lot of disputes—and particularly where the deal may have adverse consequences. On the other hand, we have had many deals where we'll scalp a deal and make seven-figure profits in a matter of weeks. Accuracy counts there too.

Recruit associates interested in sharing the success. As the demand for our services increased, it brought pressure to hire additional people. As a matter of interest, almost a third of the associates who have come to us have been former clients, contractors, or buyers who participated in one or several of our auction programs. We find ourselves constantly in the role of educator for everyone around us: owners, lenders, buyers, brokers, news reporters, and so on. Who better to hire than someone who has already been through some portion of the auction process? Consequently, we always were on the lookout for good recruits.

THE GOVERNMENT GETS IN THE ACT, TOO

Several years later we were now representing the residential and nonresidential building, investment, and lending communities. It didn't take long for the government to get in the game. Everyone else had had success with our programming, and soon Washington was calling too.

A variety of agencies were charged with selling properties under their control, and they found that our programming was a logical and viable alternative. Not only that, but because of the standardized nature of our deal structuring, time line, and bidding process, the process itself validated the results that we were achieving. Another interesting phenomenon was that these groups sought to further institutionalize our industry as a way of providing cover for themselves in the event that some type of controversy might surround the sale of any given property. Issues relating to prohibiting certain buyers from bidding, videotaping events, creating financing conduits to provide financing where it otherwise didn't exist, and other highly creative and logical iterations continued to evolve.

The hardest part of doing business with the government was dealing with the retention process. For example, clients in the private sector often buy the best service they can; the pricing of the service is secondary. Not so in the government sector. Many times contracts are let to companies that make the lowest bid, not the firm that can do the best job. Other times, nonbusiness issues relating to race or gender drive selection of contractors.

This anomaly created real problems for us. We found ourselves watching marginally qualified companies rise to prominence unrelated to their performance. To add insult to injury, when one of these companies would fail or endure a marginal event, *we* would receive fallout indicating *our* process was flawed. Consequently, we had to invest enormous energy in clearly articulating the differences in the quality of our staff, programs, and methodology.

We had made great strides in moving away from the distress business model in favor of the alternative disposition model. During this time, we rejected a number of opportunities to do business with the federal government based on the concept that we were distancing ourselves from being a distress service provider to being a high-quality provider.

This proved to be the right move. Years later, most of the companies that represented the federal government went out of business because the private sector wants *results*—it is glad to pay fees provided the results warrant the fees. An irony here is that many times potential institutional-grade sellers or sellers that seek to take an institutional approach, institutionalize their selection process and thereby fall into the same dilemma characteristic of many government contracts: Selection is made based on the contractor's being able to write a good essay answer—not the contractor's ability to do the work.

RELATIONSHIP BUILDING GOES FAR

From the outset, one of my main priorities was moving our firm from a transaction-oriented to a relationship-oriented culture. This was an extraordinarily hard thing to do, as most of our people are compensated on a commission, production-oriented basis.

A digression is in order here. Real estate brokers and salespeople are interesting phenomena—extremely social, hardworking, and committed to getting their deals done. The drawback is that unless they get their deal(s) done, they don't get paid and therefore can't buy their kids the special G.I. Joe with the Kung Foo grip for Christmas. They're also in an environment where they can do everything right—I mean everything—and still not get paid. It is because of such a situation that real estate folks can become so difficult to deal with. Unless they are getting paid, they don't want to work. On the other hand, if you tell them that the money is behind the wall—they'll walk right through the wall to get it.

When I first got into our business, it was basically every man for himself. To make money each agent had to possess a skill set of more than 20 specialties; otherwise—no money. For example, to earn a fee, agents had to be able to do the following:

- Generate a lead
- Possess a real estate license where the potential business was located
- Analyze the type of real estate
- Analyze the market in which the property was located
- Develop a detailed marketing plan to find buyers for the property
- Create a presentation in order to have the client retain them
- Negotiate the retention agreement, including relevant legal issues
- Create the budget for the program
- Develop all of the promotional literature, including brochures, advertising, public relations, and the like
- Develop all of the legal materials, including real estate sales contracts, financing documents, environmental assessments, title documents, survey, condominium declarations, bylaws, rules and regulations (where applicable), and so on
- Answer inquiries from buyers
- Track and report interest to clients
- Physically show the property to interested parties
- Arrange for due diligence agents to inspect the property and provide answers to their investigations
- Modify the offering if need be
- Prepare the auction facility
- Register bidders answering last minute questions
- Conduct the auction as the auctioneer and bid caller
- Sign up the prevailing bidder via execution of the relevant sales contract
- Accept earnest monies deposit and comply with local escrow laws
- Schedule closing, including final property walk-through and document review
- Settle/Close the transaction

Upon review, two things became clear: There was a lot agents had to be able to do and it was easy for them to make a minor mistake that could have catastrophic consequences.

It was because of the business complexity that I decided to divide job responsibilities into three areas. The first was *project management,* an area of the business for associates who are good at selling properties *once we have them.* Skill sets required for this area include budgeting, art layout and design, buyer solicitation programming, event planning, and other similar activities.

The second area was *business development,* which is a more difficult proposition, as it requires the identification, selection, and retention of the firm by potential clients. Included in this skill set are talents relating to finding customers, presenting our programming, designing disposition alternatives, arranging financing, and supervising the project management players in order to deliver the program that was originally promised the client.

The third area related to *developing managers and leaders* who would supervise the interaction between the various departments. More important, senior officers were called on to help identify our potential customers and how to reach them, and then how to best service them at the same time the officers are keeping harmony throughout and turning a profit for the firm.

Recognizing that moving the firm to a professional partnership business model was one of the most difficult tasks, I did this through a series of ways. The first way was by analyzing the character of the people who were involved with our organization. It was easy to determine who *would not* be able to make the transition; we called them lone wolves—people who had to do everything themselves. Their counterparts were team players, and they were easy to identify as well.

I started modifying our corporate culture by my example, which was often articulated—I took on partners for every piece of business that I produced. I demonstrated that leveraging my time through working partnerships generated more fees, less deal risk, and better execution than a lone wolf do-it-all-yourself program. With the use of a team, we could chase business better, present a more compelling story of why our system is superior, and grow our capacity all in one fell swoop.

Growing a Team-Building Culture

We went from one office of about 20 people to 14 offices with a total staff of about 600 people in about six or seven years. This was during a time that we were establishing our programming in previously virgin markets. It was important to have a local presence in those days, because it comforted our clients to know they were dealing with a relationship company they would see again. Consequently, the building of a corporate culture, an infrastructure brand name, and service product lines were of great importance.

The hardest part of building a team culture is determining what exactly is meant by the word *team*. It is quite a transition to go from doing everything yourself to blaming everything that went wrong on someone who is a "team" member. The key, in my view, was to create a clearly articulated philosophy, which could provide flexibility in each situation, which is important because of the broadness of our practice.

After a number of discussions, and basically through trial-and-error, we settled on running the company via a military drill (i.e., everyone had defined job tasks that, to some extent, overlapped with assignments of other team members) but with a civilian mentality. Put another way, through training seminars, luncheons, speeches, and the like we taught our folks how to march, which included avoiding marching into trees or brick walls. "Here's how we want it done, but you are free to modify the template in whichever way smartens up the deal."

This philosophy ultimately served as a touchstone for the organization because it embraced change and ongoing dialogue, which allowed our organization to evolve without great fallout.

SOMETIMES IT'S NOT CLEAR WHERE YOU ARE GOING UNTIL YOU GET THERE

Today, everyone acknowledges the applicability and breadth, in terms of variety and geography, of the programming that we offer our clientele. Being able to sell virtually any type of real estate at auction anyplace for anybody is a beautiful thing. But it's not as though there was a grand plan; it was just one thing that led to another, that led to another, and so on. The key was that we were smart and able enough to seize marketing opportunities as they made themselves available.

A recent article in *Crain's Chicago Business* summed up our profile in the business community:

> When Steven Good joined his father's firm, Chicago-based Sheldon Good & Company, in 1980, real estate auctions were something the brokerage generally reserved for a handful of hard-to-sell industrial buildings.
>
> But the Evanston native began to change that model almost immediately, helping to orchestrate a massive auction for U.S. Home Corp. that resulted in the sale of 3,000 single family homes over three years.
>
> Twenty years later, Sheldon Good & Company is the largest firm in the United States exclusively conducting real estate auctions. It's not uncommon for the brokerage to place on the block properties as diverse as a timber plantation in Chile and a vacation home in Aspen.
>
> "The idea of an auction creates a deadline where otherwise it does not exist," says Mr. Good, who has been the company's president and CEO since 1996. "The excitement it can generate in a market is unparalleled, and it can draw a wider audience than the conventional method of sale."
>
> Mr. Good eight years ago created a hospitality division, which has sold more than 8,000 hotel rooms. And four years ago, he introduced a trophy home division, handling any house worth more than $500,000. Among high-profile properties auctioned by the firm: the Barrington Hills estate owned by relatives of the late Gen. Douglas MacArthur, the condominiums in the Trump Plaza in Palm Beach, Florida.
>
> "Today, we handle every kind of real estate that can be auctioned," he says. Patricia Richardson "Bidding up: lending cachet to the real estate auction biz," *Crain's Chicago Business* 24, no. 1 (1 January 2001), 11.

In recent years we have moved toward regional consolidation and service our business on a local, regional, national, and international basis.

We are able to leverage our employee alumni base, which has eliminated the need for many satellite offices. Through a series of strategic joint ventures and initiatives with other real estate companies, trade associations, and units of local and federal government, we have evolved into a professional partnership that ebbs and flows in accordance with market demands.

Consequently, my life is right out of a movie. We have really cool deals going on all the time, all over the continent and the world.

2

SO YOU SAY
YOU WANT TO SELL
A THOUSAND HOUSES?

Sometimes I feel like Bullwinkle the Moose. You never know what is going to happen when you reach into your magician's hat and give it a pull. A couple of years ago, I got a call from Andrew Ocrant, the manager of our New York City office, reporting that he had a line on a bank in upstate New York that had over a thousand houses to sell. Andrew was very excited because the head of the bank's surplus real estate department had called him to make an initial inquiry to determine whether we could help the bank sell over a thousand homes, condominiums, co-ops, and townhouses throughout greater New York, New Jersey, Connecticut, and eastern Pennsylvania.

Andrew had joined us four years earlier and had an eclectic background. Trained as a ballet dancer, he had graduated from the Julliard School. For a short time following his graduation, he joined the New York Ballet but, as he told us, was forced to quit because of a physical problem. Every time he overheated from strenuous physical exertion, he fainted. Imagine this good-looking, six-foot-one Adonis flying around the stage at Lincoln Center and . . . boom! Out cold right on the floor.

Andrew got into selling real estate by accident. Apparently, he had met an owner of a small real estate brokerage office while he was taking

James P. DePalma
Wells Fargo

James DePalma graduated from St. Bonaventure University, a small Franciscan university in upstate New York, and began his career at Dun & Bradstreet Corporation, a New York City–based financial services company, where he was a financial analyst from 1981 to 1983. From 1983 to 1986, Jim worked at Harris Corporation, a Fortune 200 company, as a supervisor in the finance division of the RF Communications division of Harris.

In 1986, Jim accepted a position at First Federal Savings & Loan of Rochester, New York, as a senior financial analyst in the mortgage banking division. First Federal was an S&L with $6 billion in assets and one of the "Phoenix" institutions of the now defunct Federal Savings & Loan Insurance Corporation (FSLIC). First Federal was the survivor institution from the consolidation of four other troubled thrift institutions, all based in New York City: Franklin Savings & Loan, Ninth Federal, Knickerbocker, and First Federal of New York City.

Jim was promoted to assistant vice president in 1987 and held management positions in real estate appraisal, credit management, underwriting, and asset quality from 1987 to 1992. He was elected vice president by the board of directors in early 1992 and put in charge of a newly formed division called Mortgage Loan Workout and Asset Disposition. From 1992 to 1995, Jim and his division managed over $500 million of defaulted real estate loans, helping to bring First Federal's nonperforming assets ration back into line with regulatory requirements. Federal regulators praised the loan workout and disposition programs that were put together at First Federal under Jim's direction during their examinations of the institution.

In November 1995, Jim formed a new privately held corporation with several principals of The Clayton Group, Inc., one of the premier mortgage due diligence firms in the country. After his venture in New York with Clayton, Jim moved on to North American Mortgage Company, a wholly owned subsidiary of the Dime Savings Bank, as vice president of default management. North American serviced over $50 billion in mortgage loans and was the sixth largest mortgage originator in the country in 2001.

After the acquisition of North American by Washington Mutual in 2002, Wells Fargo Home Mortgage, the nation's second largest mortgage lender, recruited Jim to build a special mortgage-servicing platform designed to serve the multi-billion-dollar investment market for troubled real estate debt. Jim began this new venture in December 2002.

Jim has been a speaker at many functions of the Mortgage Bankers Association on mortgage workouts and real estate disposition and served on the Default Management Advisory Committee for the Federal National Mortgage Association (FNMA) from 1999 through 2002.

a class to get his salesperson's license. The guy took a liking to him and offered him a job as a commission real estate salesperson.

So started Andrew's career. He sold small condominium units, apartment houses, commercial buildings, and anything else that he could convince someone to list for sale with him. He became an expert in searching the newspaper and local business magazines to find potential deals and generally made it his business to try to find people who were interested in selling their real estate. Andrew had a great nose for finding people who wanted to sell. He made a substantial effort to find them, and they generally liked the ballet dancer turned real estate salesperson.

Andrew, excited about the potential business opportunity offered by the upstate New York bank, called me in our Chicago office. He had received a call from a guy named Jim DePalma, who was in charge of the default management group at First Federal of Rochester, a well-known, well-established financial concern in upstate New York (see box). Andrew told me that Jim had called us, as well as several of our competitors, and was making preliminary inquiries about the potential use of our programming to sell a gargantuan amount of residential properties. Andrew was anxious to see DePalma as soon as it could be arranged. Although I was gratified to receive an inquiry of this nature, I was also a little warier than Andrew about the likelihood of this potential account coming to fruition. I can't tell you how many times I've received a call from someone claiming to have some unbelievable business opportunity and only later to have the story change to something else and then, ultimately, come to absolutely nothing.

One of the things that I've learned is that on our nickel, everyone wants our advice, particularly when it's free. People will ask us to drop whatever we are doing, jump on a plane, run to their office, visit their property, and generate a marketing disposition plan—all in two days. Then they'll take three months to get back to us; when they finally do, many times they have read half the report, if any of it, ask us to fly back and see them and, to add insult to injury, insist that they know our business better than we know our business—but *no one* knows our business better than we do.

Consequently, years before Andrew's call to me, we had implemented a policy requiring potential clients to pay us a minimal fee for inspecting and analyzing their property, particularly if it required significant travel or time commitments. We found this approach very effective in qualifying prospective clients; in most cases, bona fide clients completely accept this practice under the thinking of "I understand you guys are busy too. Your time is obviously valuable. By the way, can I get a credit for these costs if I ultimately hire you?"

Andrew knew that I was predisposed to this approach but wanted me to dispense with it. He believed that we would earn over a million dollars in fees on this account and, being the aggressive real estate salesman that he was, wanted nothing (or as little as possible) to stand between him and this potential payday.

After a couple of minutes arguing over our policy, I suggested a compromise: Why not arrange a conference call between Andrew in New York, Jim DePalma in Rochester, and me in Chicago? By taking this tack, I could get a feel for the situation and try to determine if an exception in our policy was in order. If not, I could reinforce the rationality of our position (i.e., we can't fly everywhere in the world without the strong likelihood we'll get the business). I didn't want to lose the opportunity of getting the business suggested by Andrew, but I didn't need another wild goose chase either.

Reluctantly, Andrew agreed after I asked him the number of clients he had that were this size; the answer: none. He did have one interesting comment though: "I may not have them—but you do, which is why I'm calling you." He set the call for a couple of days later.

THE PHONE STARTS THE BALL ROLLING

My assistant, Cynthia, set the call and connected the three of us: Andrew in Manhattan, Jim DePalma in Rochester, and me in Chicago.

Andrew started the call by introducing me to Jim and explaining to Jim why he had initiated the call. I asked Jim to explain who he was, the nature of his company, how it was set up, who else was involved in this process, the size of the account, the time line, and the company's vision for our role in a potential working relationship.

He began by telling us that First Federal of Rochester was a midsize bank that had been acquired several years earlier by Canada Trust, one of the top six banks in Canada. First Federal was an aggressive mortgage lender that concentrated in providing mortgage financing throughout the greater New York marketplace. As a result of its relatively aggressive lending practices, it had taken back and continued to take back significant amounts of residential properties. Bank regulators were requiring First Federal to reserve significant funds, which limited its ability to otherwise loan the reserved funds out at a profit.

At the same time, Canada Trust, First Federal's majority shareholder, was concerned about First Federal's earnings. First Federal sought to dispose of its surplus real estate and troubled loan portfolio as a strategy to increase its earnings and hence its share price. Jim further explained that he was in charge of the First Federal unit that oversaw its problem residential real estate and loan holdings. He had several key guys under his supervision, but he reported to a senior officer who, in turn, reported to the president of the bank and its board of directors.

All in all, Jim had about $150 million on the table and sincerely thought that if he could develop a program to expedite its disposition at

---

Jim DePalma

"Prior to meeting Steve, Canada Trust, First Federal's new owner, was concerned about our rising nonperforming asset and surplus real estate balances and wanted them reduced. Canada Trust had recently purchased First Federal when the thrift was converted to a stock institution."

reasonable numbers, he could accomplish a lot. First, he would establish that the program worked and, as its architect, would greatly advance his position. Second, the incredible amount of managerial headaches that come with managing a portfolio of properties this size would diminish, the properties would become more manageable, and Jim's life would become infinitely easier. Finally, he really liked the challenge of creating a new program and pushing it through the corporate pipeline.

Jim was also very forthright in saying that he didn't understand everything about our programming but was willing to learn and give it a good college try. As for time line and methodology, he had an open mind and was convinced that if he found the right people, they would jointly develop a game plan that would work.

How could anyone say no?

TIME TO JUMP ON THE FIRST PLANE

So it was arranged. A week later, I'm at O'Hare and Andrew is at La-Guardia bound for Rochester, New York. I hadn't been to Rochester since college, when I was captain of the Syracuse University tennis team playing Rochester Institute of Technology. All I remembered was that Rochester got a lot of snow and that Kodak cameras were made there.

As my plane pulled into the gate, I was cautiously optimistic. This deal could really work. It could really fail too. Could this voice on the other end of the telephone really pull something like this off?

We had sold huge amounts of residential properties before, but they had usually been for major homebuilders who were savvy in homebuilding and management of unsold housing. Although we had also done large amounts of residential sales for banks, they were usually done one development or subdivision at a time, making the management of the real estate a lot easier.

As I walked off the jet in Rochester, there was Andrew, our answer to R2D2, a really enthusiastic guy that you could count on. I had to do everything I could to stop him from leaping out of his skin. As we continued talking, Andrew was confident the deal would be successful, but I had my doubts—we didn't even have a plan yet. It sure is nice to have someone with confidence sitting next to me, I thought, but we have a really long way to go. After all, this is just a preliminary meeting.

We hopped in a cab that took us to First Federal Plaza, the head-quarters of First Federal of Rochester. If you have never been to Rochester, New York, it's much like many older third- and fourth-tier U.S. cities. Its downtown is about 30 percent vacant with older storefronts, many of them closed, and older eight- and ten-story brick office buildings look-ing for tenants. Like most such towns, they fight the perpetual center city versus regional suburban shopping mall battle.

Enter First Federal of Rochester Plaza, a modern concrete, glass, and steel financial headquarters building second to none in the town. Citicorp Plaza is impressive, but it's in Manhattan with a lot of other impressive buildings. First Federal Plaza is in Rochester, or I should say, it *is* Rochester.

Andrew and I jumped out of the taxi and proceeded to walk briskly in our best businesslike manner—navy blue suits with white button-down collared shirts and briefcases in hand—into First Federal Plaza. After looking at all of the Ds in the directory, we couldn't find "DePalma."

While Andrew checked at the information desk, I could feel my stomach start to tighten. I sure hope this isn't a wild goose chase. How the hell did we get here and not know the guy's office suite?

Two minutes later, Andrew comes back from the information desk and leads me right *out* of the First Federal of Rochester Plaza's revolving door. We walk about a block and go into the lobby of one of the one-third empty, nondescript ten-story older brick buildings. He hits the elevator button and up we go to see Mr. Jim DePalma.

CHEMISTRIES CLICK

We walk off the elevator into a small waiting area. Although the building had to be at least 50 years old, the space of Jim's unit had ob-viously been recently renovated. One of the interesting features of being a customer's man is envisioning what your customer looks like before you meet him. In all honesty, I had no preconception of what Jim would look like. What does a guy who has a thousand houses to sell look like? The answer walked up to us a minute later. Jim sticks out his hand, gives us both a firm handshake, and tells us to follow him to a conference room where he has two of his staff people waiting.

The moment that we walk into the conference room we are warmly greeted by Jim's two associates, who said they've read all the materials that we sent and wanted to know whether we really think we can help them sell a thousand houses. I told them that, yes, I thought we could, but that it will take a lot of planning and that we'll need to be able to work together.

From that moment on, we clicked. During the meeting Jim and his associates walked us through their department's organization—particularly who did what. They further explained their interface with senior management and that they had two cultures. Theirs was informal, but senior management's was very formal; essentially, Jim's group was *research* and *development;* senior management was *results*—with a capital R.

J i m **D** e P a l m a

"My group, the Default Management Group, was assembled during the Canada Trust merger specifically to address the rise in nonperforming assets. Members of the group came from a variety of different departments around the bank. This is important to understand because we were all local people with limited real estate experience thrown into this new assignment involving properties in and around greater New York City. We could be described as a think tank because we were given the task of creating a new process that would provide a solution to the identified problem. I can see why Steve would have concluded that our group had the atmosphere of informality, because we were searching for answers and new ways of doing things.

"I may not have realized it at the time, but from Steve's perspective our group was probably very different from what he was used to when dealing with bankers. Our senior management group had a culture different from that of our default management group, as Steve pointed out. The senior management culture was built around more traditional banker protocol where any outside vendors or consultants were concerned. This more formalized process is probably what Steve was anticipating encountering.

"We knew we needed something different from the current standard operating procedure; we just didn't know what it was and how we could convince our senior management group to endorse whatever our new ideas were going to be, particularly if risk were involved—and risk is always involved when you are making a change or doing something new."

When the meeting broke several hours later, we had a game plan. We would generate a written proposal that detailed our *methodology, budget,* and *time line.* Jim's unit would review its portfolio and determine those properties suitable for our first cut of properties to be considered for our newly hatched portfolio disposition program.

At the same time, our project management team started growing. Ultimately, it consisted of over 200 people spanning five states—who'd have believed it? It was obvious that we had a tiger by the tail and we were going to ride that tiger until we either ran it to the end of the trail or it ate us, whichever came first.

We conceptualized the plan as having four stages. First, we would review all of the physical, financial, and legal materials about the various properties that made for good auction candidates. Second, we devised a marketing plan that included advertising, direct mail, e-mail, tele-marketing, signage, cooperating brokerage, and public relations that would attract buyers to the various properties in advance of the auction. Third, we developed a staffing plan that enabled us to process telephone inquiries, show the properties, answer property-specific inquiries, offer mortgage prequalification for interested buyers, and provide the relevant paperwork needed to confirm the sale of each property as it was sold at the auction. Finally, we set forth the budget, fees and costs, and logistical issues necessary to execute the auctions at their points of sale.

We shipped off multiple copies of our proposal about a week later. Two days after they were received, the telephone rang; it was Jim DePalma. With a mixture of excitement and traces of terror, I picked up the phone.

Jim said that First Federal loved the proposal and indicated that he was either going to be a hero or the fall guy if it didn't work.

We both laughed knowing that he was kidding, but kidding on the square. It wouldn't be the first time that a bank department head had been sacked for taking a chance, albeit a damn good one.

THE STAGE IS SET

About a month later, the following article appeared in the *New England Real Estate Auctioneers Journal* (see Figure 2.1). During the preauction marketing we fielded close to 20,000 calls. Not only that, but we had to call everyone back. Once we reached them, many prospective buyers

J*im* D*e P a l m a*

"Steve is correct that First Federal loved the proposal, but to be more accurate, it actually loved the *content* of the proposal. It was made clear to us after my presentation of the proposal that First Federal wanted us to do much more due diligence on Sheldon Good & Company. Steve will recall that he invited two of my managers and me to Chicago to meet the Sheldon Good team. We all went to dinner at Morton's where introductions were made, and everyone stated what his role would be in the deal. Steve brought along marketing materials and client recommendations that we reviewed before dinner.

"We had a wonderful time and fantasized how we were going to 'hit it out of the park' with our new program. That night solidified Sheldon Good as the company of choice, because we were still looking at a competitor's proposal side by side with Sheldon Good's. Leading up to that night we were certainly excited but still a little leery of moving forward with the whole deal. Steve and his team gave us the impression that night that it mattered as much to them as it did to us; in other words, it was personal, and they understood that our jobs were potentially on the line. We never got that feeling from any of the other competitors that were making proposals; somehow they all seemed more distant and didn't take the time to understand our motivations and fears. They lacked either the insight or the instincts to understand the importance of being empathetic to our position. In the end, this lack of empathy cost those competitors the deal.

"I think the lesson that was evident during the preliminary phases of this project leading up to Sheldon Good's being retained is that because each piece of real estate is unique, each evokes a lot of emotion and strong opinions, much as fine art does. This is true whether you are dealing with private sellers or individuals representing an institution, as I was. Steve was also skilled in understanding, assessing, and managing that highly emotional atmosphere. I think anyone looking to be a major player in real estate has to possess those skills."

FIGURE 2.1   *Breaking the News to the Industry*

NEW ENGLAND REAL ESTATE
AUCTIONEERS
JOURNAL

NEW ENGLAND'S ONLY WEEKLY REAL ESTATE AUCTIONS NEWSPAPER

NEW ENGLAND AUCTIONEERS SPECIALIZING IN COMMERCIAL/INDUSTRIAL REAL ESTATE

On Nov. 12 in Hartford, CT and Nov. 13 in Secaucus, NJ

Good & Co. to conduct auction for First Federal S&L

HARTFORD, CT. – First Federal Savings & Loan Assn. of Rochester will conduct the close-out sale of the remaining foreclosed properties in its residential portfolio at two public auctions on Nov. 12 in Hartford, and Nov. 13 in Secaucus, N.J.

James DePalma, vice president, First Federal, said "The accelerated marketing of real estate made possible by this series of auctions and the several other auction events that preceded it have saved the institution approximately $12 million in operating expenses."

Sheldon Good & Company's New York office will conduct the auctions.

More than 150 residential properties located in New York, New Jersey and Connecticut and valued in excess of $15 million will be offered for sale.

The property list includes hundreds of single-family homes, townhouses, condominiums, cooperatives, one to four unit multi-family dwellings and residential development sites throughout the metropolitan region, including:

• 36 Parish Rd. South, New Canaan, Conn. Located on one acre, this three bedroom 2½ bath residence has an in-ground heated pool, two fireplaces, central air-conditioning, an attached two-car garage and manicured landscaping with underground sprinklers.

• 13 Rambling Brook Lane, Warren, N.J., a five bedroom, 6½ bath single-family residence.

Steven I. Good

• 1 Farmwoods Lane, Upper Brookville, N.Y., a five bedroom, three bath single-family home.

The November auctions represent the final phase of Sheldon Good & Company's year-long assignment to sell out First Federal's real estate owned (REO), and sub and non-performing mortgage loans. By the end of November, Sheldon Good & Company will have conducted five regional auctions for First Federal, selling 350 properties for an estimated $35 million and 380 mortgage loans for an estimated $45 million.

Steven Good, president, Sheldon Good & Company, said "When complete, the 12 month series of auctions will well exceed $100 million sales of real property and mortgages. The success of this program represents the largest sale of a single residential portfolio in the tri-state area to date, within the 12 month time frame."

The first of the November auctions will take place at noon, Nov. 12, at the Sheraton Hartford Hotel. The second and final auction in the series will take place at noon, Nov. 13, at the Meadowlands Convention Center, Secaucus.

Auction seminars for all interested prospective buyers in New Jersey will be conducted by Sheldon Good & Company at Ramada Plaza Suites Hotel, 350 Rte. 3 West Mill Creek Dr., Secaucus, N.J., on Nov. 3; and Nov. 10 at 7 and 8 p.m. New York seminars will be held at New York Marriott East Side, Manhattan, on Nov. 2 and Nov. 9 at 7 and 8 p.m. Connecticut buyers' seminars will be held on Nov. 6 at 4 p.m. and 5 p.m. at the Trumbull Marriott Hotel, Trumbull, Conn.

Source: Reproduced with permission from the *New England Real Estate Journal.*

were interested in multiple properties, some located near each other, others not. Merely reaching the folks that called us was an absolutely gargantuan task. We were concerned that our telephone systems would fail from overload and we would end up with irate buyers or worse—an irate First Federal of Rochester. Jim would be a goat and I would be banished from the banking world forever.

It's a really strange feeling watching a program that you conceptualized come to life. Six weeks after our first meeting, some 20,000 people are virtually chasing us to get into the game that we created. More than 200 of our staff in addition to 25 of Jim's staff were almost overwhelmed and, of most concern, almost overrun.

One of the interesting things that we did was set up prearranged financing that not only offered attractive rates but also offered buyers a great discount if they opted to close their purchases within ten days following each auction.

The biggest problem Jim faced at this point was *his* company's having to field calls from some 20,000 people, all of whom could become borrower clients of his company. It was quite a dilemma—Jim's company was in business to make loans but had never seen the concentrated volume of calls that was being generated by the auction. The important

Jim DePalma

"One of the interesting things during the marketing period happened when my management group, as well as myself, had to go out and actually inspect the various properties: a bunch of young guys from upstate New York trying to find our way around Brooklyn, The Bronx, New Jersey, Long Island, Staten Island, and Connecticut. We were coordinating repairs on probably 50 percent of the properties and had construction crews working around the clock, actually sleeping at the properties to get the work done. We had three construction managers and also a main outside general contractor who found subcontractors for all of the work. We would send lunch in to the work sites along with pastries and such. We got to know all of the workers by their first names, many of whom came to the auctions to see how we made out."

part here was making sure that a positive point of contact continued during the pendency of the marketing program.

One of the unanticipated benefits of our program was that First Federal of Rochester was not only selling a huge amount of surplus houses but anyone involved called it to finance the deals—what a boon to an organization in the mortgage lending business. If a prospect bought one of our properties—great. If the prospect didn't—no big deal; maybe the person would finance some other deal via First Federal of Rochester. Either way, the bank won.

THE PRESHOW SHOW

Two weeks before the auction, Jim called me to say that his boss and her boss wanted to meet me. Everyone at the bank was buzzing; apparently we had everyone's attention. We were now at center stage. I told him to set up a meeting. This time the meeting at the First Federal Plaza was on the executive officers' floor.

J im D e P a l m a

"When Steve came to Rochester to present a status report two weeks or so before the events, he had no idea of the 'real' agenda behind that meeting. Steve and Andrew had assumed the meeting was what it appeared to be, an opportunity to present the status of the marketing program and to meet our executives face-to-face.

"Two weeks earlier, two members of our senior management team had called me to 'explore contingencies,' which was their way of asking what would happen if we called the whole thing off. It seemed that no matter how much I emphasized the number of telephone calls, the open house attendance, and the number of bidder kits sold, they were still nervous that we could lose too much money if the bids were too low. They wanted to 'see the whites of the auction companies' eyes' before

(continued)

the event unfolded and explore ramifications of canceling or ending the auction after a few rounds of bidding if the bids were too low.

"We reviewed all of the numbers at the meeting and, strangely enough, the subject of canceling the auction as a contingency actually never came up. At that very moment I knew we were beyond the point of no return, that we were doing it, and senior management had been convinced we had a command of the process; and, even if it were a catastrophe, it would hurt, but the bank would survive. I never felt more exposed in all my career then when I watched Steve and Andrew enter the elevator after that meeting and watched our senior management team go back into their offices without the typical chitchat that follows a meeting of this type."

When the doors to the elevator opened, Jim was waiting for me and my crew. After we were escorted to the boardroom, Jim's boss and, about an hour later, his boss's boss came in. Both of them listened attentively as

J *im* D *e P a l m a*

"It was two nights before the auction, and we had a 7:00 PM bidders seminar at the Sheldon Good office on 41st Street. The office is on the small side with three or four offices, a reception area, and a small conference room. The seminar was going to be held in an adjoining room, big enough for about 25 to 30 people, which was how many we expected. Andrew and I went for a bite to eat before the seminar started. When we turned the corner on 41st around 6:45 PM, we thought there had been an accident, a fire, or something else going on. People were milling around on the street, the lobby was jammed, and we couldn't get upstairs.

"*All of those people were there for the seminar.* We had to shuttle them up the elevators in shifts of 25, and Andrew gave the security guard $100 to not call the building manager and let us finish what we were doing. Bidders were making preemptive offers in the lobby, in the elevator, in the seminar room, to the Sheldon Good personnel. *It was an absolute zoo.* I left feeling pretty damn good that night."

Jim DePalma

"We had shuttle buses to bring the loan officers, underwriters, processors, and other staff from the Marriott to Terrace on the Park the morning of the auction. I was asking everyone if a crowd was there yet. The excitement and simultaneous tension were peaking to say the least. Some members of the Sheldon Good staff were leaving the lobby to go to the auction site; they appeared as calm as could be.

"I got to the auction site around 9:30 AM, some two hours before registration. The line had already been forming, and my attention changed from worrying about having bidders to having enough staff to handle all of the questions and tasks of taking mortgage applications and getting loans approved."

we explained the origins of our program, its methodology, its performance to date, and, most important, that we didn't expect anything to blow up.

Actually, we really thought that things would be fine. I'm not sure if the others believed me, but by the end of the meeting both senior officers were comfortable that they weren't being hustled. They believed that we believed that we were OK.

Jim DePalma

"When the entire auction was over (the third and final one) and we had run the table, Steve and Andrew met me for a drink in the hotel lobby. All of the employees, managers, bank executives, and Sheldon Good staff were in the restaurant having a great time. I remember it like it was yesterday; Andrew turned to me and said, 'It is amazing how many people come to the victory party,' referring to the large contingent of bank executives. I responded, 'If we had had a bad time, it would just be the three of us drowning our sorrows.' I turned to Steve and said, 'It feels good to win'; Steve responded, 'I never had any doubt.' I wonder to this day if that was really the case."

THE RESULTS SPOKE FOR THEMSELVES

So would we be OK? The article in Figure 2.2 pretty much summarizes it.

In a nutshell, Jim and his team hit the ball out of the park.

We did good too. So good that Prudential Home Mortgage and Citi-Mortgage followed suit.

Over a thousand houses later, our program became the standard of the industry.

I only wonder what would have happened if I hadn't invested in the plane ticket and met Jim DePalma.

J *i m* **D** *e P a l m a*

"My first day back in the office in Rochester, representatives from Prudential Home Mortgage and CitiMortgage called me to get the whole rundown on the auction. They couldn't wait to capitalize on what they had just seen. Over the next year we started having multiseller auctions with many of the big mortgage lenders. It was always satisfying to know that I was involved in starting the whole thing."

FIGURE 2.2 *Summary of the Auction Results*

New England Real Estate
AUCTIONEERS
Journal

NEW ENGLAND'S ONLY WEEKLY REAL ESTATE AUCTIONS NEWSPAPER

New England Auctioneers Specializing in Commercial/Industrial Real Estate

First Federal Savings & Loan Assn.
of Rochester, NY

Sheldon Good & Co. auction series generates $16m in sales

HARTFORD, CT. – Three public auctions held in New Jersey and Connecticut within the past six weeks have produced residential sales in excess of $16 million, according to Sheldon Good & Company, who conducted the auctions on behalf of First Federal Savings & Loan Association of Rochester and several other individual sellers.

The auction series, consisting of two public sales in Secaucus, N.J. on October 16 and Nov. 13 and one auction in Hartford, on Nov. 12, was attended by thousands of bargain-seeking prospective buyers with certified checks attesting to the seriousness of their purpose.

The overwhelmingly successful series effectively closed out hundreds of the remaining properties in First Federal's residential portfolio.

More than 250 residences located throughout the tri-state region were sold, many of them to first-time homebuyers.

More than 70% of the buyers selected Sheldon Good & Company's "quick close" option, enabling them to complete their purchase within 10 days of the auction event.

Selling prices based on winning bids ranged from $645,000 for 13 Rambling Brook Lane, Warren, N.J., a five-bedroom, 6½ bath single-family home; and $435,500 for Apt. 1B, 35 East 68th St., Manhattan, a cooperative res-

18 Water Mill Way, Ridge, N.Y.

idence to $7,250 for a cooperative apartment located at 2181 Sterling Ave., the Bronx.

Most of the "high end" properties were sold "absolute," regardless of the price, subject to minimum bids. Indeed, at the final auction in the series, more than $4 million in sales consisting of 18 homes, took place within the first 45 minutes of the auction event.

James DePalma, vice president, First Federal, said "The accelerated marketing of real estate made possible by this series of auctions and the several other auction events that preceded it have saved the institution approximately $12 million in operating expenses."

Other sellers who took part in the series were Prudential Home Mortgage

Co., Inc. – the nation's second-largest residential mortgage lender – and a handful of smaller, individual sellers.

The three-auction series was the final phase of Sheldon Good & Company's year-long assignment to sell out First Federal's real estate owned and sub and non-performing mortgage loans.

Steven Good, president, said "We have now completed five regional auctions for First Federal, selling 350 properties for an estimated $35 million and 380 mortgage loans for an estimated $45 million."

Sheldon Good & Co. is rated by Forbes Magazine as America's premier real estate auction firm and by New York magazine as the largest auction firm in the tri-state region.

3

ART DECO HOTELS GO ON THE BLOCK

Glamorous Lifestyle Included?

One of the most exciting deals in which I had the opportunity to participate was the sale of an Art Deco hotel chain in South Beach, Miami, Florida. I especially get a kick out of watching television with my kids when one of the five hotels included in the deal flashes into the background of a scene. The moment that one of the hotels appears on the screen I'm like a little kid. I'll jump up, point like a kid seeing his favorite toy at Toys R Us and tell the kids, "I sold that hotel!" By now my kids are pretty tired of my routine, but it still is pretty exciting to have been part of this historic transaction.

The story started when I got a call from the director of marketing for the bank involved in the deal. He held several different titles for three different but interrelated companies. He served as national marketing director and senior vice president of marketing for the American Real Estate Group in Irvine, California. He also worked for the Dallas-based Bass brothers, who had bought American Savings and Loan Association through a new bank—New West Federal Savings Bank—that they had started. The director was a relatively young guy for the position he held in the bank. In his mid-30s, he had an athletic build and ingratiating charm, a really bright guy who was well connected *because* he knew what he was doing. His patron in this matter was Robert Bass, who had

A *l a n* **R . K** *r a v e t s* **,** PRESIDENT
Sheldon Good & Company

Alan Kravets joined Sheldon Good & Company in 1989 as general counsel
and broker and in 1998 was named president of the firm. A founding
partner of a 25-member law firm, Alan is an FDIC-approved attorney in
private practice who has concentrated his expertise in real estate law,
banking, and turnarounds during a 26-year legal career. Throughout his
tenure with Sheldon Good, Alan has worked with developers, financial
institutions, REITs, homebuilders, the hospitality industry, health care
providers, business owners, and corporate America as a broker and
consultant.

Alan received his undergraduate bachelor's degree in business administration at the University of Michigan School of Business Administration
and his Juris Doctor from the University of Michigan Law School. He is a
licensed Illinois attorney and is also licensed as a real estate broker and
salesperson in 12 states.

To date, Alan has been actively involved in sales totaling hundreds of
millions of dollars for Sheldon Good & Company. He is widely quoted as
an expert in real estate auction and disposition strategies; he writes a
monthly real estate column and frequently lectures on real estate, brokerage, and auction matters.

a keen interest in making sure that the Florida properties were sold to
credible buyers because, as the director explained it, Bass was active in
the Landmark Preservation Council for South Beach and wanted the
legacy of the hotels to transcend the transaction.

After the initial phone call, I arranged to meet the director in his office in Irvine. I always enjoy doing business in southern California, as the
weather, food, and sights are always terrific unless an earthquake, major
fire, or riot messes things up. My plane arrived at Orange County Airport the afternoon before the meeting. I was picked up by the manager
of our Newport Beach, California, office, who had been with us for a
short time, having left a competitor to join our firm and lead our California operation.

The manager was excited at the pro[...]
Saving's successor in this transaction as Am[...]
southern California. He was also enamored w[...]
volved with the Dallas-based Bass brothers, a real [...]
own right.

Even though our manager had limited experience i[...]
we didn't. We have sold hundreds of millions of dollars of ho[...]
resorts, and hospitality properties across the United States. O[...]
ager knew that he was in the right place at the right time. If t[...]
worked out, he would serve as American's liaison from our company[...]
would serve as counsel, and our Florida guys would act as the marketing
group that would process the deal. With over $10 million on the table,
our manager had reason to be excited.

During dinner that night our manager gave me the background of
the deal as he understood it. Apparently, several years earlier, prior to
the Basses' involvement, the bank had made loans totaling more than
$35 million for the purchase and renovation of the properties, which
had been bought for pennies on the dollar when the bank was sold. The
properties had been part of foreclosure and bankruptcy proceedings in
the several years preceding our involvement and only now were at a
point where they could be sold. Our manager also pointed out, I guess
because he thought guys from Chicago would care, that one of the owners had been recently convicted of federal racketeering and wire fraud
charges and was serving a 20-plus-year prison term. I quickly pointed out
to our manager that these days Chicago was being equated with Michael
Jordan and the Chicago Bulls, *not* Al Capone and the Mob.

The next morning our manager met me in the lobby of the Westin
for breakfast. I was up early as my body clock was two hours ahead, and
our appointment at the bank was set for 10:30 AM Los Angeles time. I was
wearing the standard uniform, a navy blue suit, but instead of a white or
powder blue button-down shirt, I wore a green and blue striped shirt
with white collar, French cuffs, and a matching blue and green tie. I figured that I was in the land of the movie stars and what the hell.

Our manager was quick to notice my attire. Almost immediately he
asked me why I was wearing what I was wearing. I told him that I hadn't
really thought about it and that we were in the land of movie stars anyway. No we weren't, he countered—we were not in Hollywood; we were
in Orange County, home of California conservatism—did I have a white

cheduled to catch an af-
hirt, I explained. To this
ck an extra white or pow-
ether our manager was

ger's car and headed to-
nk was about 20 minutes
ted: a multistoried white
he odd thing was that the
igs."

office was on one of the
le saw us in his office, the
turned out, the director
rn California on a short-

pect of representing American
rican had a huge profile in
th the idea of being in-
state legend in their

selling hotels,
els, motels,
r man-
ings
I

term assignment to help the Basses put their sales plan for various portions of American Savings real estate portfolio in place. Once that was completed, his plan was to return to Texas as part of the larger Bass organization. At that point, a strange observation struck me: Why is everyone in southern California seemingly from someplace else?

With the introduction concluded, the director got right down to business. He knew of our company's reputation as a result of our having sold most of Texas and the Southwest during the previous ten years. Could we sell these hotels? Should we sell them individually or as a package? Who were the likely buyers? How would we reach them? How did we screen buyers to avoid bogus deals—a guy involved in these properties had just been put in jail? How would we report to them? What were our fees? The director was a guy who obviously knew what he was doing.

After the litany of questions subsided, I explained that we needed all of the descriptive, financial, and legal materials about the properties, and that once we received them, the guys in our Florida operation would do an evaluation of the director's portfolio. The evaluation would be followed by a full-blown written report, which would detail our programming and its methodology and attendant costs.

On the flight back to Chicago another curious thought hit me: Some guys from Chicago, Reno, and Dallas met in California to determine the fate of the Art Deco District in Miami.

The evaluation of the properties came several weeks later, after we had received the materials that we had requested from California. The deal was assigned to two of our associates who were licensed in Florida: one from our Boca Raton office and one from our Chicago office. They immediately arranged to physically inspect the properties, and their evaluation followed shortly thereafter.

One of the people involved was Alan Kravets, who had joined our firm as vice president and general counsel. He had served as legal counsel for a variety of our lender clients in a number of prior transactions. Alan had joined the firm to help us make sure that we complied with the innumerable regulatory requirements mandated by many differing state laws that govern the sale of real estate as well as brokerage and auction activities. Alan had a strong background in deals, so I invited him to be a member of the team to oversee a variety of issues surrounding the structuring of this deal.

Our analysis was multidimensional. The first thing we looked for was the physical condition of the structures themselves. We tried to determine the degree of renovation that would be required and the extent to which the needed work would impede the salability of any given property. Second, in dealing with operating hotels, we looked at their financial performance to determine their values; for example, issues of room rental charges (known in the industry as average daily rate, or ADR), the condition of the furniture in the rooms that might impact the cost of refurbishing the property, and what other properties might be available for sale in the area as competition.

The fact that the properties were in a designated Landmark District was also relevant. Any changes to their exterior facades would be closely

A *l a n* **K** *r a v e t s*

"I practiced law for many years, specializing in real estate matters and representing lawyers, sellers, brokers, and lenders. My specialty was solving deals for banks that were investors in real estate loans when something had gone wrong.

"What many people don't realize is that bankers are in the business of loaning money to people who mean to use it to make a lot more

(continued)

money than they borrowed from the bank. Of a billion dollars worth of problem real estate situations that I worked on as a lawyer, none was caused by fraud by either the borrowers or the banks. Rather, most of the problems that arose came as a result of one or more of the following:

- A negative change in the real estate markets
- The borrower and the bank mistiming the demand for the real estate
- A change in the income tax laws that materially changed the economies of the originally contemplated transaction
- A rise in interest rates that couldn't be afforded
- A change in the regulations that governed the bank that lent the money
- Some personal issue that affected the borrowers (e.g., death, business reversal, dispute, etc.)

"The talent that I brought to the table was counseling my clients to keep a level head in approaching any problems and then methodically creating the disposition strategy to maximize value for the lenders.

"Most of the loan workouts required an endgame disposition strategy and I, as an attorney for the owners, engaged Sheldon Good & Company to sell numerous properties at auction for a cross section of my clients. I learned to use the company's services to convert the real estate into cash that could then be easily managed, which was basically the strategy being followed by the lender in the Art Deco hotel deal.

"In one of my former cases, I represented a loan participation group that took over an ill-fated construction loan project for one of the most expensive hotels ever constructed on a per-room basis in the United States located in the mountains of Colorado. That's where Sheldon Good & Company and I learned about the economics of the hospitality industry and the marketing of these kinds of difficult hospitality projects. This knowledge was put to good use in the Art Deco hotel sale.

"The big question for this deal at the time was the use for which the buildings would be renovated. Hotels? Condominiums? Time-shares? Vacation club? This was an interesting intellectual proposition."

scrutinized by the various local landmark preservation groups, which meant there could be serious delays in the buyers' ability to renovate the properties. Delays cost money, so all of these factors were addressed as part of our analysis.

New West Federal Savings Bank, the successor of American Savings and Loan Association, retained us to conduct a sealed-bid auction for their Art Deco hotel portfolio.

The Miami Beach properties that were offered included:

- The Cavalier Hotel, 1320 Ocean Drive, designed by Rov. F. Fiance and built in 1936, was a three-story, 48-room, oceanfront hotel that had been previously renovated.
- The Cardozo Hotel, 1300 Ocean Drive, designed by Henry Hohauser and built in 1939, was a three-story, 46-room, oceanfront, renovated hotel known as a masterpiece of streamlining.
- The Carlyle Hotel, 1250 Ocean Drive, designed by Kiennel and Elliott, was a three-story, 44-room hotel and a showpiece of the Art Deco district with its striking vertical piers and horizontal lines that surrounded its corners. It was also home to The Whiskey, one of the Art Deco district's hottest bars and sister to The Whiskey in the Paramount Hotel in New York City, one of the nation's trendiest places at the time.
- The Leslie Hotel, 1244 Ocean Drive, designed by Albert Anis and built in 1937, was a three-story, 49-room hotel and an example of classic Deco that contrasted well with the exuberance of the Carlyle next door.
- The Victor, 1144 Ocean Drive, designed by L. Murray Dixon and constructed in 1937, was an eight-story, 97-room hotel that was a prime candidate for complete renovation.

The preauctioning marketing program targeted these properties to be marketed to a local, regional, national, and international audience. Each property was offered individually, but we made clear in the criteria set forth for bidding that the ownership had a strong preference for a buyer who would buy all of the properties simultaneously, as Bass did not want to be left with any given property.

The media plan included advertisements that appeared in a variety of newspapers and real estate and hotel trade journals as well as an extensive direct mail campaign targeting hotel operations and redevelopers (see Figure 3.1). At the same time, a myriad of brokerages that specialized in the sale of these types of boutique properties were contacted on an international basis as South Beach lent itself to a worldwide audience based on its popularity in the modeling and advertising industries.

The response to the offering was amazing. Over a thousand parties reacted to our marketing efforts, many of whom sought detailed bidder's information packages that we produced to provide substantive descriptive, physical, and legal information about each of the properties. We even drafted the real estate sales contract that all buyers were required to use if they wanted to participate in the auction. The contracts were drafted in such a way that they could be used for one, several, or all of the properties, as the case might be. Consequently, we also created the ability for bidders to bid in the alternative (i.e., building A or building B or building C but only *one,* not all). Our theory was that multiple bidders might prioritize their potential choices of properties differently. As a bidder, you could offer X dollars for the Leslie; if this was not the winning bid on the Leslie, then you could bid Y dollars for the Carlyle; if this was not the winning bid, you could bid Z dollars for the Cardozo or bid in any combination.

As part of the preauction evaluation process, we set up an on-site office at the Cardozo Hotel in order to be responsive to interested potential bidders' requests to see the hotels. One of the most unusual experiences I've had in my career was during this deal, when I visited the on-site office for the first time. Our guys had set up a four-person office in a vacant space that faced Ocean Drive and the beach. Their concept, as they explained it, was that customers who visited the office would have a stunning view of the beach, which would showcase the desirability of the property. It sounded like a good idea, and none of us thought much about it.

I made a date to visit the office a couple of weeks after it was set up to see the buildings. My trip was set for a one-night stayover, and my itinerary was set from the office in Chicago, which didn't advise the on-site office the exact time of my arrival. My plane landed at Miami International, and I caught a cab to the properties. I was wearing a suit and tie that, on pulling up to the Cardozo, I learned was an oddity in this area. I had never previously been in South Beach, Miami, and so had no specific expectations. As I stepped out of the cab, my jaw dropped. Here

FIGURE 3.1 *Advertisement for the Art Deco HotelAuction*

PORTFOLIO SALE ORDERED
SEALED BID AUCTION
Hotels and Commercial Properties in Florida

Leslie Hotel

Cardoza Hotel

Carlyle Hotel

This is your opportunity to acquire an operating hotel group in the fashionable and historic Art Deco district of Miami Beach as well as other Art Deco commercial properties and a hotel in Tampa.

MIAMI BEACH, FLORIDA

• **Cavalier Hotel,**
   48-room, 19,017 sq. ft. at
   1320 Ocean Drive
• **Cardozo Hotel,**
   46-room, 27,981 sq. ft. at
   1300 Ocean Drive
• **Carlyle Hotel,**
   44-room, 32,943 sq. ft. at
   1250 Ocean Drive

• **Leslie Hotel,**
   49-room, 22,675 sq. ft. at
   1244 Ocean Drive
• **Victor Hotel,** 97-room,
   unrehabilitated, 44,781 sq. ft. at
   1144 Ocean Drive
• **The Flambeau,** two-story,
   7,250 sq. ft. commercial bldg. at
   1126 Ocean Drive
• **Corner Parking Lot,**
   34-space lot, 90' x 140' at
   12th and Collins

TAMPA, FLORIDA

• **Ramada Airport Hotel and
   Conference Center,**
   250 rooms and 10,000 sq. ft.
   of meeting space

**BID SUBMITTAL DEADLINE:
MARCH 12**

Financing is available to qualified buyers. Cash purchasers will receive a 15% discount.

OPEN HOUSE DATES:
Miami, February 11, 20, 26 &
March 3 - Noon to 4:00 p.m.
Tampa, February 13, 18, 27 &
March 4 - Noon to 4:00 p.m.

**CASHIER'S CHECK
REQUIRED TO BID**

© Sheldon Good & Company, Inc., 1992.
All Rights Reserved.

Available in different packages.
Call for brochure with terms of sale: **(305) 538-9016**
SHELDON GOOD & COMPANY
1300 S.E. 17th Street, Suite 216 • Ft. Lauderdale, Florida 33316

Source: Reproduced with permission from Sheldon Good & Company Auctions, LLC.

before me were the best-looking people I had ever seen. I had understood that South Beach was the home of many modeling agencies, but I had never been in a place where *everyone* was gorgeous—both women *and* men. I couldn't help but feel that something was wrong with the way I looked when everyone else looked so terrific. It hit me that South Beach was to adults what Ft. Lauderdale was to college kids. Annette Funicello had grown into Cindy Crawford.

I walked into the lobby of the Cardozo Hotel—named after the famous U.S. Supreme Court Justice. I told the desk clerk (a blond Adonis) who I was, and he directed me to our office. As I opened the door, three of our associates were on their knees on two desks with their noses pressed against the front windows and ogling a group of scantily clad women filming a rock video on the beach. I heard one tell the other that this was the third video they had seen shot in the last week. It seemed as though I was standing behind them unnoticed forever when the female receptionist asked if she could help me. The moment I spoke, all three guys simultaneously jumped off the desks and we all laughed.

We relocated the office that day to a space in the back of the building that faced the alley. After all—business was business, and if you want to watch rock videos, MTV is on 24 hours a day.

The showings of the properties had been prescheduled weeks in advance so that interested bidders and their proxies could physically inspect all of the properties. This was no small task because several of the properties were operating, occupied hotels and because each of the properties, in all likelihood, were candidates for some degree of renovation.

Over a hundred parties viewed the portfolio during the several weeks preceding the auction, which required us to drastically expand the size of our staff during the scheduled on-site showing dates. Buyers came from all across the United States, Latin America, and the Caribbean. In some cases, people would initially view the properties and then create new partnerships, which would require additional viewings as they brought on potential investors/partners.

Many contractors representing undisclosed buyers also inspected the properties. They were there to gauge the amount of work needed and the attendant renovation costs their principals could expect if they prevailed in the bidding. We were careful to be sure that buyers had adequate time to fully evaluate the properties prior to the auction. This was very important because we sought to sell the properties on an "as is, where is" basis, and we knew that to generate clean, non-contingency-laden bids, potential bidders had to be comfortable with *their own* evaluations of the properties.

One of the interesting aspects of this part of our program was that, as time went on, we learned that a number of contractors who were evaluating the various properties were doing so for *multiple unrelated principals.* In fact, in several cases, the contractors were actually *pitching* the deal to parties they believed had the financial wherewithal to hire them if those parties prevailed in the bidding. They were trying to generate business for themselves, and we were the potential beneficiaries.

Another curious pattern that developed was that even though the potential buyers might be from out of the area or even out of the United States, they all sought local contractor representation—particularly when it came to trying to cost each potential deal. It would have been interesting to track who was involved with whom, but unfortunately our "radar screen" was ultimately limited to potential bidders and not their proxies.

The auction itself was one of the most unusual I have seen. Separating the lookers from the players during the exhaustive inspection process, where our office processed more than 1,000 inquiries, was one of the most challenging aspects of this deal.

We had selected a sealed-bid auction because the price of any given property was not the sole consideration in awarding either the entire portfolio or any of its individual properties. With the bidders' ability to bid in the alternative (i.e., offer different bids for any of the properties in any combinations), virtually anything was possible. We also sought to know the credibility of the buyer(s) because, despite the fact that the deals were not contingent on financing, we didn't want the properties sold to buyers who would allow them to fall into further disrepair. The goal was to sell the properties to a credible buyer or buyers of good reputation who would ultimately renovate these architectural jewels or effect their renovation.

It was really something when the bids came in. We received 42 bids in varying combinations for the properties offered. In order to present them, we ended up having a four-way teleconference because none of us were in the same city. Chicago, Los Angeles, Dallas, and Miami were hooked together as we began the arduous process of presenting the voluminous amount of materials that accompanied each bid.

Prior to the call, it took almost five hours for us to sort through the bids, checking them to see if any given bid contained terms not originally set forth in the auction's offering materials. As part of the terms of the auction, bidders were required to submit a deposit of 5 percent of their bid via wire transfer or certified or cashier's check. We were holding many millions of dollars from banks all over the world, and they needed to be catalogued regardless of whether any given bid was accepted.

A *lan* K *ravets*

"I was seriously considering making a transition from being a business lawyer to becoming a real estate disposition specialist when the Art Deco hotel deal surfaced. That's when Steve asked me to join his company as in-house general counsel and then segue into business development.

"I felt like the scarecrow being offered a trip on the yellow brick road. Even our offices were located in the same building one floor apart. How could I say no? I jumped into my new career, and as a result of my very helpful law partners, my transition went with great ease.

"I drafted the ultimate hotel purchase and sale agreement that was used in the Art Deco sale and served as the template for many deals that followed and are even used for certain deals done by us today.

"The Art Deco hotel deal was just the beginning of our hospitality group. Since that time we have sold thousands of hotel rooms representing more than nine figures in value. These include hotels that carry many well-known flags like Holiday Inn, Ramada Inn, Radisson Comfort Suites, Super 8, Hampton Inn, and many others. We have also handled many specialty, one-of-a-kind hotels, resorts, bed-and-breakfasts, and virtually every iteration of a hotel property. Sometimes the properties are sold as operating hotels, which are essentially operating businesses. Other times they are sold as real estate to be changed into something else, such as an assisted living facility for seniors, school dormitory housing, corporate retreats, or office buildings. The potential recycling opportunities are unlimited."

Our teleconference began with a recap of our original marketing plan and the attendant interest it had garnered. The director of marketing for the bank and his counterparts were already up to speed, as we had been briefing them constantly via both the telephone and written status reports. We had not been able to report the results because of the sheer volume of bids that had been received in a two-hour period right before the 5:00 PM deadline the day before. Consequently, everyone but us sat on the edge of their seats waiting to learn the winners.

When we announced the results, there were cheers by everyone on the director's team.

The *Miami Herald* reported the story the next day as shown in Figure 3.2.

FIGURE 3.2 The Miami Herald's *Account of the Art Deco Hotel Auction*

Developers' bid wins Art Deco hotels

By Beatrice E. Garcia
Herald Business Writer

A group headed by a South Beach real estate development team that has successfully renovated several Art Deco properties is the winning bidder for five hotels on Miami Beach's Ocean Drive.

The Art Deco hotels—the Cavalier, Cardozo, Carlyle, Leslie and the Victor—are considered among the most architecturally significant buildings in the city's national historic district. Their restoration kicked off the renaissance of South Beach in the mid-1980s.

The group includes Dacra Cos., a South Beach real estate development and construction firm owned by brothers Craig and Scott Robins, and Island Trading Co., the development company headed by music mogul Chris Blackwell. He is best known for discovering Bob Marley, Irish rock group U2 and Grace Jones.

The third partner is Gerald Robins, a longtime Miami Beach developer and a partner in the group that owns the Hilton Fontainebleau Hotel. Gerald Robins is Craig and Scott's father.

The Darca-Island Trading group is purchasing the five hotels, a Deco-style commercial building at 1126 Ocean Dr., known as the Flambeau, and a parking lot on the northeast corner of 12th Street and Collins Avenue. The lot is the site of the Senator Hotel, which was demolished in 1988. It is an all-cash deal, they said.

The exact price for the local properties was not revealed. But Sheldon Good & Co., a Chicago-based auction house that handled the sealed-bid auction, said the Miami Beach properties and a Ramada Inn hotel in Tampa, which went to another bidder, were sold for a combined total of $15 million. The auction house received more than 40 bids for the properties.

"We want to keep a significant portion of this portfolio and develop different strategies for operating them," Craig Robins said.

Robins said the group would like to bring in other developers, who are interested in preserving the historical character of the buildings, but in a style that differs from what Dacra and Island Trading have already done on South Beach.

Dacra and Island Trading teamed up to transform the Marlin Hotel at 12th and Collins from a crack den into a funky hotel with restaurant, modeling agency and recording studio. The two are renovating the Netherlands on Ocean Drive.

Island Trading has invested about $10 million so far in South Beach, said Wendy Hart, project manager for the company's Miami Beach properties.

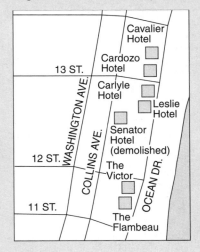

4

EVER WANTED
YOUR OWN GOLD MINE?

I have been involved in the sale of a lot of unusual properties. In fact, one of the common themes underlying the growth of our company and its programs is that auctions make a lot of sense in bringing to market properties that are not easily valued.

Did you ever wonder why in areas like fine art or collectibles it is commonplace to see a Van Gogh oil painting, Princess Diana's cocktail dress, or Jackie Kennedy Onassis's personal effects being sold to an enthusiastic bidding audience through auction? The answer is almost always that no one would know what price to pay without going through the auction process.

We had a similar situation in which the auction process was used to find and set the market for some unusual stuff: former gold mines, patented mining claims, and mineral rights that span an area about two and a half times the state of Rhode Island.

The story began with a call I received from Robert Hatcher. Bob is a white-haired guy of average build in his mid-60s who has been in the timber business for over 40 years. He is formerly the president of both the Realtors Land Institute (RLI) and the U.S. chapter of FIABCI (the International Real Estate Federation that is based in Paris, France).

R o b e r t D . H a t c h e r, ALC
Hatcher & Associates

Robert Hatcher is a real estate broker and registered forester who has worked in the forestry industry since 1961. He has also served as a university forester and has taught in the Department of Geography at the University of Southern Mississippi. He holds bachelor's and master of science degrees from the University of Georgia. Since 2002, Bob has served as director of the Forest and Natural Resource Division of Sheldon Good & Company.

Bob specializes in forestry consulting for private landowners, including all phases of forest management, timber inventory and appraisal, timber sales, forest investment analysis, land sales, and acquisitions. He has considerable consulting experience in forestry overseas and in the Americas, as well as working with foreign clients owning timberland in the United States.

Bob spends much of his time and efforts in the timberland investment field acting as broker and advisor. In addition, he is a timberland investor assembling large investment properties, arranging equity and financing for his own account and with partners. He attends trade missions abroad and at the United Nations headquarters in New York in a nongovernment organization capacity, where his investor and real estate contacts are continually increased.

Bob was the 2001 national president for Realtors Land Institute (RLI) and currently serves on its National Board of Governors. He is a past president of the International Real Estate Federation (FIABCI), Paris, France, USA chapter (Washington, D.C.), and is on the executive board (Paris). He is past president of the Georgia chapter of RLI, and in 1996 received the Georgia Land Realtor of the Year award from RLI for outstanding service to the real estate and forestry communities.

Alan Joscelyn
Gough Shanahan Johnson & Waterman

Alan Joscelyn received his Juris Doctor from the University of Montana Law School in 1975 and began his legal career as counsel to the Montana Department of State Lands in Helena, rising to chief legal counsel before deciding to hang out a shingle as a sole practitioner. During the five years that followed, he acquired a practical education in the economic delivery of useful legal advice. In 1981, Alan joined Gough Shanahan Johnson & Waterman, one of the oldest and most respected natural resource law firms in the country, becoming a partner in 1983.

Montana is a large state but a small community—the state's population is around 900,000—creating the opportunity for an enterprising lawyer to build a diverse practice. Alan has served as legal advisor to two Montana governors and represented penniless defendants in Helena City Court. He has served as chairman of Montana's Board of Personnel Appeals, as alternate chairman of the State Board of Labor Appeals, and has represented tenants seeking return of security deposits from residential landlords. He has garnered permits for major mines and watched as individual clients washed gold nuggets from sluice boxes in secluded locations. He has battled environmental activists but been instrumental in stopping the threatened poisoning of a pristine wilderness stream. He has lectured on water quality law in Great Falls, Montana, and on the needs of a workable mining law in Beijing. He has testified about water quality legislation in Helena and with respect to mining law reform in Washington, D.C. He is prosecuting a $500 million taking case but has tagged along to watch the sheriff seize a stock car for a client at the local dirt track.

Alan has served as chair of the Mining Committee of the American Bar Association Section of Natural Resources, Energy and Environmental Law, and is listed in the *International Who's Who of Mining Lawyers*. He is presently secretary of the Northwest Mining Association and on the Board of Litigation for the Mountain States Legal Foundation.

R o b e r t D. H a t c h e r

"Your findings on the auction process are as true as can be. Otherwise, you might sell a property and never know what it was really worth. When the final bid is $4,000,000 and the bid under that is $3,900,000, you know exactly where the market value is."

Bob originally approached me to start a Timber and Natural Resource Division after he heard me speak about some of the auction programs we had developed for properties that had national and worldwide audiences. He was enamored with the concept that our company could define and make markets for properties that otherwise were not definable. He routinely dealt with timberland properties throughout North, Central, and South America as a broker, buyer, seller, or syndicator. In fact, Bob, in a previous lifetime, was a college professor in the Deep South, an attribute that I especially like about him.

After numerous discussions, we developed a Timberland and Natural Resources Division that specialized in selling properties for companies that traded in a variety of timber products, mineral rights, enormous undeveloped land parcels, and any derivation of them. We developed with him a written business plan whereby jointly we would use his expertise in these product areas and our marketing abilities to offer a service not readily available in the marketplace.

A l a n J o s c e l y n

"Patented mining claims are becoming an anachronism. It used to be that when a prospector found valuable minerals on federal lands controlled by the Forest Service or Bureau of Land Management, he could get a deed, or patent, to the 20-acre tract containing the minerals if he could 'prove it up'—show it had enough minerals to make a paying mine. A dozen or so years ago, Congress said 'no more,' at least until the general mining law is reformed so that the United States keeps a royalty when it gives a patent."

Some time ago, Bob called to tell me that he had bought a tract of timberland in western Montana from a publicly traded gold mining company named Canyon Resources. He explained that the company was traded on the American Stock Exchange and several years earlier had hit the largest proven gold strike in the United States: a proven reserve of some 10 million ounces of gold valued at $3 billion. He had learned from one of his many sources that the company was interested in selling off some of its surplus holdings in Montana. As I was sitting in my office listening to Bob's story, I couldn't help but think, "What does this have to do with us?"

I really like Bob, as he has a southern gentility that manifests itself by his never immediately coming to the point. Whenever I'm talking with him, I am never quite sure whether the story he is telling me is the main subject or an interlude *to* the main subject. Furthermore, sometimes I'm not sure whether there is a substantive subject at all, because sometimes he calls me just to say "Hello." I always try to be accommodating, realizing that there are cultural differences in the way in which people do business in the United States and elsewhere.

This aspect of my relationship with Bob reminds me of what I've learned from my experiences in doing business across the continent. In the midwestern United States, a half-hour business meeting usually

A l a n J o s c e l y n

"My law firm goes back to the 1870s, and my predecessors, including Joseph Toole, Montana's first governor, represented the wave of gold miners who settled Montana.

"My personal introduction to gold miners came from representing promoters and speculators beginning in the late 1970s, when the newly unfettered gold price was creating the West's first gold boom of modern times. I soon became cynical about geologists' reports estimating thousands of ounces of gold 'in place' on a property. Fast forward to 1994 when I began representing Canyon Resources. The industry had matured and the speculators and promoters had been driven out by real miners whose claims are vetted by steely-eyed SEC lawyers."

involves 5 minutes of social pleasantry, followed by 25 minutes of business discussion, followed by a decision. A half-hour business meeting in the Deep South is usually 25 minutes of social pleasantry, followed by 5 minutes of business discussion, followed by another meeting.

A half-hour business meeting in southern California is arranged to meet the guy on a great golf course somewhere. He calls you on your cell phone three minutes before you are supposed to tee off and tells you to start without him because he is stuck in traffic, so you tee off by yourself. Around the 3rd or 4th hole, you see him talking on his cell phone while being driven out by a caddy on a golf cart. By the end of the 17th hole, he tells you that you have a deal and to meet him at his Wilshire Boulevard office at 10 AM sharp the next morning. You get to his office at 10 AM sharp the next morning, and what happens? His name has been scraped off the door, telephone disconnected, and rental car returned.

A half-hour business meeting in New York City starts with your waiting in the guy's lobby for the first 25 minutes. In the last 5 minutes you are escorted into his office, where you find him talking intensely to someone on the telephone for the first 3 of your 5 remaining minutes. With 2 minutes left, he slams down the phone and turns to you and says, "What?" You have 1 minute to answer, and in the last minute he says either OK or not OK.

A half-hour business meeting in Canada is a lot like a business meeting in the Midwest. The first 5 minutes are social pleasantry, the next 20 are business discussion followed by a decision, but the last 5 minutes are usually an admonishment that Canada is not the United States and that it has its own identity.

Back to Bob, who is on the telephone telling me that he has bought timberland from this gold mining company and then he finally comes to

R o b e r t D . H a t c h e r

"To properly continue doing business in the Deep South, dinners are mandatory and are preceded and concluded with a Jack Daniels and water at the bar. After several of these events, you might become 'family.' That is what southern hospitality is all about. In the end, we can all do business together."

A *l a n* **J** *o s c e l y n*

"Fifteen thousand votes was the statewide margin of victory for Initiative 137, which banned using cyanide in gold recovery; a similar measure had failed two years before when the environmentalists had two laws up for vote. The other one, banning corporate campaigning on ballot issues, passed. Although it was declared unconstitutional later that year, ten days before the election, the ruling came too late to let the mining companies tell their story regarding Initiative 137."

the point: He thinks the company is a perfect candidate for our Timberland and Natural Resources program. Apparently, despite the fact that it made an enormous gold strike worth $3 billion, environmentalists had succeeded in passing a statewide referendum—Initiative 137—with fewer than 25,000 votes, requiring the use of expensive mining processes that raised the costs from $200 to over $400 per ounce (gold was then selling for $300 per ounce) and that rendered the claim valueless. Canyon Resources had responded by filing a lawsuit against the State of Montana for over a billion dollars in damages that had been pending for several years. Consequently, the company had decided to divest itself of all of its surplus holdings in Montana except for the gold strike that was in dispute.

R *o b e r t* **D .** **H** *a t c h e r*

"Actually, I met with Dr. DeVoto because I had an interest in the timber on one of Canyon Resources' properties in Montana, and after discussing the timber, Dr. DeVoto said, 'Let's set that aside and talk about something else.' That is when the exciting and magical word *gold* entered our conversation. I can still visualize my daughter at the age of seven wading in a shallow stream, sitting on rocks, and panning for gold near Dahlonega, Georgia, for hour after hour. At the mention of 'gold mines,' I probably had the same facial expression as my daughter that day many years ago."

Within the next several days, Bob arranged a conference call with the chairman, CEO, and president of Canyon Resources, Dr. Richard DeVoto. Within five minutes of being on the call, I knew that I liked him. Dr. DeVoto had a Ph.D. and taught at the Colorado School of Mines. He had assumed the helm of Canyon Resources years ago and had navigated the gold mining company through a number of opportunities— some of which worked and some of which didn't. He was a modern day gold miner—Ph.D. and all.

During the course of the conversation, Dr. DeVoto explained the background of his company and its predicament with Montana. One of the most interesting aspects of his company was that it was the successor organization to the famous Anaconda Company and its predecessors, which were famous for settling and mining the western frontier during the gold, silver, oil, and copper rushes of the late 1800s and early 1900s. He was also an avid outdoorsman and historian and told of how their 900,000 plus acres of mineral rights spanned many famous places throughout Montana. Included was, among other areas, a significant portion of the famed Lewis and Clark trail, which had just celebrated its 200th anniversary. Other well-known areas where the company owned former gold mines, patented mining claims, and mineral rights included Missoula and Flathead Lake, which are connected by the famous Blackfoot River, the site where Brad Pitt made fly-fishing famous in the movie *A River Runs Through It*.

Lewistown was the city closest to the company's old Kendall gold mine, which we ultimately divided into a variety of parcels as part of the auction. The company also had an obligation to complete a remediation plan there that, Dr. DeVoto explained, was typical of most gold mining companies' procedures once they conclude mining operations at a given mine or group of mines.

R o b e r t D . H a t c h e r

"These properties are a piece of American history—the mining shafts were dug beginning in the 1860s and were mined through the 1990s. The gold-related romance as well as the environment is still there—on one of the properties we came across a moose and her calf at sundown— looking just like a postcard."

The conversation lasted about half an hour and concluded with scheduling Dr. DeVoto to come to our offices in Chicago for discussing further the idea of bringing his portfolio of surplus holdings to market via an auction.

The first group meeting occurred several weeks later. Dr. DeVoto, Bob Hatcher, and our company team met in our Chicago offices to explore the applicability of our programming to Canyon Resources' situation. It struck me with some humor that the chairman of a publicly traded gold mining company (AMEX: CAU—the chemical sign for gold) located in Golden, Colorado (of all places), along with its local Montana mining expert as well as Bob Hatcher, a timber expert from Atlanta, were coming to see us in Chicago. Had this meeting been scheduled 200 years earlier during Lewis and Clark's time, there was a high probability that someone wouldn't have made it because of fighting between pioneers and Native Americans, impossible travel conditions, disease, or even inclement weather. Being in the modern age of cell phones, air travel, and the Internet sure can be a wonderful thing.

THE EVALUATION

The meeting started with our addressing the nature and scope of Canyon's potential inventory. Dr. DeVoto had brought detailed descriptions of its various interests in the form of satellite pictures, surveys,

A *lan* **J** *o s c e l y n*

"Dick DeVoto is an unsung hero. He took a gamble, buying out Canyon Resources' joint venture partner in the McDonald gold deposit just before gold prices took a dive and environmental activists passed the unprecedented initiative prohibiting mining of the deposit. In the past three years, while the national news has been filled with stories of corporate executive wrongdoing, Dr. DeVoto has stuck out the hard times seeking justice for his shareholders as the wheels of Montana justice grind so exceedingly slow and fine."

patented mining claim drawings, and local maps, all of which he had loosely pieced together to give us as good a description as he could with minimal, if any, cost.

After some time we were able to break out Canyon's holdings into three generic areas. There were 31 separate patented mining claims totaling 641 acres, which were land ownership interests that had been acquired by the company or its predecessor(s) by filing claims on the lands by working them as gold mines. The second group of properties consisted of 44 gold mining claims totaling 845 acres for mines that were worked in and around the Kendall gold mine. The third group of property interests were 82 mineral rights interests that totaled approximately 900,000 acres.

Most people are not aware that the rights to the minerals below the surface of the ground can be sold as a separate right. In fact, throughout the United States in many western and mid-Atlantic states surface rights and mineral rights are owned by different parties. The mineral rights that were owned by Canyon Resources were subsurface rights that allowed Canyon to mine for gold and other precious ores but excluded oil or oil shale and, frankly, were more sophisticated than needs to be

A l a n J o s c e l y n

"One of the questions raised immediately was what rights somebody who bought the mineral rights would have with respect to the surface. Typically, the owner of the minerals has rights that might be surprising to the unsuspecting surface owner, for instance the right to destroy as much of the surface and surface structures as necessary to mine the minerals, subject only to paying for the actual damages.

"Actual mining is rare, though, because mineable deposits are rare. The real question was whether, how, and for what purposes the mineral owner could enter on the surface in the absence of a mine. We reported that the mineral owner could pretty much get on the property when and how he or she wanted if the purpose was surveying or prospecting for minerals."

explained here. The important thing is that the surface and mineral rights for these properties had been divided for many, many years and were being sold as a separate and discrete property interest.

After carefully discussing the various options during the course of the day and our interpolating potential strategies of marketing the properties on a local, regional, national, and international basis, we were retained by Canyon to move the potential auction program to the next level.

No Small Task

We normally arrange a physical inspection of the various properties that we are engaged to sell. Have you ever tried to view nearly a million acres, much of which is mountainous timberland with no roads or ways to access it?

In advance of the scheduled inspections, Dr. DeVoto and his staff commissioned detailed maps to be made to help clarify the locations of the various properties even though the majority of them were not accessible by land.

One tour turned into several and was conducted over the course of several weeks in order to hone the offering strategy. The strategy was discussed and re-discussed over additional weeks as the information about the various properties was developed. Months later we were finally ready to go and issued the press release shown in Figure 4.1.

R o b e r t D . H a t c h e r

"In the Canyon Resources real estate, we had truly found something that was very difficult to value. The outcry auction was the best and only way to get the best price. Every day I see large companies selling their timberland holdings in an amateur manner. Their background is in managing land, not dispersal of the land. The auction gave bidders the opportunity to see, hear, and measure their competition."

FIGURE 4.1 *Press Release Heralding Auction of Mineral Rights in Montana*

RUBENSTEIN ASSOCIATES, INC.
Public Relations

SHELDON GOOD & COMPANY Auctions LLC
Chicago, IL 60606

For Immediate Release

900,000 Acres of Mineral Rights in Montana To Be Auctioned

650 Acres of Patented Lands Throughout Western Montana and 850 Acres at the Historic Kendall Gold Mine Located in the North Mocassin Mountains Suitable for Hunting, Mining and Construction of Mountain Homes to Be Auctioned

(Chicago, IL and Golden, CO) — Sheldon Good & Company Auctions, LLC (www.sheldongood.com), the nation's largest real estate auction company, announced that it has been retained by Canyon Resources Corporation, a Golden, CO–based, publicly traded corporation (AMEX: CAU) to auction nearly one million acres of mineral rights in Western Montana. In addition, 650 acres of patented lands in the Western Montana area and 850 acres in the North Moccasin Mountains region will be offered without reserve and subject to minimum bids. **The auction will be held on August 6, simultaneously—using an audio simulcast—at the Holiday Inn, 200 S. Patee, Missoula, Montana, and at the Yogo Inn, 211 Main Street, Lewistown, Montana, at 11:30 a.m. Bidder's Seminars (Auction Information Sessions) for all parcels offered will be held at 2:00 p.m. July 13 and August 3 at the Yogo Inn, 211 Main Street, Lewistown, Montana, at 6:00 p.m. on July 15, at the Holiday Inn, 200 South Patee, Missoula, Montana.**

Steven L. Good, Chairman of Sheldon Good & Company Auctions, LLC said, "The auction format is the most efficient method of disposing unique offerings such as the mineral rights to 900,000 acres of Montana property. The auction brings the product to the forefront of the market on a local, regional, national, and global basis and the market will react to what we have to offer, in this case a highly prized and unusual offering."

Mineral Rights

The lands and mineral rights are comprised primarily of lands assembled in the early 1900s by the Anaconda Company for their timber and mineral potential. The lands are sited in 14 counties in the mountainous terrain west of the continental divide, with most of the lands being located within 50 miles East and West of Missoula and West of Kalispell to the Idaho border. The parcels range in size from 700 to 26,000 acres and include the rights to do exploratory and development work, as is necessary or convenient, and the rights to mine and extract ores from the property. Additionally, the buyer reserves the right to use such surface lands as may be

FIGURE 4.1 *Press Release Heralding Auction of Mineral Rights in Montana, continued*

required for all mining operations with appropriate compensation to the surface owner for any damage done to the surface or structures on the surface.

"In terms of acreage, the Canyon Resources offering is most likely the largest sale of its type in the history of the auction industry," Mr. Good said. "We are appreciative of the confidence placed in us by Dr. Richard DeVoto, Chairman, President, and CEO of Canyon Resources and his senior management, and are confident that the auction format will identify the market."

Mr. Good said that he sees interest in the mineral rights coming from timber companies, mining companies, conservation groups, and individual landowners.

Western Montana property:

Included at the auction will be 650 acres of patented land throughout Western Montana. The property is being offered in 13 magnificent land parcels ranging in size from 9 to 120 acres and is ideal for ranching, mountain home sites, hunting, hiking, or camping. The property provides the buyer with a number of entrepreneurial opportunities such as harvesting of timber, mineral exploration, hunting clubs, or as a base for adventure excursions throughout the area. All land parcels (except the 120-acre parcel in Lewis Clark and Clark County) are subject to a 3% Net Smelter Return royalty to Western Energy Company. The property will be sold without reserve and is subject to a minimum bid of $100 per acre.

North Moccasin Mountains property:

Also up for auction will be parcels of an 850-acre property in the Northern Moccasin Mountains (Kendall Gold Mine) with indescribable natural beauty and serenity in an area with a storied mining history. The parcels offered in this auction are patented land claims, offering legal ownership of the surface rights to the land and the mineral rights below. The property is being auctioned in parcels ranging from 48 to 85 acres. Most of the parcels are now undisturbed land with a number of streams and creaks meandering throughout the forested areas. CR Kendall Corporation is currently performing reclamation work on the property including water pumping and irrigation of re-vegetated areas, and will continue to complete all reclamation work required. The parcels will be sold without reserve and are subject to a minimum bid of $100 per acre. On-site inspections will be held at 10:00 a.m. on July 13 and August 3.

Fifty percent of all the parcels offered will be sold subject to the published minimum bids.

Exclusion:

All of the lands owned or leased by Canyon Resources or the Seven-Up Pete Venture in Lewis 8 Clark County, which includes the 10 million ounce McDonald Gold Project, will be excluded from this auction process.

(continued)

FIGURE 4.1 *Press Release Heralding Auction of Mineral Rights in Montana, continued*

About Canyon Resources:

Canyon Resources Corporation was founded by Dr. Richard H. DeVoto, Chairman, President and CEO, and Gary C. Huber, Vice President-Finance and CFO, in 1979 as a mineral exploration company. At the time, Dr. DeVoto was a Professor of Geology at the Colorado School of Mines, in Golden, CO. The Company conducted large-scale exploration programs in the United States, Australia, Latin America, and to the discovery of the world-class, 10-million-ounce McDonald gold deposit in Montana.

Canyon Resources itself became a publicly held company with its IPO in 1986 and evolved into a producing mining company with development of its Kendall gold mine in central Montana. Through acquisitions and secondary public equity offerings, the company acquired its current producing Briggs gold mine in the desert of southeastern California, the properties that host the McDonald and satellite gold deposits near Lincoln, Montana, and the million acres of mineral rights in western Montana that are the subject of this auction sale.

About Sheldon Good & Company Auctions, LLC:

Sheldon Good & Company Auctions, LLC is the nation's largest real estate auction company. Since 1965, Sheldon Good & Company has sold over 37,000 properties from coast to coast, throughout Canada and the Caribbean, for a total value of over $8 billion. Its headquarters are in Chicago, with regional offices in New York and Denver. The company is extensively involved with auction programs in both the commercial and residential real estate sectors. In addition to its new Forestry Division, the company's growth areas include a nationally oriented "Trophy Home" Division and a Hospitality-Resort Division to auction resort properties from Canada to Mexico and from Hawaii through the Carribean.

# # #

THE MARKETING PLAN

Part and parcel of the press release were the marketing efforts coordinated between our offices in Denver and Chicago. We set up the auction to be broadcast between Missoula and Lewistown, Montana, because of the great distance between the cities and thus allowing bidders to participate in the auction in either location.

We created parcels that in some cases included the interests as Canyon Resources owned them, and in other cases we bundled claims to make up logical parcels. The brochure that we produced (see Figure

R *o b e r t* **D .** **H** *a t c h e r*

"Seminars were held in Lewistown, Kalispell, and Missoula to educate the locals and potential buyers about the characteristics of the real estate being auctioned and about the auction methodology. This also gave us an opportunity to listen to the concerns of the people attending and realize their interests in owning something.

"We are certain we performed a valuable service for Canyon Resources, potential buyers, and surface owners for the ore and mineral rights. Canyon Resources had one objective—to convert real estate into cash. Potential mining claim buyers were offered properties in areas attractive to them, often adjoining, but which had not been available for one hundred years or so. Surface owners were afforded an opportunity to acquire the ore and mineral rights under their property and reassemble the bundle of real estate rights that, again, they had no opportunity to do for one hundred years."

4.2) did a good job in describing the various parcels, their locations, and the general methodology that was planned for the auction.

Our marketing plan was to market each type of property to its relevant market. It made sense to market some of the properties to local real estate developers, investors, and users as they were ideal candidates for development of resort property subdivision or hunting and camping grounds. It made sense for other surface rights to be marketed to the same types of developers, investors, and users on a regional, national, and international basis not only as development opportunities but as potential timber plays as well. It is important to remember that despite the fact we had parcelized the property, any given buyer might seek to buy multiple parcels or all of them in any given location. Consequently, we had to market the portfolio to small and large buyers simultaneously.

The mineral rights portion of the portfolio was a great challenge for the simple reason that there was so much of it and it covered an enormous surface of earth. Portions of it could be bought by a myriad of large surface rights owners, including the U.S. Park Service, the state of

FIGURE 4.2 *Brochure Describing Facts about the Montana Auction*

Montana, the Nature Conservancy, or other mining or timber companies. Consequently, we opted to market the portfolio to these segments
for the simple reason that no one could predict from where the buyer(s)
would come.

We also knew there was little likelihood we would sell the entire
portfolio. The idea was to sell as much as we could on the rationale that

FIGURE 4.2 *Brochure Describing Facts about the Montana Auction, continued*

Located in 14 Western Montana Counties

900,000 Acres of Mineral Rights on 82 Separate Parcels

TO BE SOLD WITHOUT RESERVE, SUBJECT TO A MINIMUM BID OF $5.00 PER ACRE!
Certified or cashier's checks required to buy: Parcels up to 8,000 acres: $5,000
Parcels from 8,001–16,000 acres: $10,000
Parcels over 16,001 acres: $15,000

anging in size from 700 to 26,000 acres, the mineral rights to these land parcels were acquired by The Anaconda Company in the early 1900s for their mineral and timber potential. These rights include many known instances of gold, silver, copper, barite, phosphate, and other mineral commodities.

According to the seller's deed, the mineral rights include *"the right to do such exploratory or development work as is necessary or convenient, and the right to mine and extract the same, and to use such surface lands as may be required for all operations pertaining thereto..."* with appropriate compensation to the surface owner for the value of the timber and land disturbed. The mineral rights do not include rock and gravel, nor gas, oil, or other hydrocarbon substances.

Buyers interested in purchasing parcel portions, or buyers who wish to acquire alternative parcels should contact the Project Manager at (800) 315-2199. Pre-emptive bids will be entertained. For a complete listing of the mineral rights parcels available in this auction, please refer to the property summary in this brochure.

Twelve Parcels, Ranging in Size from 8.9 to 120 Acres!

650 Acres of Patented Land Throughout Western Montana

TO BE SOLD WITHOUT RESERVE, SUBJECT TO A MINIMUM BID OF $100.00 PER ACRE!
Certified or cashier's checks required to buy: Parcels up to 50 acres: $1,000
Parcels from 51–70 acres: $3,000
Parcels over 71 acres: $5,000

his is a once-in-a-lifetime opportunity to name your price on magnificent land parcels that are ideal for ranching, mountain home sites, hunting, prospecting, exploring, hiking, camping, and fishing. Entrepreneurial opportunities include harvest of timber, mineral exploration, hunting clubs, fishing camps, or a base for adventure excursions throughout the area.

Located in seven counties throughout western Montana, these patented land claims are the legal ownership of the surface rights and all the mineral rights below. Many of the properties are located adjacent to rivers and creeks, and many have convenient access to state roads and Interstate 15.

All land parcels (except the 120-acre parcel in Lewis and Clark County) are subject to a 3% NSR (Net Smelter Return) royalty to Western Energy Company. For a detailed listing of the parcels available, please refer to the property summary in this brochure.

Source: Reproduced with permission from Sheldon Good & Company Auctions, LLC.

our program was being used to make a market where one otherwise did not exist. We placed numerous advertisements in a variety of newspapers, magazines, and trade publications that were designed to capture the attention of our targeted audiences. We also sent out some 10,000 brochures to a likewise targeted audience, which included brokerages

R *obert* D. H *atcher*

"Sheldon Good & Company advertised extensively for this auction, and those efforts gave me the greatest assurance that every prospect would be reached. How do you know who the most likely prospects are? In this auction, the contractor who had moved the earth for Kendall Mines purchased the most property. I didn't even know such a guy existed locally! Another bidder was a Silicon Valley attorney who had never even looked at the property. Also present were an asphalt contractor from South Carolina and a lumberman from Florida. Sheldon Good & Company had located our prospects."

that might have interested clients we otherwise wouldn't have found via our advertising campaign.

As a courtesy, which we virtually always do and particularly if we are selling a property that is tenant occupied, we did a postcard mailing advising the various surface rights owners that we were selling the mineral rights under their properties at the auction. Many of the mineral rights parcels we were selling were very large in scope (700 to 27,000 acres each) and in some cases were beneath many, many, many existing homes and commercial structures.

You never would believe what happened: Hundreds of surface owners started calling us to ask if they could buy the one acre or larger mineral rights below their properties. In fact, we had so many calls that Dr. DeVoto opted to publish a preauction price list for buyers for no other

A *lan* J *oscelyn*

"In usual times, mining companies would have represented the logical market for the mineral rights, but with the passage of Initiative 137 (the only law passed anywhere in the world banning the use of cyanide in gold recovery), mining companies viewed Montana in much the same light as Siberia: wonderful mineral resources, unacceptable political risk."

R *obert* D. H *atcher*

"As a person who has dealt in land all my life, I am convinced that it is of great value and importance to put the land and below-surface minerals back together whenever possible. At one juncture the small local landowners had an opportunity to do this at an affordable market price."

reason than to satisfy them. Although he was trying to be a good guy, the media hailstorm that followed was right out of a movie. Basically, the local media sought to demonize us and find a malevolent reason for our innocently offering surface owners the right to buy the mineral rights below their properties. Everyone seemed to want to get in the act.

The local newspaper, *The Missoulian,* wrote several articles about the auction. We wanted to include them in this chapter, but the newspaper refused to grant permission. It's pretty funny when a newspaper refuses to let people read its columns, when at the time it wanted *everyone* to read what it had to say.

Despite the articles that appeared in the newspapers, a number of subparcels were sold to interested surface owners who wanted to consolidate their surface and subsurface rights, viewing the auction as an opportunity that had never been available before.

A *lan* J *oscelyn*

"Part of the strategy for selling Initiative 137 to the electorate had been to demonize mining companies. Because the election campaign was conducted while mining companies were muzzled by a law prohibiting them from speaking on the issue, the debate was one-sided and mining companies generally were well splattered with mud by the end of the campaign. Canyon Resources was, as I have come to put it, politically disadvantaged. Everybody felt entitled to take a free shot at the company and took the same license with Sheldon Good & Company as with the Canyon Resources agent."

A *l a n*   **J** *o s c e l y n*

"Even though the court's reasoning mentioned the need to keep assets in Montana to ensure reclamation, its injunction tied up the funds actually being used for continuing reclamation, and it's highly doubtful the plaintiffs' lawyers would agree the seized funds can be used for reclamation, as their intent (God bless us lawyers one and all) was to try and get money set aside for their clients."

I wrote to the *Missoulian,* which was the most widely read newspaper in the region, and it published my article (see Figure 4.3) the Sunday before the auction. On the same day that my opinion article ran in the Sunday *Missoulian,* a district judge in Lewistown ordered that up to $12.6 million in proceeds from Tuesday's upcoming auction be deposited in a

R *o b e r t*   **D.**   **H** *a t c h e r*

"In my mind, a problem of perception developed with the ore and mineral rights due to, I think, a misunderstanding in the media and environmental communities that led to bad publicity for our client, Canyon Resources. I have a deep interest in the environment and represent the International Real Estate Federation based in Paris and at the United Nations in an NGO capacity. My observation is that Canyon Resources is a mining company that could bring a projected $3 billion of income to Montana in an environmentally friendly mining operation and has been denied the opportunity to bring jobs and greater economic welfare to the region because of the environmental misperception.

"As auctioneers of natural resource properties, I find there is a sensitivity involving the environment that might not be as important in the sale of other types of real estate. Many firms need to convert natural resources real estate to cash. The experience gleaned from the Canyon Resources project can be brought to bear on helping other firms solve problems in this area so they can maximize their sales when converting real estate to cash."

FIGURE 4.3 *Steve G*

Canyc
miscc

By ST

C

the n
that
on /
fro'
par...
obliged to offer ...
publication of these inaccu...

Sheldon Good & Co. was hired by
Canyon Resources to sell at auction
Canyon Resources' surplus Montana
holdings, which consist of 900,000 acres
of mineral rights and 2000 acres of surface rights located throughout the state.
After analyzing the portfolio, it was decided that it would be sold in 700- to
27,000-acre parcels for the mineral
rights and 7- to 120-acre parcels for the
surface rights. A decision was made
that the auction would serve to accommodate a bulk sale of these holdings;
consequently, affording investors the
opportunity to buy these parcels and
subdivide them as they saw fit.

Though neither our company nor
our client was obligated to, we mailed
brochures to those affected individual
landowners that we could find informing them that the mineral rights to these
properties would be offered for sale in
bulk at auction on Aug. 6 and that
ownership would transfer from Canyon
Resources to the winning bidder.

Almost instantaneously we began to
receive calls from parties wanting to buy
the mineral rights under their proper-

to our sale, ...

It was never part of ...
our client's plan, to contract on an individual basis with the almost 3,000 affected landowners. Canyon has elected
to sell these mineral rights in bulk,
with thousands of acres being sold at
once to what we anticipate will be a relatively small group of investors precisely to avoid the lengthy process of
negotiating with 3,000 individuals on
price and executing contracts, a
process that could take years to finish.

Canyon Resources is not using the
"threat" of an auction as a tool of in-
timidation, nor is our company being
used as a fundraising vehicle to incite
fearful landowners to pay Canyon Resource an excessive value for these
mineral rights. These mineral rights
will indeed be auctioned in bulk
acreage on Aug. 6, which will create
extraordinary buying opportunity for
those who participate in it.

*Steven L. Good is chairman and chief
executive officer of Sheldon Good & Co.*

njunction, which he later made

al families that had filed suit against

ing Canyon's mining operation had

ce and property. The money was to be

ts at the Kendall mine.

g today.

THE AUCTION

ction marketing had drawn hundreds of calls from bid-
the country and the world. We had set the mechanics of the
that bidders could attend the auction in either Missoula or
wn, Montana, thinking that buyers for the Kendall mine proper-
were likely to bid in Lewistown and the other bidders, particularly
ose from out of the area, would fly into Missoula and bid there.

We had identical staffs at each auction site and had the auctioneers linked by satellite technology, soundboards, and all. Each room could hear the other and in real time. When bidders placed bids in Missoula, the auctioneer chanted in Missoula. When bids were placed in Lewistown, the Lewistown auctioneer cheered them on. Whichever room won—the gavel came down there and the winning bidder selected the parcel or parcels he or she wanted, signed the contracts for them, and deposited the earnest money.

About 200 people attended the auction, split 125 in Missoula and 75 in Lewistown, of which about 100 had come to bid. A number of bidders were locals but other prevailing buyers came from all over the country,

R *o b e r t* **D .** **H** *a t c h e r*

"The Sheldon Good & Company group often travels to the auction site several days in advance to become familiar with the area and the people. During this advance period, some of them went on a float trip; their attorney hiked in Glacier Park; and Steve and several others went fishing on the river. It is always good to see the land being enjoyed."

R *o b e r t* **D .** **H** *a t c h e r*

"Steve had a dozen of his people at each site for the auction. Sheldon Good & Company had shipped crates of equipment and supplies in advance of the auction so that each person had copies of all the documents, calculators, folders, staplers, and so on. In Sheldon Good & Company, there is a specific way to execute every single piece of paper. All of the staff and I wore hunter green Sheldon Good & Company shirts so we were easily recognized to answer all questions regarding the auction process. Dr. DeVoto was so impressed that he asked for a shirt too.

"Personally, my organizational abilities are limited to a tattered, green, pocket-sized notebook that is always with me. People laugh at its appearance but are amazed at the information I pull from it."

including Denver and as far away as Florida. Even the director of the University of Montana's Lubrecht Experimental Forest came to watch.

At the end of the day, including preauction interest, bids were received on 14 of the 82 mineral rights parcels totaling 24,416 acres and all 27 gold mine and patented mining claims parcels sold. When the auction was over, I received a nice letter from Dr. DeVoto thanking us and appreciating "the professionalism, diligence, and experience that your fine team brought to the recent auction of our Montana lands and mineral rights."

We had successfully created a market for real estate products that sell outside of those that fit in traditional real estate marketing methods. The deal had worked because we had properly predicted the type of

A *l a n* **J** *o s c e l y n*

"Seeing the Sheldon Good & Company crew create an upbeat, electric atmosphere at the auction out of the icy cold unwelcome visited on both auctioneer and client in the preceding weeks made me a believer. If they did it here, they can do it anywhere."

products that the market would buy. No one could have predicted the reaction of the judge or of the community at large. We had been part of a true human drama.

SUMMARY: ALAN JOSCELYN

The Sheldon Good & Company chapter of the Canyon Resources story is another chapter of a developing epic. The story of Canyon Resources Corporation and its troubled McDonald gold project reaches deep into Montana's rich mining history, the story of a bonanza lying undetected until modern times, of capricious near discovery and perseverance, and finally the reward of discovery. It is the story of glittering promise turned into richly deserved expectancy by dint of hard work and money, and finally of expectations dashed and expropriation.

When Marcus Daly's Anaconda Company ceased its separate existence, the company's extensive ownership of mineral interests across Montana transferred to Western Energy Company, the mining subsidiary of Montana Power Company, another legendary name now relegated to history. Among these interests were mineral lands located east of Lincoln near the junction of the Landers Fork and Blackfoot Rivers.

Western Energy Company geologists explored the area in the late 1980s, drilling two core-drill holes east of the Landers Fork and north of Highway 200 in an area generally known as McDonald Meadows. These

R *o b e r t* **D .** **H** *a t c h e r*

"I grew up in central Georgia where the basic industries were kaolin mining and timber. I developed a keen interest in geology and forestry as a youngster, choosing forestry for my professional education, and have practiced it for some 40 years. In addition, I have a great interest in history and geography—I like to travel. So the national auction circuit is attractive.

"For the past four years, I have been involved in land and forestry investments in Montana, making monthly trips there from Georgia. On one of my summer trips I heard that the Zortman gold mining properties in the Little Rocky Mountains were going up for a bankruptcy sale in three days. I immediately went to reconnoiter it for an investment group but determined that the potential liabilities that came with the property were greater than my group wanted to shoulder. It worked out that the mine was facing a projected 60-million-dollar reclamation.

"In the discussions with the Zortman bankruptcy representative, he made mention of the former Anaconda Copper ore and mineral holdings in western Montana of almost a million acres, and I made a mental note to research and target the owners as potential auction candidates.

"Later in the year I became aware of timber on Canyon Resources' Kendall Mine and visited the property. I decided that I needed to talk with the president of the company whose offices were in Golden, Colorado, about buying the timber. I called Dick DeVoto, founder and chairman of Canyon Resources. We discussed his timber, and I told him I wanted to come by his office for further discussion. Realizing that I lived in Big Canoe, Georgia, DeVoto asked me if I knew where Golden, Colorado, was located, and I told him I was an old geography teacher. I had considered going to the Colorado School of Mines at Golden so was very familiar with its location. Now I had an opportunity to meet a real mining expert and former professor.

"As soon as I got off the phone, I put together a package of information about my credentials and projects that I was involved in and, more specifically, Steve Good's auction material. On my next trip to Montana I arranged to fly into Denver and drive up to Golden to meet with Dick DeVoto.

"When I arrived at DeVoto's office, we spent some time talking about his interest in selling timber and how we might consummate a deal. He then pointed to a stack of materials at the end of the conference table and said, 'I have another project I would like to see if you can help me with.' The materials and maps he then showed me turned out to be the Anaconda Copper Mining Company ore and mineral package of almost a million acres. So much for being a good researcher!

"My contact with DeVoto led to further discussions and the eventual actuation of the Sheldon Good & Company auction of the Canyon Resources' mining claims, ore, and minerals. The message I want to share is that activity, circulation, and preparation generate business."

two exploration holes, as it turned out, stopped just a few feet shy of the exploration geologist's dream—a previously unknown body of gold-bearing rock containing literally millions of ounces of recoverable gold.

Soon after the two holes turned up a bust, an unknowing Western Energy sold its Montana mineral interests to a company called Addwest Gold, thus beginning the series of events leading to the discovery of the fabulous McDonald deposit.

The rarely achieved dream of gold-mining ventures is to discover and develop a gold deposit with the size and potential of the McDonald deposit. The rareness of the event stems directly from the fact that few deposits like this exist anywhere in the world. When a venture is able, by dint of persistence, savvy, know-how, risk taking, and, yes, sometimes luck, to achieve this, its need and expectation is reward—financial reward sufficient to justify the risks and investments in exploration projects that never result in discovery of an ore body.

Expectation of reward was justified on Canyon's part. The state itself leased portions of the deposit to the venture, with incentives to achieve production of the gold. It accepted the venture's applications for mining permits, charging millions of dollars for processing the permits and justifying the venture's expenditures of many more millions to third parties to advance the permitting.

The McDonald project story is not, however—at least as yet—a story of expectations rewarded but rather a story of expectations dashed, investments nullified, and property expropriated. Antimining activists, who saw mining of the deposit as a threat, procured passage of a ballot initiative prohibiting the use of cyanide to extract the millions of ounces of gold and silver from the McDonald deposit. Cyanide is an enigma: On the one hand, it is one of the world's most widely used industrial chemicals and the equivalent of alchemic magic in dissolving gold and silver from encapsulating rock; on the other hand, it is the agent used to carry out sentences of death in gas chambers. The latter claim to renown predominates in the public psyche, making the banning of its use by miners an easy task, notwithstanding no one has ever died in Montana from the use of cyanide in mining. The name is enough.

The passage of the ballot initiative changed everything for Canyon Resources—one minute designing the mine that would recover the precious metals without being an insult to the surrounding lands and ecosystems, the next forced to prosecute a takings claim against the State for the golden opportunity wrested away as a sacrifice to the intentionally fanned flames of groundless fear. (Believe me, you never want to see the despair in the faces of mining engineers and geologists forced to turn from the joyful labor of developing their once-in-a-lifetime bonanza to watching helplessly over their lawyers' shoulders as their discovery is dragged profanely through the courts, slipping even further from their reach.)

What happened? In a way, the Canyon-Montana saga reflects a struggle being played out throughout our nation between those who produce the food and materials necessary to our lives and those who consume the food and materials but are remote from the production. The now famous red and blue map of our nation illustrating the Bush versus Gore popular election results is, in my view, explained by the distinction between those who are close to primary production and those who are not.

Fewer and fewer of us actually have to deal with the hows and whys of the production of our daily bread and comforts. Many of us live more and more in an antiseptic, high-tech virtual world in which there is no obvious connection between the comforts we enjoy and the price paid to produce them. Our main connection with the outdoors is for recreation.

The result is that antiproduction activists have an easy time of it when they focus the attention of today's public on the unlovely aspects of production—mines, farms, ranches, logging, factories. There's an old saying that if you want an omelet, you have to break a few eggs. Likewise, you have to disturb nature if you want the products that are the result of applying human knowledge and capabilities to the natural world.

As a society, we will eventually find the right balance between environmental regulation and the need to produce. This grand experiment in government we call the United States of America has always required that someone like Richard DeVoto and his shareholders be on the front lines of conflict as we as a people deal with new and evolving issues. As Canyon Resources' relationship with Montana plays itself out, the only real question is whether understanding of the need for balance will come sooner or later.

The Sheldon Good & Company role in the story? It came along when things looked darkest for Canyon Resources and applied its own version of alchemy to turn a nonproducing asset into cash that will allow Canyon to persevere in the struggle.

5

NOTHING BUT NET

Everyone knows Michael Jordan. His basketball talent has not only reenergized the sport but also redefined the meaning of branding and sports marketing. You can hardly watch television or walk through a store without seeing Michael Jordan—his likeness, his picture, his logo. Underwear, breakfast cereal, shoes, golf clothes—you name it—his name is on it. I read some time ago that Michael is one of the most recognized people in the world.

It's no wonder that a group of entrepreneurs decided to create a restaurant in the heart of Chicago's downtown named, of all things, Michael Jordan's Restaurant. During the Chicago Bulls' unprecedented run as world basketball champions, this restaurant was the place everyone wanted to be.

Our involvement in the story started in a roundabout way. One of our associates walked into my office one day and showed me an article in *Crain's Chicago Business,* a local publication extensively read by the business community. The article indicated that the owners of the building housing the famous Michael Jordan's Restaurant were in a serious dispute with their lender, Northern Trust Bank, a well-known and highly respected lender. The article detailed that the restaurant operation was owned and operated separately from the group that had purchased the

M *a r k*   **A .**   **H** *a l e ,*   SENIOR VICE PRESIDENT
Hinsdale Bank & Trust Company

Mark Hale has an A.B. in economics from the University of California at
Berkeley and a J.D. from DePaul University College of Law. Mark has been
involved in Chicago real estate since 1983. Shortly after the Michael
Jordan deal, Mark left The Northern Trust Company and now can be
found at Hinsdale Bank & Trust Company in Hinsdale, Illinois, dispensing
commercial loans to clients and giving advice to those who will listen.

building and renovated it for its use as a restaurant. There was apparently
also a dispute between the restaurant and the building's ownership, which
accelerated the building ownership's default on its underlying mortgage
obligation. Consequently, the holder of the mortgage and lender, Northern Trust Bank, was pursuing its collection rights via the court system
and taking steps to take the building back through foreclosure.

This was really big news as the parties to this dispute included some
of the highest-profile people in Chicago. One of the building's owners
was formerly the chairman of the mayor's election finance committee.
The group controlling the restaurant partnership also owned one of Chicago's most popular high-fashion clothing store operations. The Bulls
had just won three National Basketball Association championships, and
the restaurant was where Michael Jordan, his family, and his buddies
regularly hung out. In fact, a separate, private glass-walled dining room
had been built exclusively for Michael's use. If you wanted a chance to
see Michael or watch a Bull's game, everyone knew Michael Jordan's
Restaurant was the place to be.

Our company had represented The Northern Trust Company and
its subsidiary, Northern Trust Bank, for more than 20 years. In fact,
we had recently conducted an auction for the company on a troubled
downtown Chicago office building that had sold for more than a million
dollars over its original opening bid. The Northern was a good customer
of ours, and as a result of our relationship we were confident that if it
opted to go forward with an auction marketing approach, we would get
the call.

Nonetheless, I called one of my friends at The Northern, who worked as an officer in the Trust Department and was often called in to help with real estate problems by any of The Northern's related companies; I asked him about the deal. He told me that everyone in the bank was aware of the article that had appeared in *Crain's,* but my call was premature. He further assured me that if the situation, in The Northern's view, was appropriate for our services, we would be given every opportunity to present a proposal, the key part of the comment being "in The Northern's view."

I hung up the phone and put the deal on the back burner. "Que sera sera—Whatever will be will be. . . ."

SERENDIPITY STRIKES AGAIN

When I was in high school I had a girlfriend whose family and I became friends. Although I went to public school, my girlfriend, her sister, and her brother went to a prestigious private school in downtown Chicago. Her father was the president of a bank and took a liking to me at an early age.

Every once in a while I would have dinner at their house with the family and argue with her father whether there should be a dress code in school, he arguing "for" and I arguing "against." During one of our dinner discussions about education and its applicability to life, he said something that has stayed with me to this day: "I have found that as I got older every single thing I learned in school I ultimately used in some way."

Boy, was he right. Who'd believe this lesson would shine through 20 years later? I graduated from the DePaul University College of Law and

M a r k H a l e

"I was in downtown Chicago at my desk at The Northern Trust Company staring out at some fine Chicago real estate when my reverie was interrupted by the distinctive ring of my telephone. In my ten years at The

(continued)

Northern, I had looked at a lot of real estate—and my phone rang a lot. I was the person charged with selling real property owned by trusts and estates. I was not popular because the properties were so terrific (and some extraordinary). It was the siren song of a potential bargain that kept my phone ringing. People are convinced that the representative of a trust or estate is either desperate to sell assets, unconcerned about the price, or just plain ignorant about the real estate market.

"The Northern, however, was well aware of the tendency for people to think of it as an easy mark. Over its 100-year history, The Northern had assembled a Trust Real Estate Division of about 15 people who devoted themselves to obtaining the best outcomes for The Northern's clients. From farmland to entire golf courses to office buildings, The Northern's Trust Real Estate Division worked to maximize the value of real estate assets and was willing to assert itself inside and outside the organization in the process. My role was to sell commercial property for The Northern's clients, and I was sometimes loaned out to the banking side of the business when it had a troubled situation. Consequently, any real estate with The Northern's name on it led to a call to me. Given the tendency of people to seek bargains, most phone calls were an opportunity to tell or be told that someone had a moronic view of a proposed deal. I looked forward to the verbal skirmishes—they tended to be good-natured battles as well as opportunities to meet people and make deals.

"This time my admiration of Chicago's Civic Opera Building, which was the view from my window, was interrupted, not by an outside real estate broker or investor, but rather by one of the officers from the banking side of Northern's business. Old, staid trust companies erect 'Chinese Walls' between people from the banking and trust sides of the businesses. To avoid potential conflicts, trust people don't share details on files or clients, a separation that creates a little 'us-them' feeling inside big banking and trust organizations. Real estate permits a greater-than-average fraternization between the two sides, so I was happy to hear from my colleague on the 'other side.' My friend from banking was not too happy, however. He wanted to talk about the bank's loan secured by Michael Jordan's Restaurant."

won the American Jurisprudence Award in the field of real estate transaction. The award is given to the student who scores the highest grade on the one (and only) exam given for the class at the end of the year. I won the award by demonstrating the best understanding of the workings of the state's Mortgage Foreclosure Act—*the law that governs the procedure by which foreclosures are conducted.* Little did I know at the time that I would revisit this topic in a future life.

Several months after my discussion with my banking friend, my company received a call from the head of the troubled loan department of Northern Trust Bank, who asked that representatives of my company meet him in his office.

The Northern Trust Company's headquarters is located in a famous marble-columned limestone, eight-story mansion-style building on the corner of LaSalle and Monroe Streets in the heart of Chicago's central business district. It was founded by one of Chicago's well-known Lake Forest families. The institutional, marbled interior exudes old wealth and true class. Originally known as a world-class trust company, its sister company, Northern Trust Bank, is known as the bank for well-established and very wealthy clients.

Nonetheless, sometimes deals and loans have problems as do all successful banks. As a result, the bank has a department that specializes in dealing with its problem loans. The goal of the department is to either solve the problems causing the borrower to default on the loan or to collect the amount due on the loan by taking back the collateral supplied to guarantee payments.

AVAILABLE ALTERNATIVES

A lender has a number of options when a loan falls behind. Restructuring or refinancing the loan is an alternative whereby the bank rewrites or replaces the loan and is usually done through a negotiation between the bank and its borrower customer. Lawyers may be used in complicated situations, but in the majority of cases the business terms are negotiated between the principals, and the terms are then codified by lawyers in a variety of writings.

Items that are regularly restructured include:

- Changing the rate of interest paid
- Extending the term or amortization period during which the out-standing balance will be paid
- Increasing the collateral that is used to guarantee the perform-ance of the loan
- Finding additional guarantors to help the underlying borrowers either make the payments or supply additional collateral
- About a hundred different iterations of the above

Bankruptcy is an alternative available to both the lender and the bor-rower. The lender uses involuntary bankruptcy to force the borrower to surrender the collateral through a federal court proceeding. Sometimes the lender will ask that a trustee or receiver be appointed by the court to take over the management of the property during the pendency of the dispute with the borrower. At other times the borrower will use bank-ruptcy as a way of halting any collection efforts the lender has under way in state court.

The important aspect of bankruptcy is that at any time prior to the state court's issuing a judgment of foreclosure *on the mere filing* of the bank-ruptcy, the borrower can stop the lender's collection efforts in its tracks.

Foreclosure is a state court remedy whereby a lender asks the court to enforce the provisions of the loan that allows it to collect the unpaid amount. There are usually several components to a foreclosure, includ-ing the request to collect the unpaid balance due on principal, the un-paid interest, any penalty interest or costs, attorney fees, and any and/or all of the lender's claims. The things for which a borrower is ultimately liable are usually negotiated at the inception of the loan.

As part of the proceedings, the court is asked by the parties to de-termine the amount that is due the lender as a result of the borrower's default. The lender argues *everything* is due and the borrower argues *nothing* is due, with each party usually explaining away why it is not the party to be held financially responsible for the default.

Ultimately, the court makes a ruling and then issues a judgment of foreclosure. Once the judgment is entered, the lender can then ask that the sheriff *or* some other party sell the property in a forced auction sale. The lender reserves the right to bid at the foreclosure auction; because these types of sales are *not* designed to find the ultimate market for the property, the lender usually ends up buying the property by bidding an amount lesser than or equal to the judgment amount granted to it by the state court.

THE NORTHERN TRUST'S PERSPECTIVE

The Northern had filed a foreclosure action against the owners of the Michael Jordan's Restaurant building as the owners had stopped paying on the building's mortgage prior to our being called.

M a r k H a l e

"Chicago couldn't stop talking about Michael Jordan even though he was (temporarily, it turned out) out of basketball and out of Chicago. The building that housed Jordan's restaurant had failed to sustain a solid restaurant or related concepts and uses for years before getting the Jordan name. Most people in the business community were convinced that when His Airness lent his name and fame to the building, the troubles were over. The banker who called me was dejected at the prospect of another failure for the parcel of property. A failure for Michael Jordan's meant a failure for the bank and somehow a failure for Chicago. I reflected on the situation for a few moments and knew there was a solution if people had the courage to implement it. Courage is not always plentiful in the conservative world of banking, but I knew the answer was Steve Good and his organization, even if I didn't see precisely how at that moment.

"Steve and I had been friendly for a long time. His firm, Sheldon Good & Company, had a long association with The Northern and a real flair for accelerated sales. I had seen Steve's firm perform at some extremes in our business. Using an auction technique, the Good firm sold a portfolio of nearly dilapidated Chicago apartment properties at record prices as they capitalized on gentrification, which was occurring in the neighborhood. Likewise, Steve and his colleagues made sense of a tricky ground lease deal with more than ten separate property owners. In that instance, Sheldon Good & Company took a downtown Chicago building from almost a local joke to a product that multiple bidders were fighting to buy."

M *a r k* **H** *a l e*

"The Michael Jordan's Restaurant deal was a real puzzle. Ownership was at odds with the tenant; the bank was at odds with the ownership; and the high profile star the restaurant was named for was out of town and reportedly cool to the concept now. I hung up the phone after finishing with my colleague from banking and called Steve. After exchanging some pleasantries, I brought up the topic of Michael Jordan's Restaurant. We chatted briefly about the particulars that we knew. That telephone conversation ended with Steve's telling me, 'Stay tuned. My secretary just handed me a note that says Tom Walvoord (then The Northern's director of special assets) and I are going to get together next week.' "

A meeting was set in the office of Tom Walvoord, senior vice president of Northern Trust Bank, in a new high-rise skyscraper that had been bought several years earlier to handle the enormous growth the bank had experienced. Although the skyscraper had a walkway to the main building, Tom's unit had about half a floor in the new building and a corner office for him that was meticulous. Tom was a guy in his late fifties who lived in the country and commuted an hour and a half by train each way every day. He was tall—over six feet—and wore Brooks Brothers suits and tortoise-shelled glasses, and he looked like George Will's twin brother.

I had met Tom several years earlier and enjoyed working with him. He was a no-nonsense guy who always came right to the point. You always knew where things stood with Tom, a quality I like about him. He also never forgot what he said, promised, or meant, and he had a long memory.

Tom invited one of his associates to attend the meeting whom I had never met and began by explaining that the foreclosure was proceeding in the standard way. He anticipated its taking some time before he had a judgment of foreclosure as the owners-borrowers had competent legal counsel who could drag things out for some time. He was also concerned that the borrowers could file bankruptcy at any time, which could further delay The Northern's efforts to collect its loan.

At this point a light bulb went off in my head. Law school revisited—my old law school exam—the state's Mortgage Foreclosure Act allowed the hiring of a *special selling agent* instead of the sheriff to sell the property in a statutorily mandated auction sale. This was a role that *we* could play and shortcut, to everyone's benefit, the massive legal proceedings that would ensue if things continued along the traditional path.

Tom was already ahead of me. He had The Northern's lawyers check the act, and although they had never utilized this provision of the law, he was intrigued with the possibilities. Within half an hour we had mapped out a working game plan. Our company would inspect the property and generate a proposal. If, after our analysis, we thought it feasible, we would propose that the parties, both lender and borrowers-owners, agree to have us retained by the state court as the special selling agent and sell the property for a fair price through a stand-alone auction.

For this plan to work, the owners-borrowers would have to agree. As it turned out, we knew both individuals, and they had a high regard for our experience and track record. They were well-respected members of the business community and had just gotten into a deal that went south.

THE PROPERTY

The Michael Jordan's Restaurant building was a three-story, 17,700-square-foot renovated loft structure just north of Chicago's Loop about six blocks south on LaSalle Street from The Northern Trust's headquarters. A giant basketball with Michael's signature was on the roof with a two-and-a-half story mural of His Airness flying through the air palming a basketball over the entrance.

On entering the building, one saw a gigantic bar on the right side and a small kiosk (maybe 10 by 20 feet) that served as a concession stand selling Michael Jordan jerseys and other MJ stuff. It was rumored that the kiosk did more business than the restaurant and its operator was exempt from paying rent.

The place was so crowded most of the time that it could take an hour and a half to get a table. So it was designed to capitalize on its patrons' desire to drink and be like Mike by wearing his jersey. The main restaurant was done well and looked like many restaurants in renovated loft buildings with lots of exposed brick and track lighting. The draw, of course, was not the restaurant; the draw was the magic of Air Jordan.

We received all of the substantive legal and financial information and quickly analyzed why the deal had gone south. The restaurant revenues were down because Michael had opted to retire immediately following the murder of his father. Despite a valiant effort on Scottie Pippen's part to lead the remainder of the Bulls, the team lost most of its luster. Consequently, the busload of tourists who had flocked to the restaurant in previous years to pay homage to His Airness were finding other ways to enjoy themselves while visiting Chicago.

The restaurant lease provided that the owners-borrowers-landlords received a percentage of the revenues, and with significantly lower revenues the rent had dropped to a point where it could not sustain the monthly mortgage payments due Northern Trust Bank.

Two other aspects were looming in the wings for the owners-borrowers-landlords. First, they were each personally liable for any deficiency (i.e., the difference between the building's price and the amount due on the mortgage plus accrued interest and penalties). The longer the court case dragged on, arguably the more they would owe to Northern Trust Bank and the larger the deficiency would grow. Second, the tenant–restaurant operator had joined the foreclosure suit claiming that the owners-borrowers-landlords had breached certain provisions of the lease and therefore the restaurant's tenant should be released from paying the full rent that would otherwise be due.

THE COURT HEARING

As planned, we submitted our proposal to The Northern and the owners-borrowers and proposed that our auction program be used to expedite the sale of the building. We recommended using a stand-alone (i.e., a one building–one auction) program that was designed to market the property on a local, regional, and limited international basis. We advised that we would need a 75-day lead time before the auction and set closing about 45 days following the acceptance of the winning bid. Included in our proposal was a promotional plan detailing print and electronic advertising, direct mail, public relations, and brokerage activities

M a r k **H** a l e

"Every broker in town was calling (even one of Steve's brokers who was sniffing out the deal but hadn't yet been clued in), a multitude of investors called, and even the restaurant operator called through an intermediary. I was only too happy to send them off to Steve at Sheldon Good & Company when the bank's arrangements were made public. I wasn't sure how the bank was going to extricate itself from the quagmire of relationships between owner and operator, not to mention the relationship between marquee name, adoring public, and creditor—but I did know that they picked the right people. Like Michael Jordan every time he stepped onto the court, this was going to be fun to watch."

that would lead to a fair, as opposed to a distressed, price being generated from the property.

The foreclosure laws required that the lender and borrowers agree to a settlement on the amount due the lender; once agreed on, the lender would be allowed to bid up to the amount owed at the auction.

The matter came before the state court, and the circuit court judge swiftly ratified the plan. He thought that it was a great idea and a good solution to a relatively ugly situation. Consequently, the motion to have us retained as the special selling agent was granted—it was now time to go to work.

MARKETING MJ'S RESTAURANT BUILDING PROCEEDS

Virtually simultaneously with the entering of the court's order employing us, our marketing plan kicked into high gear. We immediately issued the press release shown in Figure 5.1.

The press release set off a wave of stories about the auction, which was covered by the *Chicago Tribune* and then retold in a variety of other papers (see Figure 5.2).

FIGURE 5.1 *Press Release Announcing Auction of MJ's Restaurant*

TAYLOR JOHNSON
A S S O C I A T E S

FOR: Sheldon Good & Company

FOR IMMEDIATE RELEASE: Building Housing Michael Jordan's
Restaurant Goes on Auction Block

Want to be landlord to the restaurant operation bearing the name of NBA superstar Michael Jordan? The three-story, 17,700 sq. ft. loft building just north of Chicago's Loop, at 500 N. LaSalle St., that's home to the spectacularly successful Michael Jordan's Restaurant will be sold, without reserve, to the highest bidder in a public auction February 13.

The suggested opening bid is $1 million.

The sale, ordered as part of a decree in a foreclosure suit, will be subject to court approval. It also will be subject to the restaurant's lease, which runs until 2003, but will have no effect on restaurant operations, other than to change landlords.

To be conducted by Sheldon Good & Company, the open outcry auction is expected to attract bidders nation-wide. Steven L. Good, president of the firm, said the auction "gives every prospective owner a full and fair opportunity to participate in the sale of this exceptional property."

Good added that "combining the auction terms—the building is being sold without reserve—with this particular high profile tenant, and the building's attractive annual net operating income, an exciting afternoon is almost guaranteed."

An Illinois limited partnership which defaulted on a nearly $2 million mortgage owned the building. Last summer, The Northern Trust Co., which held the mortgage, filed for foreclosure in Cook County Circuit Court. As a result of a court order, the parties to the suit consented to a public auction of the building to expedite the sale.

Good said interim financing, two years at a half-point above the prime rate, will be available to the successful bidder. The restaurant lease, which will have approximately seven years remaining at the time of the auction, can be extended by the current tenant for an additional five years, he added.

The restaurant, Good said, is "wildly successful. Revenues have increased every year and they're still growing." The building received a $3.5 million renovation before the restaurant opened in 1992.

Sheldon Good & Company, the nation's premier real estate auction firm, has sold more than $6 billion of commercial and residential real estate, more than any other real estate auction firm, since its founding in 1965.

For more information about the auction and the building, contact Sheldon Good & Company, (312) 630-0915.

###

Source: Taylor Johnson Associates Advertising & Media Relations.

FIGURE 5.2 Chicago Tribune *Reports Legal Issues and Auction*

Building housing Jordan eatery on the block after owners default

By Steve Kerch
Tribune Staff Writer

Maybe you can't block Chicago Bulls superstar Michael Jordan's jump shot, but you may be able to take a shot at being his landlord.

As part of a decree in a foreclosure suit, the building at 500 N. LaSalle St. that houses Michael Jordan's restaurant is being ordered onto the auction block. The repository of Juanita Jordan's macaroni and cheese is safe, however; the pending sale will be made subject to the eatery's existing lease, which runs until 2003.

"The restaurant is wildly successful. It continues to grow [in revenue] every year. The 1995 sales should exceed $7 million," said Steven Good, president of Sheldon Good & Co. Auctions, which will conduct the sale in mid-February.

But the building's owners, an Illinois limited partnership, were not so fortu-nate. Paul H. Stepan and Gerald S. Kauf-man, who according to court documents personally guaranteed the partnership debt, defaulted on a nearly $2 million mortgage held by Northern Trust Co., which filed for foreclosure in Cook County Circuit Court last summer.

Good said that, in an agreement among the parties to the suit, his firm has been hired to sell the property to the highest bidder. But Good said the build-ing, given its high-profile tenant and its annual net operating income of $350,000, should garner national attention.

As to who will eventually be the les-sor to Michael Jordan, Good would not speculate. "But I told my son that if Den-nis Rodman buys it, he'll probably change the color of the roof."

We also produced some 10,000 colored brochures that gave an at-a-glance description of the terms of the auction and attributes of the prop-erty. You can see what the brochure looked like in Figure 5.3.

As is usual with celebrity restaurant properties, we had an enormous response. We fielded hundreds of calls from all over the world—every-one wanted to find out about the deal on Michael Jordan's Restaurant building.

Problems Develop with the Tenant

As mentioned earlier, the tenant–restaurant operator had joined the state's lawsuit claiming breaches of various sorts by the owners-landlords.

FIGURE 5.3 *Brochure Describing Auction*

500 N. LaSalle Street • Chicago, Illinois

**OFF SITE DUE DILIGENCE
MATERIAL REVIEW:**
You may review all of the due dili-
gence material at the offices of
Sheldon Good & Company, 333 W.
Wacker Drive, Chicago, Illinois on the
following dates:

9:00 – 11:00 a.m.
Tuesday, January 16
Wednesday, January 24
Tuesday, January 30
Friday, February 9

You must sign a confidentiality agreement and purchase a Bidder's
Information Packet prior to inspection
of the property. Please call
(312) 630-0915 to arrange an
appointment for inspection.

BIDDER'S INFORMATION PACKET: The Packets include the Purchase & Sale Agreement, Terms of Sale and other due
diligence information. Packets are available at $35 each and may be obtained (a) at all Off and On Site Inspections or (b) via
mail or fax (312) 346-1233. Shipping is available via Federal Express second day at an additional cost of $15 per Packet.

Almost immediately on our being retained, we received a telephone call
from the lawyers representing the tenant demanding various things.
First, they wanted us to make it clear in our promotional materials that
we were selling the Michael Jordan's Restaurant *building,* not the restaurant itself. Second, they wanted us to inform all interested buyers that

FIGURE 5.3 *Brochure Describing Auction, continued*

17,725 Sq. Ft. Loft Building
Currently Leased to Michael Jordan's Restaurant

Suggested opening bid: $1 Million

TO BE SOLD WITHOUT RESERVE SUBJECT TO COURT APPROVAL

Certified or cashier's check required to bid: $100,000

The quintessential armchair investment, this prime three-story commercial building is leased to Michael Jordan's Restaurant as sole tenant through December 31, 2002, with one five-year renewal option. The property was completely renovated by the tenant in 1993 at a cost of approximately $3.5 million. Situated in the popular River North area, the building's previous tenants include Ireland's and Burhop's restaurants. The 'restaurant row' location is part of the regentrification of River North, which has flourished since the 1970's. The area is replete with loft buildings that have been adapted for commercial, residential and retail use. The Michael Jordan Restaurant prop-

erty is close to prestigious Michigan Avenue and the busy Merchandise Mart. Ontario Street, just to the north, has now replaced Rush Street as the hot new nightclub district and is extremely popular with both Chicagoans and tourists.

NET OPERATING INCOME:
(1994) $332,000

LANDSITE: .141 acres or 6,168 sq. ft., L-shaped

FLOOR AREA RATIO: 2.87

ELECTRICAL: Three-phase, 240 volt, 1,200 amps

BASEMENT: Partial utility with 275 sq. ft.

HVAC: Rooftop forced-air, three-zone system

SPRINKLERS: Fully sprinklered

ELEVATORS: 2 new 2,500 lb. capacity cars

PLUMBING: Men's and women's rooms on each floor, finished with quarry tile

ZONING: C3-5, Commercial Manufacturing District

REAL ESTATE TAXES:
(1994) $128,640.36
17-09-245-014 PIN

FINANCING: Excellent non-recourse financing is available to a qualified purchaser through the Northern Trust Company, with a downpayment of 40% of the purchase price or $800,000, whichever is greater, for a two year term, interest only, at a floating rate of prime (as established by the Northern Trust Company) plus 0.5%. Please see the Bidder's Information Packet for details.

Source: Reproduced with permission from Sheldon Good & Company Auctions, LLC.

the tenant had a lawsuit pending that if not settled prior to the auction would transcend the closing and be the new buyer's problem. Finally, they agreed to otherwise cooperate with us fully as they, too, saw the immense benefits of our auction program to all concerned.

As part of our development of the preauction descriptive materials, which included the sales contract the prevailing bidder would sign on winning the bid, we decided as a strategic matter to bring an action before the court as the agent of the court. We had our counsel bring a motion to compel a settlement of the tenant's grievances in order to create stability in the transaction. Without this matter's being settled, we couldn't accurately forecast the rent that would be paid, and that would have disastrous consequences on the bidding. The court agreed. Ten days later, about 45 days prior to the auction, an order was entered resolving the landlord-tenant dispute.

At this point all of the loose ends had been tied.

Interest Builds

Because we were garnering interest from all over the country and the world, we scheduled a number of preauction viewings of the property, all of which were very well attended.

An interesting part of our business is that because we sell most properties on an "as is, where is" basis, buyers conduct their due diligence in advance of the auction. Consequently, we often get a lot of feedback, particularly from bidders who ultimately decide not to bid.

In this case our prospective bidding audience saw the deal as having great potential but also great risk. Although Michael Jordan had retired, speculation abounded that he would come out of retirement soon and return to the Bulls. If that happened, the auction would be a great opportunity to buy the property; its cash flow had been down based on Jordan's retirement. Arguably, if and when he returned to the Bulls, the revenues of the restaurant would go up as would the corresponding value of the property.

The perceived drawbacks to the deal also surfaced. First, the deal was a restaurant deal, and most restaurants fail within five years of opening. Would this restaurant survive? Second, if the restaurant closed, there would be enormous costs to retrofit it for another restaurant, as most operators seek to change the theme of a failed restaurant. Larry Levy, the famous restaurateur, once told me that the trick in the restaurant business is keeping your customers coming back—a lot of new restaurant themes are coming online every day intended to draw them away.

Finally, although the building was well designed, it lacked its own parking, a drawback requiring valet parking that caused patrons added expense.

THE AUCTION

I served as the auctioneer and had a great time doing it. We had previously arranged to conduct the auction in the Assembly Room at The Northern Trust Company's LaSalle Street headquarters building. The facility is used for large gatherings and is incredibly impressive. We had had an enormous response, and our phones rang off the hook with preferred clients asking if they could come and just *watch* the auction.

As part of our registration procedure, any bidder who wanted to participate had to either bring or put on deposit with us $100,000, which served as earnest money should they prevail in the bidding. At the same time, each bidder had already received a bidder's information package that contained all of the financial and legal material about the property, including the real estate sales contract that governed the terms of the auction. We would open the bidding, and on the gavel's coming down announcing the property as sold, the winning bidder would execute the preapproved contract as would I as the official agent of the court.

The auction was set for 2:00 PM, and our staff started setting up for the auction before noon. We set up the room theatre style with a podium and microphone in the front and seating for about 150 people.

Tom Walvoord and his associate, a delightful Austrian chap who was having a great time with his first auction, met with me and another senior member of our company hours before the auction in Tom's office. Because it was lunchtime, the four of us decided to grab a bite to eat, and we walked via the walkway to the bank's cafeteria in the main building.

Once we went through the cafeteria line, got our food, and were seated, a funny thought struck me: "Why aren't we eating at Michael Jordan's Restaurant?" The thought passed quickly and it was back to business.

Tom wanted to receive a last-minute briefing on the exact details of how I was going to conduct the auction. He was charged with potentially bidding on behalf of The Northern Trust and asked many of the questions that bidders normally ask. I explained to him that the bidding was slated to open at one million dollars; from there it was just a matter of who held up his or her hand the longest. I also told him that because The Northern Trust had the right to bid, it would own Michael Jordan's Restaurant by day's end if he held up his hand the longest.

We started registering bidders at 1:00, and by 2:00 the Assembly Room was packed. One set of bidders was a group of Mexican nationals who had flown in to try their hand at buying a famous place. Other bidders had come to try to take advantage of what they perceived to be a great buying opportunity. Several television camera crews, including superstation WGN, were there covering this truly newsworthy event.

This was going to be fun.

After the normal introductions, which included explaining the procedure for bidding, the terms of sale, and a practice round of bidding, we were ready to start.

"Do we have an opening bid of one million dollars?" I cried out, slamming the gavel loudly against the podium to commence the horserace. Four hands shot up.

"How about a million one?"

"A million two?"

"A million three?"

Seven minutes later the bidding closed.

"Sold, one million nine hundred seventy thousand dollars."

Tom Walvoord of The Northern Trust Company never raised his hand, although he did get back all of the company's money plus interest.

6

NEED A GENTLY USED CHURCH?

One of the areas of our practice that I relish is representing nonprofit, religious, and/or philanthropic organizations. In fact, we have sold over a $100 million of surplus facilities to, and for a variety of, these organizations. They include public and private elementary, middle, and high schools; colleges, either a portion of or their entire campus; synagogues; libraries; social service agency properties; parks; and one of my personal favorites—churches.

I enjoy a lot of things about representing this constituency. First, I like working with people who are involved in church organizations. Unlike most business situations, these organizations are usually volunteer driven. The people running the organizations are there because they *want to be* not because they *have to be*. True, in many cases there may be a professional staff in place to help manage the organization, but my experience is that the altruistic nature of the organization ultimately shines through everyone involved. Second, the nature of the properties are usually good candidates for our auction programming because they are unusual and therefore not easily valued. More easily valued properties are handled through our conventional/traditional brokerage company and usually fall outside of my direct involvement, as I gravitated from the brokerage to the auction area some 15 years ago. Last, the buy-

The Reverend Frederick Aigner, PH.D., PRESIDENT

Lutheran Social Services of Illinois

The Reverend Aigner was elected president of Lutheran Social Services of Illinois (LSSI) in June 1997. Founded in 1867, LSSI is a statewide not-for-profit social service agency of the three Illinois synods of the Evangelical Lutheran Church in America (ELCA).

LSSI provides a broad array of community-based and residential services to people of all ages, races, and beliefs, and touches the lives of thousands of people annually. LSSI's services include counseling, mental health programs, substance abuse treatment, residential treatment for children and adolescents, early childhood education and childcare services, programs for adults and children with developmental disabilities, foster care and adoption, housing and services for older adults and individuals with disabilities, nursing care, and programs for prisoners and their families. LSSI has an annual operating budget of nearly $90 million and employs approximately 1,900 people.

Pastor Aigner came to LSSI with a long history of personal commitment to the church and social services. From 1983 to 1997, he served as senior pastor of Our Savior's Lutheran Church in Arlington Heights, Illinois. Prior to his work at Our Savior's, Pastor Aigner served Christ the King Lutheran Church in Florissant, Missouri, and Christ the Shepherd Church in Altadena, California.

He is a graduate of Wittenberg University, Springfield, Ohio. He received a master of divinity degree from the Lutheran Theological Seminary at Gettysburg, Pennsylvania, and a doctorate from Graduate Theological Union in Berkeley, California. Pastor Aigner served on the LSSI board of directors from 1990 to 1996, and he is also president of the G.J. Aigner Foundation, Inc. Currently, he serves on the board of the Chicago Alliance for Collaborative Effort and the Governor's Families and Children Leadership Subcabinet.

ers who are attracted to these properties are often some of the best people you are ever going to meet. Most of them, like their selling counterparts, are volunteers, interested in helping their cause or organization for no other reason than to give something back to the community in which they and their families live.

My wife and I have always believed in volunteerism and from the time we were married in our mid-20s have always served on some type of philanthropic, community, or religious board of directors. We have embraced the philosophy that if people like us don't help, who will? Some of the more notable groups with which we have been involved include United Cerebral Palsy, Easter Seals, the United States Holocaust Museum in Washington, D.C., Lincoln Park Zoo in Chicago, DePaul University College of Law, Syracuse University, our local public school district charitable foundation, and an ongoing list.

We also became involved conducting fundraising auctions for charities by accident when we attended a black-tie gala ten years ago with some friends; I was spontaneously asked to fill in for a good-natured volunteer, who was trying to be an auctioneer and failing miserably. Here we were at a black-tie, $500 per seat, blue-blooded event at the Ritz Carlton Hotel with friends of ours who were on the board of directors of the charity. My wife's friend was in charge of the live auction part of the evening, which was scheduled for after dinner, basically as the floor show and main fundraising event. Within the first two minutes of the volunteer auctioneer's taking the podium and asking for bids, it was clear that the rest of the evening was in big trouble.

If you have ever attended a fundraising auction where the auctioneer is lousy, all I can say is that it is a truly painful and embarrassing experience, especially when 30 volunteers put in a year's worth of work to plan a "kickin'" party.

Out of complete desperation, my wife's friend turned to me and asked if I would substitute for this poor guy before someone threw a rock or tomato at him. I had had a couple of drinks and, being good-natured, empathetic, and a little tipsy, agreed to do it. I got up on the spot and took over. I asked the audience to give him a round of applause before he departed the podium, and they politely complied. I'm not sure whether it was courtesy or relief to see him go.

Anyway, I picked up where he left off. All I can say is a good auctioneer makes for a good floor show; when the auction was over, I had made friends with 30 board members who knew I had helped to save their event. (As a footnote, some ten years later, we do almost 100 charity events and raise over a million dollars a year as our pro bono community service.)

"What does this have to do with real estate?" you are probably asking yourself. The answer is that a couple of years later one of those heretofore unknown board members suggested to the local Lutheran Church bishop that the church hire us to sell eight churches in one crack—the largest single portfolio of churches sold at one time in the greater Chicago area.

We Get the Call

I returned to my office after lunch on a late summer day and looked in my telephone message box. Among about ten messages was one from a lady, which read, "Got your name and want to talk to you about selling some churches." Obviously, I was intrigued, as I didn't often get messages like that, so I called her back immediately. It took a couple of tries as she had left home and office phone numbers. I called her number at home first and got an answering machine, then called the office number and learned that the office was, in fact, in a church.

A day or so later we connected. By the sound of her voice she was an older woman, a volunteer, who had been involved in her church for many years. She held a trusted position in the church as its Church Council president and had great authority to sway her group to her views. She had called me because she had heard of me through the bishop, who had heard of me through some friends that had seen me at a fundraising event and also knew of some of our real estate disposition activities for other nonprofit organizations, including Lutheran Social Services.

She told me that she was the president of one of the congregations that were part of a group of small Lutheran congregations that had decided to merge into one larger congregation. This was being done as a result of many of their former congregants moving from the city to the suburbs over a prolonged period of years. Her group owned eight neighborhood churches that they wanted to sell because no one church was large enough to house the entire consolidated congregation. The game plan was to sell the eight churches and build a new facility with the proceeds that would house the consolidated 1,000-member congregation. Not only did they need a church but they also needed office and Sunday school facilities—a building that would be hard to find and probably have to be built from scratch.

Another problem was that they couldn't *buy* anything until they *sold* their existing churches because they needed the cash from the existing churches as a funding source for the acquisition and construction of the proposed new facility. Have you ever tried to figure the value of a 40- to 90-year-old neighborhood church with no parking? Until recently, they hadn't either.

Before we hung up, we made a date to get together at the central church, which was being used as the headquarters for the seven other congregations.

THE INITIAL MEETING

Doing business with religious organizations and nonprofits is a much different experience than doing business with their private business sector counterparts. Sometimes things are decided by committees, sometimes by single individuals. The problem most of the time is understanding the decision-making chain of command. Our first meeting was held at St. Andrews Lutheran Church (recently renamed the United in Faith Church), which was the largest and most central of the eight churches.

The church was located in an older, well-established working-class city neighborhood that could have been in any older city in the United States or Canada. A local bakery, bar, and automobile repair shop were right down the street from the church. There were several main thoroughfares of seven or eight blocks in each direction, and most of the local homeowners were part of the thrifty working class that George Baily, in the famous Christmastime movie *It's a Wonderful Life,* fought so hard to defend.

St. Andrews was the only neighborhood church that had a parking lot, albeit a very small one. As I parked my car on this summer afternoon and walked into the church, some white-haired ladies were coming out just after having sponsored a Golden Diner (city of Chicago Department on Aging congregate dining site).

I asked for the church office and was immediately directed to the right place. The office consisted of a front office with a secretarial area and a private office for the pastor. The office was circa 1955 and reminded me of Clark Kent's and Lois Lane's offices in the old *Superman* television reruns.

As I walked into the office, the president of the church immediately recognized me and greeted me warmly. She was a stately, white-haired, soft-spoken person with steel in her words who I guessed to be in her late sixties or early seventies. She had retired some time ago from her private sector job, taking a volunteer position with the church and having been a congregant for more than 50 years.

She showed me into the pastor's office where the pastor was waiting. He was a tall, good-natured-looking fellow in his midforties with rosy cheeks that reminded me of the guy in high school from homeroom that everyone liked.

The meeting began with the pastor and the president reiterating the situation for which they had called us. Their plan was to retain us to help them find a new church or a site on which to build one and also have us try to sell their eight churches on a conventional brokerage basis.

I asked them for background information that would help provide a framework for us to put together a plan that would work. One of their congregants was a local real estate broker and had provided them with some guestimates as to the value of their churches. They had a ballpark idea of the size of the church they sought to build, but they lacked the financial wherewithal to move forward without the monies from the sale of the existing churches.

After about an hour of background discussion, I put a working theory on the table that I thought was better than their current approach, which can be very dangerous in this type of setting. Many times, these types of groups, while soft spoken, want *their* plan executed for no other reason than that they have obtained a consensus within their group— typically no small task. Organizations that work through consensus have a very hard time in situations that require creativity for the simple reason that their decision-making process results in a decision with the *lowest common denominator* and not the *best idea presented.*

I have met many people in service businesses that adhere to a "give the customer what he wants" philosophy even when they know that the customer is being shortchanged. I had made a philosophical choice years before to always say what I *really* think, as relationships have to be grounded on a mutuality of approach. People have to buy into the same way of solving a given problem. I also believe that intelligent minds can disagree intelligently, and the dialogue that flows through the process often produces superior results.

THE PLAN

I explained I thought that, while not wrong, a better approach could be used than the one they were contemplating. I suggested a three-step plan.

Step 1: Sell the Real Estate First

Irrespective of their broker's opinion, it was clear that the value of the properties could vary widely. It was also clear that the congregation's ability to buy or build a new church was directly dependent on the proceeds that would be garnered through whatever sale process was ultimately adopted. Consequently, I urged them to delay their search for a new facility and focus their efforts on selling their existing ones.

Step 2: Lease Back One or More of the Churches Once They Were Sold

The congregation needed to quantify *with specificity* the total dollars needed to achieve their ultimate goal. They were already operating out of their largest existing facility, St. Andrews Lutheran Church (now the United in Faith Church), where, coincidentally, the meeting was taking place.

Our recommendation was to sell *all* of the churches on an individual basis *simultaneously* and arrange to lease back St. Andrews for a period sufficient to buy or build a substitute facility. The initial problem was determining the length of time they would need to stay via the lease, as it was speculative at best when their new facility would be available.

We discussed several alternatives and ultimately chose to have them write a three-year lease that would survive the closing with the rent set at the market and where they had the right to cancel the lease on six months' prior notice to the new buyer/owner. In this way they would have enough time to find what they needed while avoiding being encumbered with a long-term financial obligation should they find something right away.

We also reasoned there was a high probability that the invested returns of the proceeds of the sale of the churches were likely to be equivalent to the rent that would be required under the lease.

Step 3: Find or Build a New Church

Once they had the cash in hand, this part of the proposition would be easy. Many of the congregants had lived in the community for decades, and because we were dealing with a very limited geographic area, it was clear that in all likelihood they would find a site and build a new church because there was no other church in the immediate area available for sale. In fact, they told me that they already had their eye on something else but didn't want to discuss it at that time.

The meeting broke with the idea that we would be given the substantive descriptive, legal, and financial information about the properties and then put together a detailed proposal that would address their disposition options consistent with the three-step approach that I had presented to them. We would also arrange to physically inspect the properties as part of our due diligence process.

THE PROPOSAL

It took about two weeks from the time that our meeting concluded for us to review the due diligence materials and inspect the churches.

Based on our analysis, we recommended a program that had not been contemplated by the leadership of the congregation: a sealed-bid auction. We made this recommendation knowing there was a risk that they would reject the idea because it was unfamiliar to them and not consistent with their original wishes. We argued that this was a better alternative for the following reasons:

- The properties were not easily valued, and our experience was that a sealed-bid auction would draw the entire spectrum of potential buyers to each property and yield prices that were in line with the market.

- Each property would be offered individually, and all bids on *all* the churches would be fielded *simultaneously*. This had the enormous benefit of creating a bulk sale without giving a bulk sale discount.
- Being neighborhood churches, the properties were all within several miles of each other. If other religious organizations were in the market, odds were that they might have an interest in more than one church. We could set up our sealed-bid auction so that bidders could bid in the alternative and prioritize their choices (i.e., if we don't get church "A," then we want church "C"; if not church "C," then . . . and so on and so forth).
- We could prestructure the sale of St. Andrews to provide for the leaseback of the property and thereby avoid a lengthy and perhaps fruitless negotiation.
- We could examine the financial strength of every bidder part and parcel to the auction to make sure that we were dealing with *only* qualified parties. This was enormously important because our selling group was going to have a continuing presence in the community and wanted to make sure that the successor/owners of the churches would act in a way that would benefit the community at large.

After reviewing the proposal, the president of the congregation called to tell me that they absolutely loved it. She explained that even so, we would need to make our case to the church's council—a group of about 20 elected church leaders—which she chaired. If the Church Council approved, we would then have to make a similar presentation to the entire consolidated congregation because according to their bylaws, the sale of the churches needed a two-thirds vote to pass. Furthermore, the bishop would have to bless the program as these safeguards were in place to avoid someone's making a horrific mistake.

In a word, my thoughts were, "You go, girl!"

THE APPROVAL MEETINGS

One interesting aspect of representing nonprofit organizations is that most meetings occur on weeknights and weekends because most of their leadership are volunteers and have full-time day jobs. Consequently, my full-time day job requires nighttime and weekend work.

We met with the Church Council about a week later and walked the members through our proposal and thought process. One member was a broker; another an accountant; another a carpenter. It became clear in short order that we were dealing with a true cross section of the community and all of these people shared at least one thing in common: They cared about their community and wanted to do the right thing—whatever that was.

The meeting took about 90 minutes. We explained that *in this case* we thought the market would be essentially local in scope but wanted to do some limited regional marketing just to play it safe. We reasoned that based on the nature of their properties being community churches, we thought the primary market would be other religious or neighborhood-based organizations. The secondary market could be developers or homeowners of some kind as several of the properties included a parsonage (i.e., a house for the local pastor) and we had previously seen these smaller churches retrofitted for residential use.

I have to tell you that at that meeting I was proud to be an American, because I was being judged on what I had to say—not where my ancestors came from. I'm not Lutheran, nor did anyone care. They cared that we had a good, albeit unorthodox, solution to their situation. When the presentation was over, they thanked us, excused us, and called us the next day to tell us that they enthusiastically and *unanimously* voted in favor of going forward. By the way, were we available in a couple of Sundays to address the congregation after their scheduled church service?

They retained us shortly after our meeting with the Church Council, and we implemented the multifaceted marketing plan that we had proposed. We produced print advertisements, a direct mail program, a public relations program, and a brochure for the church portfolio shown in Figure 6.1.

Shortly after our retention I received a call from the bishop's office inviting me to meet him at St. Andrews. Although the meeting lasted only 30 minutes, the bishop was entirely supportive of our efforts and of the Church Council's decision to move forward with the program. We had his blessing.

Several weeks later, the Sunday meeting occurred at St. Andrews chapel immediately following the Sunday morning service. I hadn't real-

FIGURE 6.1 *Brochure Advertising Church Auction*

PERFECT FOR RELIGIOUS ORGANIZATIONS, COMMERCIAL, RESIDENTIAL
AND CONDOMINIUM DEVELOPERS, MUNICIPALITIES OR PRIVATE BUYERS

Eight Magnificent Lutheran Churches

Certified or cashier's checks required to buy: 5% of bid price

heldon Good & Company is pleased to represent United in Faith Lutheran Church in the sealed bid auction sale of these fine properties, which are ideal for a multitude of development or conversion opportunities.

Constructed in an era when craftsmen and artisans created one-of-a-kind works of architectural art, these magnificent churches are adorned with fabulous woodwork and attention to detail rarely found in structures built today. Many of the churches feature soaring ceilings of richly-hewn hardwood, with exquisite brick, stone and woodwork, leaded stained glass windows, balconies and pipe organs in the worship areas. Many of the church buildings have huge finished basements, perfect for community functions and copious auxiliary rooms that are ideal for a multitude of potential uses, including offices, classrooms and meeting facilities.

These properties give religious organizations an outstanding assortment of options for the relocation of their congregations into a first-class worship facility. With their excellent location in Chicago's Portage Park, Irving Park and Jefferson Park neighborhoods, these properties offer a host of exceptional possibilities for developers, whether residential or commercial. These properties would also lend themselves well to municipalities for public use, for private schools, healthcare organizations or private day care facilities.

This sealed bid auction represents a once-in-a-lifetime opportunity to name your price on one, several, or all eight of these distinctive, highly versatile properties.

SEALED BID SUBMITTAL DEADLINE:
5:00 p.m., C.S.T., on Thursday, December 10, 1998, at the offices of Sheldon Good & Company, 333 West Wacker Drive, Suite 450, Chicago, Illinois 60606.
Attention: Project Manager, Lutheran Churches Auction.

AUCTION LINE: (312) 630-0915
FAX: (312) 346-1233

Please use specific property numbers when calling the Auction Line for additional property information.

BIDDER'S INFORMATION PACKETS: Detailed Bidder's Information Packets have been assembled for each property offered in this auction, and include pertinent information related to each property, the auction and the Terms of Sale. The Packets will be available at on-site inspections for $30.00 each, or are available via FedEx second day express for $40.00.

TERMS OF SALE:
This auction is being conducted subject to the Terms of Sale, as stated in the Bidder's Information Packets.

BROKER PARTICIPATION INVITED:
A 2% referral fee will be paid by the ownership to the Realtor®/Broker whose registered buyer closes on a given property. Please contact the Project Manager at (312) 630-0915 for complete buyer-broker registration requirements.

ized it until then, but the two-thirds vote that was required meant two-thirds of *all* of their registered congregants. Said a different way, unless at least two-thirds of the congregants *showed up,* even with 100 percent of their votes the sale would be killed.

The pastor had arranged for the meeting to start a half hour after services had concluded. Buses started pulling up to the church unloading

FIGURE 6.1   *Brochure Advertising Church Auction, continued*

PROPERTIES 6220A AND 6220B

Available in Two Distinct Parcels, or in its Entirety

Nebo Lutheran Church and Former Parsonage

PROPERTY 6220A

Nebo Lutheran Church

3914 North Menard Avenue,
Chicago, Illinois

Originally built in 1913, with a two-story parish hall added in 1936, Nebo Lutheran Church stands as a beautiful example of the era's fine architecture and outstanding construction standards. The richly adorned sanctuary area of the building totals 4,560 square feet, including a 720 square foot balcony and the church has a versatile 3,480 square foot, finished basement. The church seats up to 320 people, including 40 in the balcony. The 6,244 square foot parish hall features three private offices, a reception area, overflow and media rooms, a large hall with stage and a 3,122 square foot finished basement. Total square footage of the church, parish hall and basements total 17,766 square feet.

ZONING: R-3, General Residence Dist.

LANDSITE: Approximately 15,286 square feet.

PROPERTY INSPECTIONS: *By appointment only,* on October 28, November 5, 11 and 17, at 3:00 p.m.

DIRECTIONS: The property is located at the southwest corner of north Menard Avenue and west Dakin Avenue, just east of Austin Avenue.

PROPERTY 6220B

A Beautiful Four Bedroom Brick Residence

Former Church Parsonage

5815 West Dakin Avenue, Chicago, Illinois

This handsome, two-story brick residence, formerly a parsonage for Nebo Lutheran Church, is ideal as a single family residence, or can be used for social services, municipal uses, as a pastor's residence, or other options available under current zoning. The four bedroom, 2.5 bath residence features a generous floorplan, large living and dining rooms, a home library, fireplace, bay windows, rear deck and separate two-car garage.

LOT SIZE: 48' x 123'.

ZONING: R-3, General Residence District.

PROPERTY INSPECTIONS: *By appointment only,* on October 28, November 5, 11 and 17, at 3:00 p.m.

DIRECTIONS: Please see directions for Property 6220A. The property located adjacent to Property 6220A to the west.

Source: Reproduced with permission from Sheldon Good & Company Auctions, LLC.

seniors who were in wheelchairs, walkers, and whatever. These folks had grown up with the churches, which had played an integral part in their lives, and along with their grandparents, parents, and children were here to help—even if that meant just raising their hands (or not) when the vote was taken.

I got to the church about 15 minutes before the scheduled meeting and was escorted to the pastor's office. By now it was a very familiar and very friendly place. When the time came, the pastor led me to the podium in the front of the church after introducing me and my associates as well as the members of the Church Council, all of whom were in attendance. I was awed by the spectacle, but by then everything had fallen into place, and we were convinced that we had a winning program. It was easy to argue for their support—I believed in the merits of it.

Forty-five minutes later, we received a unanimous yes vote with the exception of one congregant who, I was told later, always objected to everything. I don't know his name but figured there is always at least one fly in the ointment.

By this time we had concluded seven weeks of marketing and were having a phenomenal response—literally hundreds of people involved with *other* religious organizations were flocking to see and, we hoped, bid on the properties. They came from everywhere and represented over 25 different religious groups, many of whom I had never heard of. It struck me that we had set in motion the same process that St. Andrews sought, namely, finding a new home for people seeking to worship in freedom.

THE AUCTION

An interesting aspect of sealed-bid auctions is never knowing who is going to bid what; in this case, having eight churches involved, the issue was eight times as complicated.

The terms of the auction allowed bidders to *bid in the alternative*—bidders could bid for more than one property but were not obliged to *buy* more than one property on which they prevailed—and required a certified or cashier's check in the amount of 5 percent of each bid to accompany the approved real estate sales contract that had been distributed in advance. The bids came into our office in all different types of packages: Federal Express, UPS, DHL, hand delivered—everyone who wanted a church had their bid by the 5:00 PM deadline. The bids remained unopened, and by the time they were to be opened, we had almost three feet of bids. In fact, one of the local television stations sent a camera crew to our office to film us opening the bids and were disappointed to learn that we opened and cataloged the bids in *private*. To help them out, I did slit open one of the envelopes for the camera but didn't remove the bid from the envelope until the camera crew left.

One of the nice things about sealed-bid auctions is that many times the bidding is done in private, which, believe it or not, is favored by certain types of bidders. We had scheduled a sales subcommittee of the Church Council to come to our offices at 7:30 PM—two and a half hours after the bids were due. It was also the earliest time the group could see us after their workday was over.

Our staff needed every bit of the time allotted to open and catalog the bids. Although the contract forms we had developed for the property were not complex by comparison with some of our other deals, we had a voluminous number of bids, and several religious groups had opted to bid on different churches in the alternative—just as we had predicted!

More than 40 parties had submitted almost 70 bids. Each property had received anywhere from 4 to 12 bids, with the majority of the bidders being other groups. Many minidramas were unfolding right before us, and there we were right in the eye of a bidding hurricane.

Within the first hour of the meeting, we were able to present all the bids and determine that there were clear winners for three of the eight churches. The remaining five churches required serious discussion. One of the five churches had a curious problem: The highest bidder was a real estate investor who had told us of his intention to demolish the church and put up a convenience store on the site, whereas the second highest bidder was the son of a Baptist minister and had submitted a bid in the hope of buying the church for his father. The second highest bid was significantly below the highest bid, but the Church Council representatives were anguished nonetheless. They also knew that the Baptist minister's dream was to have his own facility, and that dream was being determined right here in our conference room.

The decision? The minister won—better for the church to remain a house of God than a 7-Eleven; hallelujah!

Three other churches had another peculiar dilemma: The top several bidders had submitted bids that were so close in price as to make it unfair to accept the top bids. The last thing we wanted was to have any of the losing bidders later learn of the closeness of the bids and then cry foul on grounds that had they known the winning bid amount, they could have easily beaten it. In these cases there were three choices: (1) award the bid on the spot; (2) invite the bidders to bid openly against each other; or (3) advise the bidders that the bids were extremely close and, as a courtesy, invite them to *voluntarily* increase their bid with the understanding that there would be no further opportunity to bid. If they lost by $1, that would be that. A further complication developed as a result of each of the three churches involved having several parties *bidding in the alternative,* so this process iterated itself threefold.

The decision? Voluntary increase option—all three churches sold.

The final and most discussed decision involved none other than St. Andrews church. As predicted, the bid came in at a number at which the interest income that would be garnered by the sale of the portfolio would easily offset the rent on St. Andrews.

The result? Two days later, after close scrutiny by the church's accountants and Investment Committee, the church was sold—subject, of course, to the lease we had designed months earlier.

All in all, seven of the eight churches were sold to other congregations that reflected the changed demographics of the community; denominations included eastern Europeans, Greeks, Koreans, Philippinos, and a host of others.

Several days later we called a press conference at St. Andrews to introduce the press and the community to the new owners of the churches. No clergy wore the same garb, and everyone in attendance cheered when we took a picture of all of us.

God Bless America.

EPILOGUE

All of the deals closed, and the congregation garnered several million dollars. The congregants were very appreciative and told us they wanted to catch their breath before advising us when they wanted our help in finding a new location.

About a year later, at Christmastime, one of the associates who had worked on the deal stopped me in the hallway of our office to say he had read an article in a weekend newspaper reporting that the congregation had bought an old industrial building in the neighborhood, renovated it, and moved in with cash to spare. I never did see the article but nonetheless reveled in the outcome.

S u m m a r y :   T h e   R e v e r e n d
F r e d e r i c k   A i g n e r ,   Ph.D.

. . . you also, like living stones, are being built into a spiritual house to be a holy priesthood. 1 Peter 2:5

When the apostle Peter wrote these words to members of the early Church, there were no Christian "churches" per se. Two millennia later, it might appear that we are as much in the real estate business as the business of saving souls and serving others—particularly when the need to create positive margins in order to enable mission requires a church property to be sold.

We are the Church (with an uppercase "c"—that is, spiritual houses built of living stones; the church buildings of brick and mortar in which we gather for worship, fellowship, and service are decidedly lowercase). There is, however, a "spirit of place" that tends to take residence in edifices that become important parts of our lives—especially our spiritual lives. Divesting ourselves of such buildings can be daunting.

Having been a Lutheran pastor called to serve three congregations in my 23 years since ordination, I thank God that I never had to oversee the sale of a church. But while serving in the Metropolitan Chicago Synod of the Evangelical Lutheran Church in America (ELCA) since 1983, I know the parties involved in the sale of the church properties that Steve Good writes about in this chapter. I know how difficult it was for some people to part with those properties. At Steve's invitation, permit me to share some thoughts on real estate transactions I have been involved in—either as a board member of Lutheran Social Services of Illinois (LSSI), a capacity in which I served in the early to mid-1990s, or as president of LSSI, a position in which I have been privileged to serve since June 1997.

What would LSSI, a ministry of the three Illinois synods of the ELCA, do with a luxury hotel donated to the agency by a generous benefactor? Sell it, you're probably thinking. And you're right—we ultimately did. But for more than 25 years, in keeping with the donor's wishes, the needs of the community, and a fundamental part of our mission, LSSI operated it as a residence for seniors.

The Hotel Baker in St. Charles, Illinois, was built in 1928 by Colonel Edward J. Baker at a cost of $1 million. When Colonel Baker died, ownership of the hotel—a beautiful Spanish revival building along the banks of the Fox River—passed to his niece, Dellora Norris. She and her husband, Lester, unable to find a suitable buyer for the property, donated it to Lutheran Social Services of Illinois in 1968. With the help of craftsmen, volunteers, and donors, our renovations preserved the architectural integrity of the "crown jewel of the Fox Valley," as the hotel was known, while providing a quality retirement environment for seniors.

But by 1995, despite annual six-figure expenditures on building maintenance and preservation, it was estimated that as much as $3 million would be needed for structural and mechanical improvements that would allow services to continue in an increasingly competitive marketplace. Rents—limited by competition from other, larger senior residences that had since become available—combined with a lack of economies of scale in a 47-unit building and the increasing availability of in-home services enabling seniors to remain in their own home longer led to operating deficits. KPMG was brought in to evaluate potential options. After all options were explored, an informed decision was made to sell.

The "spirit of place" was firmly entrenched in the hotel: Colonel Baker had lived in its penthouse for nearly 40 years; the Baker and Norris families played a vital role in the life of St. Charles; many community residents had held their wedding receptions or other family celebrations in the hotel's Rainbow Room for generations; and the hotel was listed on the National Register of Historic Places. Everyone wanted to make sure that, in ensuring a fair valuation, both the place and its spirit survived the sale. No one wanted it more than LSSI. Happily, Sheldon Good & Company delivered! The new owners wound up investing a reported $10 million in restoration of the Hotel Baker, for which they were recognized by the Landmark Preservation Council of Illinois in the late 1990s. Since then, the challenges of operating a hotel in the postmillennium downturn—in a town devastated by the demise of Arthur Andersen and its St. Charles training complex—apparently led to financial difficulties, with

(continued)

Steve's company ultimately being retained to sell it again—only this time as a completely renovated jewel.

Our sale of the hotel came in the middle of the booming 1990s, when the rising economic tide seemed to raise all boats except those that served the neediest of our citizens. In an ideal world, private-pay revenue from a viable Hotel Baker, like revenue successfully generated by our P.A. Peterson Center for Health in Rockford, Illinois, and St. Matthew Lutheran Home in Park Ridge, Illinois, should have subsidized our other ministries, such as foster care and adoption, maternity services, Head Start and day care for families with low incomes, group homes for people with chronic mental illness or developmental disabilities, substance abuse treatment, counseling, affordable housing, and services for prisoners and their families. In the real world, those other ministries were subsidizing the hotel, a reality that we could not allow to continue.

In an ideal world, the state pays the actual cost of doing business when it contracts with private, primarily private-pay agencies like LSSI to care for the poor and infirm on the state's behalf. In the real world, the 1990s saw the start of an ongoing contraction in state funding of human services that has led to a reduction in our staff by more than 50 percent, the closing of programs, and the auction of several properties just to balance our budget. Closures included Augustana Center in Chicago, where we cared for children and adults with developmental disabilities; Salem Village in Joliet, where we provided skilled nursing home care; and Edison Park Home in Park Ridge, where we provided residential treatment for troubled adolescents. Sealed-bid auctions served us well in the sale of these difficult-to-value facilities. But the value beyond price rightly ascribed to the properties by our supporters made them difficult transactions to announce.

"The Lutherans in the area expressed deep disappointment at the loss of this very visible sign of the caring ministry of the church," wrote the Reverend John P. Petersen in a history of the agency. Although he could have been describing the reaction to any of the divestitures of the mid-1990s, he was writing about the sale of our first facility, the Children's Home at Andover. Founded in 1867 to house children orphaned by a cholera epidemic, it was the first Lutheran charitable institution in Illinois. For 100 years the facility adapted to the evolving needs of children in a changing world. But as a result of the decreased use of institutions for housing dependent and neglected children (in favor of more homelike settings) and the growing problems of maintaining a century-old campus, the program was merged in 1970 with another facility, and the building was eventually sold.

Today the legacy of that caring ministry continues in the form of more than 200 programs at more than 100 sites across Illinois (some leased, some owned). They are places where we put into practice our mission—responding to the Gospel, Lutheran Social Services of Illinois brings healing, justice, and wholeness to people and communities. Each site is endowed with a spirit of place that endears it to our clients, donors, volunteers, and staff.

Current forecasts for the fiscal years state unprecedented deficits and an approaching storm for human service providers—a "perfect storm," some have called it. Our agency and others like us may again be buffeted. But bolstered by the support and advocacy of people of good will—the "living stones"—and with faith in Jesus—the cornerstone on which our agency is built—the spirit of place will continue to watch over LSSI and the people of all faiths we serve.

7

THE WORLD IS
OUR STAGE

Up to now I've talked a lot about a variety of properties that we have handled on a transactional basis. I thought that for no other reason than to change the pace a little, it might be interesting to discuss a really cool deal that we engineered without talking in detail about the properties that were involved. Suffice it to say that some of them sold and some of them didn't, netting our clients millions of dollars.

The important part here is that the legacy of the deal made our company a worldwide player and propelled us into a new league.

TRADE ASSOCIATION WORK

Our company has always been big on involvement in trade association work. Like most service companies, visibility in the business community is the lifeblood of our revenue pipeline. Although it is also true that much of our business comes as a result of past customers as well as their business and legal counselors, absent *new* customers learning of us and believing that we are the premier company in *today's* world, we would have an uphill battle in landing business.

Terrence M. "Terry" McDermott
National Association of REALTORS®

Terrence McDermott is the executive vice president and chief executive officer of the National Association of REALTORS® (NAR), America's largest trade association representing over 850,000 members involved in all aspects of the residential and commercial real estate industries.

Before coming to NAR, Terry was executive vice president and chief executive officer of the American Institute of Architects. The institute is a 65,000-member professional society founded in 1857 to represent the nation's architects.

Terry has more than 27 years of experience in the publishing and media professions. Before taking the top post at the American Institute of Architects, Terry was with Cahners Publishing Company, America's largest business and special interest magazine publisher, for 24 years. He was president and chief operating officer at Cahners from 1987 to April 1993. Terry was the publisher of *Building and Design Construction* magazine from 1976 to 1984 and group vice president of its Electronics and Computer Division from 1983 to 1987.

Terry attended Loyola University, Chicago, and received a bachelor of arts degree in organizational development from the National College of Education in Evanston, Illinois.

He is vice chairman of the board of the National Building Museum in Washington, D.C. He is an honorary member of the American Institute of Architects and the Society of American Military Engineers, and a member of the Urban Land Institute and Lambda Alpha, the land economics society in Washington and Chicago. He is past president of the board of the American Architectural Foundation.

Consequently, we put together a plan every year about the trade associations in which we are going to participate. I mentioned earlier that we handle more than 70 different types of real estate spanning virtually all of North America. Deciding with whom and in what area we are going to invest our time, money, and energy is, therefore, no small task.

We also have to determine the length of time that we are prepared to spend in trying to break into a new trade association, because we have learned that more times than not, particularly with larger groups, it may take a while to learn your way around. Furthermore, some groups are less accepting of new recruits than others, and some groups are not accepting at all.

Another relevant aspect in determining the selection of a given trade association is whether its membership or its sphere of influence is likely to be a source of business for us. Issues like membership composition, geographic dispersion of properties likely to need our services, and the location of the group in the economic cycle also impact our selection process. For example, the trade associations we like the most are ones containing members who either control or advise real estate disposition decisions. Said a different way, it makes absolutely no sense for us to involve ourselves in trade associations composed of members that cannot help us get or do business.

SELECTING THE RIGHT REPRESENTATIVES

Once we have determined where and with whom we want to be, we also need to choose who from our company should participate. Even though this sounds relatively easy to do—it isn't. Our experience is that the individual chosen to represent our company in the trade association at a minimum must *like* the trade association's cause and, more important, the people in it. Absent believing that the meetings are interesting and the members engaging, the new recruit will quickly become a recent alumnus.

We encourage associates' self-selection of trade and professional associations. We have found that although we can provide guidance for the general landscape of these groups, our associates are usually better at determining where they believe their best fits lie. They can also tell, within a meeting or two, whether their personality, experience level, and chemistry are well suited to the group. If so, they carry on. If not, they look for another group until they find one that's a good fit.

We make a philosophical distinction between trade associations and philanthropic organizations: The former are about generating business and professional development; the latter about giving back to the community. Sometimes people get confused. Other times people get lucky and find that the group they become involved in gives them both. I got lucky with the Chicago Association, Illinois Association, and National Association of REALTORS® (NAR).

OPENING ACT

I graduated from the DePaul University College of Law about 20 years ago and passed the bar exams, which admitted me to practice law in Illinois and Florida. In addition to my formal training, a close friend and legal mentor gave me a great piece of advice one summer during law school when I was working in his law firm: Go into the real estate business; you'll get a whole lot further a whole lot faster. It's kind of funny because 20 plus years later, that same guy represented me when I bought out my father's remaining interest in our company.

Having come into the business with a formal legal background, I immediately gravitated to trade associations composed of lawyers. At the outset of my career this was a great fit. We could easily relate to each other; we were *not* competitors and consequently could happily refer business to each other. Just like everyone else in service businesses, lawyers *love* client referrals, and we generate lots of client deals for lawyers to service. I joined a ton of legal trade associations, including the Chicago, Illinois, Florida, and American Bar Associations and made friends with everyone that had any commonality with me. I also made friends with a bunch of folks that had nothing to do with our business that I met through these groups as well.

Our company had always been a member of the Chicago Association of REALTORS® (CAR) as were all the leading real estate companies when I first got in the business. On joining the local real estate board, you *automatically* join the state and National Association of REALTORS® as well. CAR was founded in 1883 and currently has over 10,000 members. NAR has over 850,000 members; however you slice it, that's a lot of members. In fact, it's the largest trade association in the United States.

These groups offer their membership a myriad of goodies: great educational programs, the opportunity to meet individual peers, property information resources, and the largest political lobby in the United States. The national conventions draw an average of 20,000 members annually. REALTORS® are truly a force to be utilized, and the best thing for us is that NAR is based in Chicago—our hometown.

I always knew of these groups but never became active in them. Once in a while I was invited to give a speech or write an article for them or one of their affiliated groups (there are many) and attend the national convention that was usually where the speech was given. One of the fun things about NAR conventions is that because they are so well attended and annually move the host city, attendees are guaranteed to have a great time. Honolulu, San Francisco, New Orleans, Chicago; NAR conventions took me to all of them.

THE PHONE RINGS OUT OF THE BLUE

I was calling into my office late one early fall morning to ask my assistant, Cynthia, for my messages. I am out of the office a lot for meetings, viewing real estate, or traveling and rely on my assistant to schedule everything and talk to everybody. In fact, when we converted the company to a professional partnership some years ago, Cynthia was offered some stock; she bought it and now I'm not quite sure who works for whom.

Anyway, Cynthia was reading me my messages and noted that I had received a call from John Andrus, who identified himself as the president of CAR. Neither of us could figure out why he had called me as my involvement with CAR had been limited to having given a couple of speeches through the years and attending its annual Board of Directors Installation Banquet, which draws 1,000 of its 10,000 members. I had also served as an arbitration judge in one case that lasted a day, but that had been years ago and would hardly be a reason for him to be calling me.

It took a couple of tries, but Cynthia finally reached him. John was high-tech and always on the road. We theorized that if he got caught in a rainstorm, he'd probably be electrocuted by his beeper, cell phones, and other strapped-on electrical gear.

He quickly introduced himself and explained why he was calling. As president of CAR, it was his job to select chairpeople for various committees, and several of the officers had suggested he call me. His call struck me as odd because my dad had been president of CAR ten years earlier, and no one else had ever called me with a proposition either before or after my father's term expired. John explained that he wanted me to accept the position of the chairman of CAR's Commercial Committee and suggested that we get together over dinner to discuss it.

I told him that I was flattered to be the object of CAR's attention but couldn't understand why he was calling me for this position as I had never even attended a meeting of this committee. He persisted in his request for a dinner meeting and, as is usual in life, his persistence paid off. Who was I to summarily dismiss the president of CAR?

DINNER FOLLOWS THE CALL

About a week after our phone call, I walked over to the restaurant, a dimly lit popular Italian place in the basement of a former private downtown city club turned into an office building. I was right on time, and when I checked in with the hostess, she told me that my party was already seated. When she walked me over to the table I immediately saw that it wasn't a table for two—it was a table for seven with six people already seated and one open chair right in the middle of the table reserved for you know who—me.

I recognized only one of the people at the table—Jim Ascot, the immediate past president of CAR. I didn't know him well but had always liked him. Within two minutes I was introduced to everyone else: John Andrus, the current president (the guy who had called me to arrange the dinner); Jim Ascot, the immediate past president; David Hall, the president-elect; Darcy Dougherty, the chief executive officer; Bob Dougherty, the deputy chief executive officer; and Dennis Gano, the director of technology, who also doubled as CAR's Commercial Committee staff liaison.

By the time dinner was over, it was unanimous. I was the new chairman of the Commercial Committee, which meant serving a two-year term. The ambush had worked.

LUNCH IS SERVED

Being the chairman of this committee was fun. I have a great Rolodex and within a short time had organized a bunch of my friends, associates, and colleagues to serve as speakers and roundtable participants for a variety of preset committee luncheons. I also found myself meeting people in the industry that I had read about or whose For Sale signs I had seen on buildings. I was matching up names and faces and having a great time doing it.

As summer rolled around, I got a notice that CAR was interviewing for people interested in joining its board of directors. I figured that since I had another year left as chairman of the Commercial Committee, I would give the interview a try. The board meetings were scheduled for half a day once a month with no meetings scheduled during August and December. Many accomplished guys and gals I knew had loved the board, so—why not?

I received a notice from CAR several weeks later indicating that my application had been accepted after a Spanish Inquisition–style interview. I wasn't quite sure what I was getting into but I was having such a good time with my Commercial Committee guys and gals that I thought it would be a broadening experience at a minimum. I had previously served on a number of other boards of directors, so I was not intimidated by the idea of being on this board.

A couple of weeks later Cynthia told me that a luncheon date had been arranged at the 410 Club, which is a leather-chaired private dining club complete with white linen table cloths in Chicago's famous Wrigley Building (named after the chewing gum folks). She said that it had been arranged by CAR *and* NAR to discuss our Commercial Committee programming. I wasn't quite sure what to make of it but I had learned from my dinner experience a year earlier that the REALTORS® at least fed you well *before* they bushwhacked you.

Anyway, I was already doing what they had asked, and I welcomed the opportunity to share my thoughts and experiences with CAR's national association counterparts.

When I walked into the club, I was the last to be seated. We were sitting in a U-shaped booth with two chairs forming the U of the booth. Two of the people were from CAR—Darcy Dougherty and Jim Ascot. The other two people where from NAR.

I immediately recognized Terry McDermott, the chief executive officer of NAR, from previous conventions and speeches that I had given. He introduced me to his associate, NAR's Chief Financial Officer Dale Stinton, although I had not previously met Dale.

Terry is one of the most charismatic guys I have ever met. He has a way about him that, within the first 30 seconds of talking to him, makes you wish you'd have gone to college with him. He seems to be in his late 50s with smart, horn-rimmed glasses, and is always impeccably dressed in well-tailored and well-pressed suits and custom (at least they look it) shirts; and he ties his tie in a perfect knot. Terry grew up on Chicago's West side, which at the time was Chicago's answer to the Bronx in New York. He loves to talk about Old Chicago politics and, being the next Chicago generation, I always loved hearing his stories. It's too bad Damon Runyon is dead; Terry would have made a great character in a Runyon short story.

The first half of lunch consisted of the other folks talking about their CAR and NAR roles and experiences. Being the newcomer, I did what smart newcomers do—I watched and listened. Then came the main course—me. Except this time I wasn't being bushwhacked; I was being courted. Terry and Dale explained that the leadership of NAR had decided to expand its appeal to commercial real estate practitioners and were in the planning stages of a major convention event. They sought to create a unique educational and marketing event that would attract people from all over the world. The idea was to provide an annual central commercial forum for transactional commercial real estate professionals to meet and do deals *in person*.

I loved it. I thought, "What a great idea. I'd go. We'd all go." Best of all, they wanted to have it in Chicago every year. I paused, then remembered something about watching out for bushwhackers and thought, "But where do I fit in?"

Terry, among his other talents, must be telepathic because just as the voice in my head finished the word *in*, he delivered the punch line. He wanted me to design a worldwide commercial real estate auction forum specifically designed to auction properties that lent themselves to national and international buyers. NAR had been watching our company's commercial real estate programs for years and had purposely chosen us because of our success in selling major properties to national and international buyers. The members thought they would use an auction as one of several permanent forums that would be hosted at their annual commercial conventions. They would promote it via their formidable public relations machine, which reached over a million real estate professionals—both commercial and residential practitioners alike.

NAR had come quite far in its planning for this convention. It had already entered into a joint venture arrangement with the Urban Land Institute (ULI), America's premier trade association for the real estate development community, and the ULI had enthusiastically endorsed the idea of the auction. This was because, as Terry had learned, the ULI had retained us several years earlier, and we had successfully auctioned its former headquarters building at 18th and Connecticut in Washington, D.C., in the heart of Embassy Row. I had been the auctioneer with the winning bidder—Jeane Kirkpatrick, the former U.S. ambassador to the United Nations—who was bidding on behalf of a charitable foundation seeking to occupy the former ULI headquarters building.

These two powerhouse trade associations—NAR and the ULI—had taken the process even further. They had lined up virtually *all* of the who's who in the real estate trade association world to get behind the program. A partial list at the time included:

- Commercial Investment Real Estate Institute (CCIM)
- Counselors of Real Estate (CRE)
- Institute of Real Estate Management (IREM)
- Realtors Land Institute (RLI)
- Society of Industrial and Office Realtors (SIOR)
- American Institute of Architects (AIA)
- Auction Marketing Institute (AMI)
- FIABCI International (the International Real Estate Federation based in Paris, France)
- Lambda Alpha International (the International Land Economics Society)
- National Association of Real Estate Investment Trusts (NAREIT)
- National Auctioneers Association (NAA)
- National Realty Committee (NRC)

In addition were NAR's 39 cooperating real estate associations in 34 countries worldwide. (I had previously either written for or given speeches before many of these organizations.)

As Terry continued talking, all I could think of was how amazing all this was. A year earlier I had been a civilian sitting in my office doing our business. Today, a year later, I had been transformed into a trade association battlefield general. I hadn't even had a plan.

MOMENTUM BUILDS

NAR had a great idea and we had a tiger by the tail. The idea was, as we spoke, iterating and evolving itself. Both Terry and I were good concepts guys, but I was the guy being called on to make our part of the program work. CAR's role was to roll out the red carpet and make the convention attendees feel as comfortable as possible. That they could do in their sleep. But make a worldwide forum where none existed before—that might make *me* lose sleep.

When lunch concluded, we had a deal—a multiyear contract that would stay in place with the understanding that NAR might seek to move the convention event elsewhere if circumstances warranted it; if that happened, then the continuation of our program would be up to the new event organizers. Our lawyers would paper the deal, and NAR would assign a liaison to our auction program. We were off to the races.

When I got back to our offices, I was pumped. I'm a pretty good storyteller, but who would believe *this* story? It was unbelievable. I immediately called a meeting of our senior officers. It took me about 90 minutes to explain what had gone on at lunch. The guys listened and disbelief turned to elation. We have always been opportunistic, out-of-the-box thinkers not constrained by geography, but this proposition was more than even we had ever contemplated.

Years later one of our major investment clients expressed his frustration in marketing a portfolio of four investment properties valued in excess of $15 million via conventional methods. The concept of creating an auction forum for properties with worldwide markets had never been done before, and here we were having the most powerful trade associations in America ask us to partner with them to accomplish this goal. Each participant would win as would our clients, provided we could execute the plan.

THE CHALLENGE IS TAKEN

I really give credit to our guys. Even though it took 90 minutes to explain the deal to our key guys, 45 minutes later we had the deal analyzed and staffing assignments set. If a deal came in from anywhere between the North and South Poles, we were ready.

The First Step Is: Get the Telephone to Ring

I had already discussed during our lunch with Terry the way in which NAR was going to help promote the auction. NAR's plan included four solicitation approaches.

The first approach was via a direct mail letter campaign that went from each sponsoring organization to its respective members. The letters would be authored by each organization's leaders and would be accompanied by a brochure that outlined the conference as well as our worldwide auction program. NAR's liaison coordinated this effort with us, designing the promotional materials needed to succinctly explain our auction programming.

The second approach targeted limited speaking opportunities that were arranged as available through the sponsoring associations. We sent our people to talk up the NAR conference and the auction at events that were being held by the cosponsors. It was impossible to hit everyone, but we made an effort and did speak before a goodly number of them.

The next aspect was a worldwide advertising campaign that we cosponsored with the *Wall Street Journal*. We had a great relationship with the *Journal* that transcended our relationship with NAR and any of the trade associations. We were its largest real estate auction advertiser and, in fact, were one of its advertised corporate endorsers. Figure 7.1 is an advertisement the *Journal* recently ran worldwide in its real estate section.

We had a very close relationship with the advertising people at the *Journal* and on learning of our participation in the conference, they asked to be included as a cosponsor. This was a great opportunity for them to expand their global marketing presence. We all knew we were in good company. Finally, the NAR public relations machine kicked into high gear.

THE PHONE RINGS ALL THE WAY FROM THE SOUTH POLE

The telephone started ringing. Our idea had caught on. Owners of properties that lent themselves to worldwide markets jumped at the chance of being able to include their property in a forum that had never existed before.

FIGURE 7.1 *Advertisement in* Wall Street Journal, *2003*

Over Three Decades of Success

"Since 1965, *The Wall Street Journal* has been our international marketing partner. Having sold some 40,000 properties valued in excess of $8 billion at auction and conventionally across America, the *Journal* is where buyers and sellers find us and some great deals.

"Whether it's a trophy home in the Hamptons, hotels in South Beach, condos in Chicago, development deals in Denver, or any of the 70 different types of real estate that we handle from coast to coast, the regional, national, and international exposure has helped build our company into a household brand name. The *Journal* works for us and will work for you too."

■ *Steven L. Good*
Chairman and Chief Executive Officer
Sheldon Good & Company International

SHELDON
GOOD
&
COMPANY
www.sheldongood.com

We now put our plan in action.

Calls that came in from the western United States were handled by our guys in that region; same with calls that came in from the middle and eastern regions. Owners of properties outside the United States were serviced by specialists in our company that had handled non-U.S.

properties before. The only difference was that all the calls were coming in *simultaneously,* and we had to filter the properties in such a way that their marketing could be done simultaneously. Properties that fell outside of the program were directed to other existing auction forums that were available through our company.

A number of properties surfaced that we felt didn't lend themselves to our auction programming at all. Owners of those properties were directed to conventional brokerages we felt could best service them.

At the end of the solicitation and evaluation period, which lasted about 100 days, we issued the press release shown in Figure 7.2.

We also produced brochures (see Figure 7.3).

After two years of sponsoring its own commercial real estate conferences, NAR and its marketing partners opted to merge its program with a high-technology conference, which was controlled by another organization. The joint conference has served as the premier commercial real estate *technology* event and is attended by some 3,000 practitioners annually.

Chicago was selected as the site for the new and improved conference with the CAR acting as the host REALTOR® Association for this event.

Terry McDermott's contract as CEO of NAR was extended past the date of his scheduled retirement.

I was elected as CAR's 121st president and sworn in at its 120th Inaugural Event.

FIGURE 7.2 *Press Release Announcing International Auction by Global Simulcast*

SUSAN L. BERMAN
ASSOCIATES, INC.

For Immediate Release

NATIONAL ASSOCIATION OF REALTORS SELECTS CHICAGO AS SITE OF FIRST GLOBAL REAL ESTATE AUCTION OF INTERNATIONAL COMMERCIAL REAL ESTATE VALUED AT *$100 MM;* SHELDON GOOD & COMPANY TO CONDUCT LIVE AUCTION DURING INTERNATIONAL REAL ESTATE CONFERENCE

Sept. 24 Auction of Properties in U.S., Mexico, Chile & Caribbean Simulcast in Dallas, Miami, London; Five Prominent Keynote Speakers at Conference; Urban Land Institute, The Wall Street Journal Are Sponsors

CHICAGO—The National Association of REALTORS® (NAR) has selected Chicago as site of the world's **first global commercial real estate auction** and a Chicago-based company, Sheldon Good & Company Auctions, to conduct its live, international event in America's heartland. During what is expected to be a 1½ hour bidding frenzy, Good & Company, one of the nation's leading real estate auctioneers, **will auction an unprecedented $100 million slate of prime international real estate** in the U.S., Mexico, Chile and the Caribbean.

The inaugural global auction forms the cornerstone of "TRANSACT '99," the nation's first international real estate conference developed jointly by NAR and the Urban Land Institute (ULI) with major sponsorship from *The Wall Street Journal* and 50 other national and international trade organizations. Approximately 1,000 delegates from around the world are expected to attend TRANSACT '99, which culminates in the global auction, co-sponsored by *The Wall Street Journal* and NAR.

The event takes place from **2:30–4 p.m., Friday, September 24** in the Sheraton Chicago Hotel and will be simulcast in **Dallas, Miami, and London,** announced Steven L. Good, chief executive officer of Good & Company.

"The Dallas and Miami simulcasts will make it easy for buyers from the Caribbean and Mexico to bid, while London will be convenient for English and German institutional investors," Good said.

The premium and unusual real estate offered for sale at the global auction includes corporate office buildings in **McHenry, IL, Mexico City, and Kansas City, MO;** recreational and resort properties in the **Caribbean, Mexico, Utah, and Michigan's Upper Peninsula;** timberland in **Chile;** mineral rights to

595 Braeside Road • Highland Park, IL 60035-5263 • (847) 681-9030 • (847) 681-9912 (Fax) • sbhsba@aol.com

FIGURE 7.2 *Press Release Announcing International Auction by Global Simulcast, continued*

300 million tons of marble (100 years' supply) in **Nevada** as well as retail and industrial properties in **Texas.**

The properties are as follows:

- A new, 240,000-square-foot, eight-story office building, net leased for 15 years to PricewaterhouseCoopers, in **Mexico City;**
- **Caribbean** resorts in the Turks & Caicos Islands, Salt Cay, and Ocho Rios, Jamaica;
- 300,000 acres of timberland in Chiloe, **Chile;**
- A "European-style" corporate headquarters and light manufacturing facility of a Swiss-owned company in **McHenry, IL;**
- Mineral rights to a mountain containing 300 million tons of marble (100 years' supply) and possibly some gold, in Northeast **Nevada;**
- A vacant, 32-story, 300,000-square-foot former federal office building, listed on the National Historic Registry and featuring state-of-the-art renovation, in **Kansas City, MO;**
- Resort and residential development land in San Carlos, **Mexico,** and in Iron River on **Michigan's Upper Peninsula;**
- Recreational acreage in Salina Canyon, **Utah;** and
- Retail and industrial property in Ft. Worth, San Antonio, and Hearne, **Texas.**

Explaining how the properties were selected for the global auction in Chicago, Good said that his company prepared a "short-list" of 13 premier properties throughout the world, each meeting one or more key auction criteria. "We were highly selective when we assembled the final list," he added.

"This selectivity enables us to maximize the promotional impact of each property, creating drama for the real estate and selectively marketing it to specific types of buyers. We accepted the assignment believing we would have a $5 million group of properties; $100 million speaks strength and credibility of the auction vehicle to move product," he continued.

"We created TRANSACT '99 to encourage the formation of international real estate partnerships and to promote the negotiation of commercial real estate transactions worldwide," said Sharon A. Millett, president of NAR. "We are confident that this $100 million auction of international properties by such a widely recognized real estate auction firm will serve as the ideal centerpiece for the conference." During the past several decades, Good & Company has sold at auction some 38,000 properties valued at some $7 billion.

Sheldon Good & Company's familiarity with global real estate markets and relationships with key players on the global scene weighed heavily in NAR's selection of the Chicago-based real estate auction firm.

In addition to the September 24 auction, Sheldon Good & Company has entered into a multi-year, co-marketing arrangement with NAR to conduct an

(continued)

FIGURE 7.2 *Press Release Announcing International Auction by Global Simulcast, continued*

ongoing series of global auctions. A **second global auction** by Good & Company takes place in **Orlando on Thursday, November 11,** during the **annual REALTORS® National Convention & Expo** in the Peabody Hotel. The annual NAR convention draws some 20,000 delegates, 1,000 of whom travel from 33 foreign countries. Property listing deadline for the November 11 auction is late August.

Good said that a number of the sponsoring trade organizations are soliciting global property listings for the November 11 auction in Orlando. High-end residential properties, "trophy" homes, and other estates throughout North America and the rest of the world are likely to be selected for that event.

In Chicago, TRANSACT '99, which focuses on executive networking, real estate sales, and education, features internationally known speakers and moderated panel discussions. Prominent real estate and finance executives participating in three general sessions include:

- Samuel Zell, chairman and CEO of Equity & Financial Management; Jack R. Rodman, managing director, Global Financial Services–Asia Pacific, E & Y Kenneth Leventhal Real Estate Group; and Bill Rothe, executive managing director, CB Richard Ellis. The three will participate in a panel discussion during the closing luncheon entitled: "Deal Makers' Forecast: Where's the Smart Money Going Next?"

- Kenneth Courtis, first vice president of Deutsche Bank Capital Markets Asia Group, will discuss "The Global Economy"; and

- Bill Emmott, editor-in-chief of *The Economist,* will speak about "Finance and Business."

NAR-affiliated sponsors of TRANSACT '99 include the: Commercial Investment Real Estate Institute (CIREI); Counselors of Real Estate (CRE): Institute of Real Estate Management (IREM); REALTORS® Land Institute (RLI); and Society of Industrial and Office REALTORS® (SIOR).

Other sponsors are the: Auction Marketing Institute (AMI); American Institute of Architects (AIA); International Real Estate Federation (FIABCI): Lambda Alpha International; National Auctioneers Association (NAA); National Realty Committee (NRC); and National Association of Real Estate Investment Trusts (NAREIT), in addition to 40 cooperating associations in 34 countries.

For a brochure, terms of sale, and other information about properties slated for Good & Company's unprecedented global auction, call (800) 315-2199, send e-mail to: stevengood@sheldongood.com, or visit the Good & Company Web site at www.sheldongood.com.

###

Note to Editors: List of properties slated for auction at TRANSACT '99 is attached.

FIGURE 7.2 *Press Release Announcing International Auction by Global Simulcast, continued*

PROPERTIES SLATED FOR $100 MILLION GLOBAL AUCTION AT TRANSACT '99

2:30-4 P.M., FRIDAY, SEPTEMBER 24 IN SHERATON CHICAGO HOTEL

CORPORATE HEADQUARTERS—MIDWEST

- **McHenry, IL**—A 60,000-square-foot, "European-style" corporate headquarters of Medela, Inc., a Swiss-owned maker of breast pumps. Medela, which has grown to become its industry leader, will move to larger headquarters in the same McHenry Corporate Center.

  The white, two-story Medela office building in the McHenry Corporate Center contains 26,000 square feet of office space featuring rounded walls and expansive views of open, rolling farmland. Build on 4.75 acres in 1990 and 1994, the property also offers industrial and warehouse space, parking for 150 cars, 24-foot ceilings, three docks, and adjacent child care center.

  According to Vern Reizman of Medela, the company decided to stay in McHenry to retain its stable work force as well as the state economic incentives it receives. In McHenry, Reizman added, employers can hire from a pool of well-educated, non-transient employees, ranging from assembly line workers to professionals.

  The McHenry Corporate Center is 50 miles northwest of downtown Chicago (between Route 31 and the Union Pacific Railroad tracks, and northwest of Route 176). A Motorola plant is also located in the Center. 4610 Prime Parkway. Seller financing. Sealed bid deadline: September 15.

- **Kansas City, MO**—The 32-story, 300,000-square-foot vacant downtown landmark building is listed on the National Historic Registry. A former federal office building, it features Neo-Classical Revival architecture with pyramidal copper roofs. Vacant with complete state-of-the-art renovation. Suitable for residential redevelopment. 911 Walnut. To be offered without reserve subject to a minimum bid of $2 million.

PRIME INVESTMENT OPPORTUNITY—MEXICO CITY OFFICE BUILDING NET LEASED TO PRICEWATERHOUSECOOPERS

- **Mexico City, D.F.**—A new, eight-story, 240,000-square-foot office building, net leased for 15 years to PricewaterhouseCoopers, with an initial net operating income of $6.15 million USD. Suggested opening bid: $30 million.

HOSPITALITY—CARIBBEAN

- **Turks & Caicos Islands, Salt Cay**—Windmill Plantation, a boutique Caribbean Resort, features oceanfront with 1,100 feet of white sand beach. Very private with only eight guest rooms, it can be operated as is or can be modified into a family or corporate retreat or expanded by purchasing an additional 10 acres of development land. The entire property is zoned for either 20 condominium units or 20 hotel rooms per acre (total of 200 units possible). To be offered with reserve, subject to a minimum bid of $1.5 million USD for hotel and $500,000 USD for additional land.

- **Jamaica, Ocho Rios area**—Hotel Casa Maria, a 20-room Jamaican hotel 15 miles from Ocho Rios in Port Maria, has oceanfront with 1,800 feet of beach on 21+ acres. Ideal for resort redevelopment. The property faces east on a protected

FIGURE 7.2 *Press Release Announcing International Auction by Global Simulcast, continued*

cove and is adjacent to Noel Coward's former home, "Firefly," now a museum. Seller financing. Suggested opening bid: $1.5 million.

TIMBERLAND AND MARBLE RESERVE—CHILE AND NEVADA

- **Chiloe, Chile**—A 130,000-hectare (300,000 acres)—about three-quarters the size of Rhode Island—"freehold interest" (ownership) forest on the southern tip of the island of Chiloe in the Xth region of Chile in the Pacific Ocean. The virgin Southern Chiloe Forest contains hardwoods suitable for veneer, lumber wood-based panels, and wood chips. Property has valuable landscapes and places of unparalleled scenic beauty. Suggested opening bid: $3 million.

- **Nevada (North East)**—Mineral rights to a mountain of marble with an estimated 100-years' supply of high-grade marble and possibly some gold. (Mountain is adjacent to a gold mine.) Rights consist of 60 "lode claims" equaling 1,200 acres. This marble and mineral reserve has more than 300 million tons of high-grade marble, a quality of marble not normally found in the U.S. in the volume. Located in White Pine and Elko counties, 60 miles south of Wendover. Favorable water source. Sealed bid deadline: September 15.

RESORT & RESIDENTIAL DEVELOPMENT LAND—MEXICO & MICHIGAN'S UPPER PENINSULA

- **San Carlos, Mexico**—Two adjacent development sites in Playa Pelicanos approved for hotel and condominium development with 300 feet of frontage on the Sea of Cortez. Suggested opening bids: Parcel 6230: $1.1 million USD, Parcel 6240: $400,000 USD.

- **Iron River, U.P., MI**—An approved 1,400-acre development site with much of the infrastructure in place for a multi-use property featuring marina, hotel, golf course, single-family homes and campground. Seller financing. Sealed bid deadline: September 15.

RECREATIONAL ACREAGE—UTAH

- **Salina Canyon, UT**—Children's Foundation, a charitable organization, is selling a 3,400-acre recreational ranch ideal for camping, hunting, and horseback riding. Spectacular vistas, rock outcroppings, and waterfall. Surrounded on three sides by Fish Lake National Forest. Only 17 miles from Salina, I-70 access, and 2½ hours to Salt Lake City. Sealed bid deadline: September 15.

RETAIL & INDUSTRIAL—TEXAS

- **Ft. Worth, TX**—A 95,000-square-foot warehouse facility on 8.5 acres, 70% leased to Pierce Leahy—a credit tenant. Vacant single-tenant space of 28,500 square feet available. Projected gross income: $147,000 at 100% occupancy. 318 E. Long Street. Seller financing. Suggested opening bid: $300,000.

- **San Antonio, TX**—A retail center at a busy traffic intersection with 63,000 square feet on 6.85 acres. One 49,000-square-foot, single-tenant space is vacant. 1707-1735 South WW White. Seller financing. Suggested opening bid: $250,000.

- **Hearne, TX**—The 40,900-square-foot Hearne Shopping Center on 6.5 acres is 80% occupied and anchored by IGA. Fifty miles south of DFW. 1998 net operating income of $52,100. 901-921 Brown Avenue at Live Oak. Seller financing. Suggested opening bid: $150,000.

FIGURE 7.3 *Brochure for International Auction*

FIGURE 7.3   *Brochure for International Auction, continued*

PARCELS 6140 & 6150   North Beach Road, Salt Cay, in the Turks and Caicos Islands

AN INTIMATE BOUTIQUE CARIBBEAN RESORT & CONDO/HOTEL DEVELOPMENT LAND

Windmill Plantation

Hospitality/Resort Properties

TO BE SOLD WITHOUT RESERVE,
SUBJECT TO MINIMUM BIDS OF:

Parcel 6140, Resort: $1.5 million, USD

Parcel 6150, Development Land:
$500,000, USD

Certified or cashier's check
required to buy:
Parcel 6140: $150,000 USD
Parcel 6150: $50,000 USD

The only resort on tiny Salt Cay, Windmill Plantation was envisioned as the ultimate island getaway, a singular destination where serenity, intimacy and sophistication reign supreme. Windmill Plantation has received worldwide acclaim, and is recognized as one of the Caribbean's 100 best resorts, as featured in *Travel & Leisure*, *Travel Holiday*, *Caribbean Travel and Life* and the *New York Times*.

Eclectic in concept, operation and design, Windmill Plantation offers guests a singular opportunity to enjoy unfettered lifestyle and simple elegance in an unspoiled Caribbean paradise. Occupying 4.5 acres, the resort features eight charming guest suites, a marvelous owner's apartment, and wonderful ambiance, reflecting the exquisite tastes of its present owners, renowned architect Guy Lovelace and his interior designer wife, Pat. The resort's design is a unique union of West Indies-style buildings and Neo-Classical flourishes, gardens, a colonnaded L-shaped pool which ends in a charming pavilion, and a variety of sculptures.

The development property consists of two non-contiguous, five acre parcels. The first parcel has been approved for a 20-unit condominium. Plans, construction documents and permits for the development are in place, providing builders infrastructure for immediate development of the parcel. The second five acre development parcel is presently leased from the government, and can be purchased from the government at a later date.

Windmill Plantation also presents buyers a once-in-a-lifetime opportunity to purchase a fabulous family compound or retreat.

Salt Cay, a 4.5 square mile islet in the Turks and Caicos archipelago, once the Caribbean's salt capital, presently has only 193 residents. Nature has reclaimed the island and surrounding waters; diverse exotic wildlife and flora are omnipresent; sea turtles lay their eggs on the pristine beaches; humpback whales return each winter to calve. Offshore to the west, is the famed "Wall", a magnificent coral reef that plunges to 7,000 feet, a fishing and diving enthusiast's heaven.

Access to Windmill Plantation is excellent. American Airlines schedules two flights daily from Miami to the Providenciales, where scheduled charters are available to Salt Cay. Salt Cay is a tax-free, British dependent territory, located 575 miles southeast of Miami, 80 miles south of the Providenciales, and 90 miles north of Hispaniola.

Azure waters gently meet pristine white sand beaches, palm fronds rustle softly in the soft tropical breeze, the finest beach in the Caribbean is yours alone...

GETTING TO SALT CAY:*
Salt Cay is easily reached by making travel arrangements to the Providenciales, and calling Windmill Plantation directly at (649) 946-6962 to book overnight accommodations. When calling to book your stay, please indicate that you will be inspecting this Transact '99 auction property. Cost for the first night of accommodations is $480.00, additional nights, $330.00. The cost of accommodations include room, round-trip charter flight from the Providenciales, ground transportation on Salt Cay, and three meals per day, including non-alcoholic beverages.

NOTE: To reach Salt Cay on the same day of departure from the continental United States, visitors MUST be booked on the 1:20 p.m. American Airlines flight from Miami International Airport to the Providenciales.

4

FIGURE 7.3 *Brochure for International Auction, continued*

PARCEL 6160   Port Maria, Jamaica

WITH 1,800 FEET OF SPECTACULAR BEACH FRONTAGE

20-Room Hotel Casa Maria on 21 Acres

Suggested opening bid: $1.5 million USD • Certified or cashier's check required to buy: $110,000 USD

Ideally situated on 21 acres (8.46 hectares) in Jamaica's Ocho Rios area, this outstanding property features 1,800 feet of spectacular beach frontage, the perfect site for the astute developer/investor to build a world-class resort complex, or expand and improve the present facilities.

The property radiates star quality; it is adjacent to Noel Coward's "Firefly" and Bob Marley's recording studio, and minutes from Ian Fleming's "Goldeneye". Nestled in a protected cove, the east-oriented hotel commands breath-taking views of the Caribbean and basks in a pleasant sea breeze that keeps the property approximately ten degrees cooler than the rest of the island.

Sold in coöperation with Paradise Real Estate Brokers, Jamaica broker.

Hospitality/Resort Properties

HOTEL CASA MARIA SUMMARY:
• Three-story, 20-room hotel, with reception area, office, television lounge and conference room.
• Rooms have fabulous ocean views, balcony and full bath.
• Two restaurants and three bars.
• 25' x 50' swimming pool.
• Four-unit, 1,590 square foot retail building.
• 1,600 square foot beachside bar/restaurant facility.
• Garage/laundry.
• Public restrooms.

GETTING TO HOTEL CASA MARIA: Fly to Montego Bay and travel east on Queens Highway (along the shore) approximately two hours to Casa Maria. Visitors can also take Air Jamaica from Montego Bay to Ocho Rios. The property is 15 miles east of Ocho Rios. For information regarding lodging and ground transportation, please call (312) 630-0915, extension 342.

5

Source: © National Association of REALTORS®. Reprinted by permission.

A *fterword:* T *errence* M *cDermott*

During the bull market in the late 1990s but in the prebubble stock market years, which were also backed by a strong commercial real estate market, the National Association of REALTORS® launched a renewed focus on its commercial members. Led by former NAR Presidents Russ Booth and Martin Edwards during their respective terms, both of them commercial REALTORS® from Salt Lake City and Memphis, respectively, NAR sought the right market niche to position its new commercial services initiative.

Niche and *focus* were critical as NAR's commercial affiliates have enjoyed a preeminent position in the real estate world for decades. The Counselors of Real Estate (CRE), the Commercial and Investment Institute (CCIM), the Society of Office and Industrial Realtors (SIOR), and the Institute of Real Estate Management (IREM) serve thousands of commercial practitioners and have a well-earned prominent status in the real estate community. Their professional designations are eagerly sought and highly respected in the business community. Our goal required incorporating the increasing value of their affiliation with NAR along with serving our commercial members and boards with greater vigor and visibility.

The prosperity of the Realtors Commercial Alliance (RCA) and our outreach has been successful, and more commercial REALTOR® boards are forming. Steve Good is now vice chairman of the NAR Auction Committee and the 121st president of the Chicago Association of REALTORS®, one of our largest boards with more than 10,000 members.

I fondly remember the challenge, the sizzle, and most of all the auction. I'm confident the entrepreneurial spirit and incredible energy of Steve Good will keep him at the forefront of real estate for many years to come. If you ever need a can-do guy, call Steve Good. If it's a breakfast meeting, a little Valium slipped into his orange juice will help you conserve your energy for the rest of the day.

Our first effort was to launch the Realtors Commercial Alliance in which all of our commercial affiliates and commercial committees and boards would have a strong voice. We would also increase our industry outreach by offering a seat at the table to large commercial brokerage firms that may or may not be active REALTOR® members. Expanding our scope would make us collectively a stronger voice for commercial real estate, especially with the inclusion of the Real Estate Roundtable and the National Association of Real Estate Trusts.

To give the alliance proper support and a cohesive center of management, we created the first senior vice president for commercial real estate in our 90-year history with the addition of Bonnie Gottlieb. Bonnie is a former executive vice president of SIOR and a real estate attorney in Washington, D.C.

As we approached the millennium, we were ready. The commercial world was prospering and the RCA was meeting effectively, but there were few headlines other than "The REALTORS® held another meeting." Our 800,000 member organizations have more meetings than the United Nations. After many "where's the sizzle?" meetings with Frank Sibley, our senior vice president of communications, and productive discussions with Rich Rogane, FAIA, the high-energy leader of the Urban Land Institute, one concept did begin to sizzle a bit. ULI, which ironically had been founded by NAR decades before, was willing to help us launch and comanage a commercial REALTOR© conference as long as it didn't overlap or compete with ULI's own hugely successful efforts in the spring and fall. This cosponsorship gave us a big leg up in credibility in the industry with ULI and our affiliate sponsorships.

The sizzle wasn't quite high enough though, because the purpose of the conference was to announce to the industry that we were staking a claim and were very serious about the commercial market. Transact 99 would be a good launch, but it needed seasoning and the hotter the better. Frank Sibley had recently met the chairman of the Chicago Association of REALTORS® commercial group, and he recognized his potential as a good partner. Frank said this chairman not only had great energy and an idea a minute but also what an old friend used to call terminal *shpilkes,* "ants in your pants" for the uninformed.

(continued)

This unique Chicago-style dynamo, of course, was Steve Good, CEO of Sheldon Good & Company, so at Frank's invitation, we met over lunch with Steve. During lunch, I was thankful the good nuns had hammered home sentence diagramming and the Jesuits their love of logical form and analysis. Otherwise, coping with Steve would have been impossible. *Shpilkes* is one thing; this guy is the eye of a hurricane.

The clarity of the opportunity Steve presented was unquestioned. Let's add the sizzle and uncover NAR's international strength by holding a live auction of property during Transact. This was certainly beyond the offering of any other conference and added the sizzle to the intellectual equity brought by ULI.

Unlike a lot of high-energy guys, Steve's also a producer with a fine staff, and he and his organization literally developed, programmed, and conducted an auction of $100 million in commercial property holdings. The event was blessed with good press coverage and all 700 of the initial Transact attendees were jammed into the Sheraton Chicago Ballroom for the event. The biggest smiles were on Steve's face as head auctioneer and NAR's for holding the auction, which nicely contributed to the success of our first Transact conference.

The next year, we changed the conference from a seminar format to a research symposium that presented organizational research from some of the biggest names in real estate academia. Of course, we asked Steve to repeat the auction, which was again a commercial success and the highlight of the second Transact Conference.

Even though we convened over 1,200 attendees in two years and the auction gave us the sizzle factor we needed, the commercial real estate market was on a record-breaking pace and we needed to consolidate our efforts to ensure a place on the successful commercial REALTORS® calendar. With the calendar already crowded with great offerings from our affiliates, the Urban Land Institute, Lambda Alpha, and others, we merged Transact with RealComm, a highly successful technology conference that continues the tradition we started prior to the start of the new millennium.

8

UN-UNITED HOMES

Referral clients, as previously noted, are the lifeblood of every service organization. You can cold call customers until the cows come home, but unless you have good references based on a great track record, you and your company are as good as dead.

A long time ago I got into the habit of asking clients to write letters of recommendation for us at the conclusion of a transaction. I learned that we could tell potential customers that we are a great company until we are blue in the face, but a good letter of recommendation often gets us to the place we intended a lot faster than a bunch of sales talks.

After we had concluded a significant transaction that came from a bankruptcy case we handled, one of our clients wrote me a terrific letter (see Figure 8.1) that was intended to serve as a reference.

I received other reference letters from participants in the case, but this was one of my favorites. So is the guy who wrote it.

BACKGROUND

We have worked hard over the past several decades to dispel the myth that auctions are a tool of last resort in the sale of real estate. We

B *arry* A . C *h a t z*
Arnstein & Lehr

Barry Chatz is a partner in the bankruptcy group of the law firm of Arnstein & Lehr. His major practice areas are bankruptcy, creditors rights, and commercial litigation. Barry represents lenders, unsecured creditors, corporate debtors, and trustees in numerous matters around the country.

Barry is an active member of the Illinois, California, and American Bar Associations and the American Bankruptcy Institute. He also serves as a panel bankruptcy trustee for the U.S. Bankruptcy Court for the Northern District of Illinois. He served with the office of the U.S. Trustee for the Central District of California from 1987 to 1990 through the U.S. Attorney General's Honors Program.

Barry has been published in numerous trade publications and has spoken before many legal organizations, including the Commercial Law League of America and committees of the American Bar Association, as well as private businesses.

Barry is a graduate of DePaul University College of Law (J.D., 1987) and the University of Wisconsin (B.A., 1984).

have been remarkably successful in this regard, and as a result, most of our clients view our company as being to the real estate business what Sotheby's or Christie's is to the fine art and collectibles business—a comparison made at the beginning of Chapter 1. Consequently, although we do handle properties in bankruptcy, these properties account for less than 5 percent of our business annually. In fact, most clients in bankruptcy cases retain our firm to *avoid* bankruptcy-style auctions associated with court-ordered sales.

The U.S. Bankruptcy Code was designed to give borrowers and lenders a *federal* right to settle their issues in court. Even though state laws can govern these matters, for all intents and purposes federal laws control. Consequently, law firms that have significant corporate clients usually have a bankruptcy group because, as we've learned in the last several decades, no company is bulletproof. In fact, I remember attending

FIGURE 8.1 *Letter from a Satisfied Client*

February 7

Mr. Steven L. Good
Chairman and CEO
Sheldon Good & Company Auctions, LLC
Chicago, Illinois

> RE: *320 Property Portfolios*
> *United Homes, Inc.*
> *Arizona, Illinois & Michigan*

Dear Steve:

We wanted to write you to express our appreciation for the terrific job you did in selling the above captioned portfolio of properties.

By way of background, our company was a construction lender to United Homes. After United filed for bankruptcy your firm was retained to sell this portfolio. You came to us via strong recommendations and, in hindsight, we sure are glad that we followed that advice.

The portfolio consisted of approximately 320 properties in 14 subdivisions in the three states. The subdivisions were in various stages of completion that included raw land, partially completed homesites, fully completed homesites, partially completed townhouses, townhouse sites, and houses with various levels of completion. Your initial inspection and offering recommendations for the properties with us proved invaluable. You segmented each property and then marketed it, pre-auction to its relevant markets. The response was unbelievable, thousands of interested buyers surfaced in the six-week period that proceeded the one-week, four-auction, series.

Despite having the right to buy any property that we thought could be sold for more, every property sold at the auction due to the strong demand that your firm generated for the properties. More impressively, every property actually closed, netting $19.3 million in sales proceeds.

Suffice it to say that you earned yourself a new client. Please feel free to use us as a reference to your potential other clients. Your service has an invaluable *value-added* aspect to it that I only wish that we could have used your services sooner.

Thanks again for your help and congratulations on a job well done.

Sincerely,

Managing Director

---

a black-tie dinner where Microsoft's Bill Gates was the featured speaker. Because Gates was arguably one of the wealthiest people in the world at the time, the dinner was packed with business tycoons.

Two things in Gates's speech stuck with me. First, he had prepared his presentation by means of a computer-generated format, and when he flipped the switch, the whole program crashed; so much for technology wizardry. Second, he stressed in the body of his speech that the markets for his company's products changed so rapidly that one of the points he always stressed to his employees was that without their ability to innovate, the company could fail in a mere 18 months.

If Bill Gates was right, it's no wonder that so many law firms have bankruptcy departments.

This story starts with an urgent call I received from an old friend, Barry Chatz, who along with his father *was* the bankruptcy department of a major law firm. Barry called to tell me that he had been appointed the chairman of the unsecured creditors committee for a residential real estate building company. He was both excited and nervous because this was a case in which his clients stood to recover some of the monies that the company had been unable to repay if he was able to engineer a sale of the company's unsold properties at a good price. On the other hand, without a sale of the properties at a good price, everything would go down

B *arry* A . C *h a t z*

"Prior to the forming of our perfect union in 1776, debtors who didn't pay their bills in *the days of Merry Olde England* were thrown in jail. Now debtors file bankruptcy cases in a commercial corporate context, and their creditors fight like savage dogs over the remaining business corpse. The fights are reminiscent of the Old West, where every creditor is represented by a gunfighter seeking to either receive some limited dreg of money or, instead, is happy to kill the debtor if the client is unhappy with the outcome.

"Understanding the foregoing as well as that senior secured lenders perceive their loan documents are always without flaw and they should not be held accountable, notwithstanding their tacit involvement in the creation of unsecured debt for their benefit, the battles begin."

the tubes, and not only would his clients get nothing, but he wouldn't get paid either. I thought to myself, "What a way to make a living."

My relationship with Barry went back a long way. I first met him when I was 16 and a junior camp counselor at Camp Ojibwa in Wisconsin's North Woods. He was one of my campers, and even at age 13 he couldn't sleep at night. I'd come back to the cabin after midnight and all of the other kids would be asleep except Barry. Knowing this, I would regularly stop at the late-night burger joint, and Barry and I would munch on burgers and A&W root beer. We fell out of touch after that camp season and didn't see each other again until almost 20 years later.

We rekindled our friendship when a local bankruptcy trustee called me to help sell a large vacant landsite; Barry was at the initial meeting representing the bank that held the mortgage on the property. The deal ultimately worked out great for Barry and his client, and the good old days for Barry and me were back again. We started doing a number of deals together, and I was excited for him when President Bill Clinton appointed him to be a federal bankruptcy trustee.

Barry made an appointment to see me the day after a telephone call to say he urgently needed our help. When we met the next day, he explained the situation. More than 30 creditors had been stiffed when a well-known residential building company called United Homes opted to put itself into a Chapter 11 bankruptcy. The company owned in excess of 500 properties in three states. It had gone from more than 200 to a mere 5 employees; and the two secured creditors, Bank of America and United Home's primary construction lender, were bearing down hard on the company. Furthermore, Barry believed there was a high likelihood that the value of the properties owned by United Homes was exceeded by the accumulated debt so that the company really had no motivation to do anything because there was no money in it for the company. I had remembered reading an article about the company's problems in *Crain's Chicago Business* several months earlier, but it wasn't until Barry explained the situation to me in legal terms that I really understood.

He was also very concerned that time was his client's enemy because the loans with the secured lenders were in default and, as a result, were accruing interest at an accelerated rate. If it took six to eight months to sell the surplus properties, which could easily be the case, his client's potential recovery would be wiped out. He was likewise concerned that if he pushed to have the properties sold in bulk, they were likely to be sold at a deep discount, which again would leave his client with nothing. Barry had come to our company because he believed we could put an auction sale program in place that would solve his problem by offering the properties individually to be sold to their corresponding retail markets within a 75-day time frame. He further reasoned that even if the properties sold at a slight discount, the saving in carrying costs (i.e., the monies that would be expended while waiting to sell each property) would more than make up for any discount given by shortening the selling period.

B *a r r y* **A .** **C** *h a t z*

"As Steve said, I represented and continue to represent the Official Committee of Unsecured Creditors for United Homes, Inc. (UHI), an Illinois corporation. The committee is owed in excess of $20 million. Many of the unsecured creditors were tradespeople who failed to properly perfect liens based on inducements provided to them by the debtor and other parties, and the creditors include unpaid bondholders with debt in excess of $8 million.

"The lender in UHI was content to take its secured property and go away, leaving the unsecured creditors no money and the potential of no recovery other than through litigation. The unsecured creditors were unable to evaluate the value of the real estate given the divergent locations and different nature of the properties. The debtor was less than inclined to take any actions for the benefit of the unsecured creditors, as certain of the debtor's principals had agendas relating to mitigation of guaranties in settlement with the secured lender, as well as other desires to not be concerned with the plight of the unsecured creditors.

"The key element in my view for the success of the auction program occurs through the ability of Sheldon Good & Company to manufacture and create a market and to maximize values for the properties. The buyer that Steve Good previously found for the former Al Capone manufacturing facility that we handled together in a previous transaction was ultimately an entity whose principal had a very strong interest in the history of Al Capone and his impact on the nation. A premium was paid by the purchaser because of this personal interest."

We discussed the situation at great length, and I told Barry that I thought he was on the right track. Although his facts and familiarity with the properties were very sketchy, our open outcry/sealed-bid portfolio sale auction program was an ideal solution if his numbers were right. For us to follow up, he'd have to get us connected with a representative of United Homes so we could get our arms around its inventory of unsold properties and thus make the necessary analysis to confirm that our initial gut check was right.

Barry called his contact at United Homes from my office, and we made a date to get together the very next day.

GATHERING THE CRITICAL INFORMATION

The downsized office of United Homes was located in a one-story, suburban, multibuilding complex composed of numerous small companies. Barry had told me the company's size had been drastically reduced; when I walked into the offices with two of my associates, it was obvious the company was going through tumultuous times.

The offices consisted of five or six private offices, and there was no receptionist to greet us. We wandered around for a moment before being met by the person with whom Barry had made the appointment for us. The representative showed us into his office, and with three of us on the other side of his desk, we were sitting in pretty cramped quarters. Packed cardboard boxes were everywhere, and our host turned the ringer of his telephone off after we were all seated.

It turned out that he was a lawyer turned builder and had been brought on prior to the bankruptcy as a senior officer to handle the company's various legal matters. Before joining the company, he had worked for a very prestigious downtown Chicago law firm; although we hadn't previously met each other, we had a ton of mutual friends in the law business. In fact, he began by telling us that he had represented a custom homebuilder who had sold a property in one of our auctions but had then backed out of the deal after he accepted the bid at the auction only to resell the property for hundreds of thousands of dollars *less*. At the time I wasn't sure if he was telling his story as a compliment or a complaint but later learned that he meant the story as a compliment.

After we shared the first five minutes of social pleasantry—typical of business meetings in the Midwest—our host got down to business and gave us his take on the United Homes story. He explained that the company had downsized itself to a point where basically none of the remaining executives had any substantive idea as to the status of the remaining properties. All of the line people had been fired, and because the remaining executives didn't believe the value of the properties exceeded the debt against them, his view was that there was no sense in United Homes doing *anything* other than cooperating with the bankruptcy court's appointed trustee. As previously noted, United Homes had two secured lenders: Bank of America and United Home's primary construction lender (which asked not to be named because it is still in litigation). United had agreed to return Bank of America's collateral of 200 properties as a negotiated settlement of United's debt with the bank; the other lender, the primary construction lender, was fighting it out in the bankruptcy court for the right to collect monies owed it from the remaining 320 properties in United's portfolio.

Our host was as pleasant as he could be but made it clear that other than giving us the names and places where the properties and their corresponding descriptive materials were located or stored, he would *not* commit any other resources to this project. He had given us the basic information about what they owned, where it was located, and what dollars they had in it but was at a loss about the status of any given project. This was basically because United Homes had abruptly filed for bankruptcy, thus causing everyone working for them to be dropped overnight. It was like being in the middle of a neutron bomb explosion. He wished us luck in getting the assignment because he knew that we would do a good job and, it was hoped, earn a significant fee.

THE INITIAL PROPOSAL

We had received all the information that was readily available from United Homes. When we reviewed it, we learned that the portfolio consisted of about 320 properties evenly distributed around suburban Chicago (Illinois), Scottsdale (suburban Phoenix, Arizona), and suburban Grand Rapids (Michigan). We also learned there were three United Homes, one for each state, and each company had filed for bankruptcy in its own state separately. Fortunately, the three bankruptcies had been consolidated into one courtroom, so for all intents and purposes we could deal with everything simultaneously.

As I've said before, we have handled virtually every type of real estate that exists in many different procedures. As it turned out, United Homes had the following types of properties spread out in the previously described locations:

- Vacant land
- Vacant land platted but not subdivided
- Vacant land subdivided with and without utilities installed
- Subdivisions with unsold homesites
- Subdivisions with unsold homesites and some finished homes
- Subdivisions with unsold homesites, some unfinished homes, and some finished homes
- Townhouse subdivisions with unsold townhouse sites, individual finished townhouses, and unfinished townhouse buildings

There were also numerous legal problems having to do with the unfinished nature of many of the properties. Some of these included:

- Environmental issues
- Drainage problems
- Building code violations
- Hazardous building conditions
- Mountains of unspread topsoil on unfinished subdivision sites
- Leaking roofs, unfinished electrical systems, and the like

In writing the proposal, I *knew* we had the ability to ultimately answer a number of unanswered questions once we were retained. Furthermore, because we had handled numerous properties like these before, we *could* generate the marketing plan, general timeline, and staffing requirements, which would provide the parties to the bankruptcy a solution and its corresponding cost. This was a true "value-added" solution for everyone, as the alternative was to continue duking it out in court, during which time the properties would continue to deteriorate and everyone's equity in the properties would erode further.

What we brought to the table was the ability to sell *everything* and convert the properties into *cash,* which could be invested in something else and earn interest. The parties could then fight about their share in the proceeds, which ultimately the court could easily divide.

Good plan, huh?

The proposal we submitted was a smorgasbord of overlapping approaches that mirrored the smorgasbord of properties we were being asked to sell. Vacant properties were going to be marketed to investors and other residential developers. The unfinished townhouse development was being positioned to be sold to the townhouse development community. Individual homesites were earmarked to be sold to homebuilders, individual potential buyers who would have homes built for themselves, and investors. Finished and partially finished houses were going to be targeted to individual homebuyers who would occupy or complete them. The scope of marketing was planned on a local, regional, and national basis—particularly the Scottsdale product, as Scottsdale is a world-class resort community.

SELLING THE PROPOSAL TO THE LENDER AND THE CREDITORS

Simultaneously with the submission of our proposal, Barry Chatz was busy negotiating a deal for the unsecured creditors. He had been up front with me and made it clear that his goal was to get his group paid *something.* After a few weeks of wrangling with the primary construction lender's lawyers, a deal was struck. The lender would get the first $15 million in proceeds and the unsecured creditors would get some portion of the rest. At this point it was impossible to determine the exact amount each creditor would receive because each group would be required to formally prove the amount it was due in court. It made no sense to prove anyone's claim if the properties didn't generate enough cash to pay them. As I mentioned earlier, they could duke it out once they knew there was money to fight over.

The hardest part at this point was convincing the lender's various representatives that our program would work. Their company was one of the premier construction lenders for the homebuilding industry, and it had never been involved in a deal this size that had gone bad. They were great businesspeople on unfamiliar ground. I knew that if they'd give us a fair chance to present our program and company credentials, we'd have a good chance of going forward. The challenge at this point was to take the dialogue from the lawyers to the businesspeople.

The lender was lucky to have its managing director on its team. He was the business decision maker, but it took a while for him to surface. We originally submitted our proposal through the lender's lawyers; the lender had an army of them dispersed throughout the country, many of whom had converged because of this case. Ultimately, our proposal ended up in the managing director's office, and shortly thereafter we met with the managing director and several of his colleagues in our offices in Chicago.

I liked the managing director the moment that I met him. He was a residential builder specialist, and his client base read like a who's who in the residential building world. We knew a ton of the same people, as both of us had been doing business in this community for many years; we just worked different sides of the same street. He was the construction lender and I was the guy who got his clients out of trouble. What a great fit. Within a short time he saw the merit of our concept; he would support it *provided* he could review our methodology as we developed its application on a subdivision-by-subdivision basis.

THE COURT APPROVAL PROCESS

Once the lender approved, Barry Chatz and the lender's lawyers orchestrated the bankruptcy court's approval. United Homes had hired a well-respected lawyer who was extremely capable to represent them; he could read, write, and count and enthusiastically supported our business plan. He filed the necessary motion before the bankruptcy court that would lead to a hearing before the judge.

I remember sitting in the gallery of the court waiting for the United Homes case to be called. There must have been 40 or 50 people packed into this small courtroom. When the judge entered, everyone stood up as is customary and then seated themselves once the judge was seated. When the first case on the judge's docket was called, two lawyers stood and argued their motion before the judge. When they concluded, another case was called with the same protocol prevailing.

About 20 minutes later, the United Homes case was called. I was surprised to see *30* people jump up and approach the judge. As they went around introducing themselves, I learned that each of them was a lawyer, and each announced the name of his or her client and the role the client had in the bankruptcy. One lawyer represented a bank, another the concrete supplier, another the carpentry company, another a landscaper. This went on and on. I remember thinking to myself, "Is there anyone left in this business that doesn't hold a claim?"

United Homes's lawyer addressed the judge first and explained the deal that had been proposed and why he thought the court should ratify the motion to employ us. The judge asked a number of questions that related to the cost, time frame involved, and probable outcome of the program. The lawyer asked that I be sworn in as a witness to give testimony as to our credentials, program, and tentative methodology. The court approved, and I took my seat in the witness box, which was next to the judge's bench.

I explained to the court the information we had provided in our written proposal. All of the lawyers and the judge had received a copy of our proposal, as it had been attached as an exhibit to the motion. The important part of the questioning revolved around the fact that we would be developing the specific auction disposition strategy for each property once we had been retained via court order; until we were retained and finalized the research, we couldn't answer the court's detailed questions. The judge understood and asked if anyone, the lender in particular, had an objection to the terms of our retention. With none being heard, the judge granted the motion.

It was time to learn just how much hair there *really* was on this deal. The first step was developing specific property strategies. Have you ever physically inspected 320 properties in 14 subdivisions in three states in five days? I have. Twice. First with our staff and then with the lender's managing director to make sure that he concurred with our recommendations.

Gathering Further Information

Prior to the property inspections, I dispatched a team of people from our Chicago office to gather all of the property-specific information we could find about the various properties. The main problem was that none of the people at United Homes knew anything about the properties. All of the documents about them had been boxed and shipped to self-storage lockers or put in an attic. It took our people days to retrieve the materials, sort them so that they could be used, and update them (some of the information had become stale). Our people told stories about the exorcism they went through when they were forced to retrieve information from non-air-conditioned storage lockers in Arizona, where the heat exceeded 100 degrees; or worrying about falling out of a non-air-conditioned attic in Grand Rapids after a United Homes secretary told them she had been instructed *not* to help them so they were on their own.

Be that as it may, our people got the materials and the fuzzy picture began to clear. All the properties were well located in desirable suburban locations. Some portions of them were problematic, but all of the problems were solvable by their respective markets. The property inspections would further clarify this challenging situation.

Inspecting the Properties

Our team scheduled the initial viewings of the properties, no small task as all of the finished properties had to be opened by locksmiths. We ultimately rekeyed them as well to make them accessible to our staff. During the inspections we sought to match up the written information that we had garnered with each particular property. We were concerned that we could potentially misinform the market on any given property, which would further complicate an already complicated situation. We didn't want any buyers' lawyers joining the entourage of lawyers already involved in this case.

We learned a lot during the inspections. First, some of the properties we thought United Homes owned we found it didn't. In other cases the addresses were wrong; in still others, the descriptions of the properties were wrong. Several homesites had construction and/or sales trailers on them that would have to be removed. The problems went on and on, but we are a large company and assigned people to address and correct problems and offer solutions as part of our methodical development of the property databases. Within three weeks we were ready to make strategic offering recommendations.

THE OFFERING RECOMMENDATIONS

We addressed each subdivision and the variety of properties located in each as though the subdivision contained the only properties being offered. We knew that because 14 different subdivisions were involved, we would be able to create certain economies of scale in the areas of print and electronic media advertising, direct mail solicitation, public relations opportunities, solicitation of the brokerage community, and the auction events themselves.

Certain properties were slated for sealed-bid auctions and others for open outcry auctions. All in all, we planned to conduct four auctions within eight days: two in Chicago, one in Grand Rapids, and one in Phoenix. One of the auctions held in Chicago overlapped a worldwide auction we were conducting with the National Association of REALTORS® and Urban Land Institute and 39 of their cosponsors. Our entire plan was written up and submitted to United Homes, which immediately gave its OK. The lender responded through its managing director, who wanted a personal tour of all the properties to make sure that he concurred with our advice.

Our company planned the second inspection trip, the one that included the managing director. The two of us went from city to city and were met by our staff in each place. It was during this inspection trip that the two of us got to know each other. Interestingly, we still make it a point to call each other every once in a while to exchange notes or just say, "Hello, I'm passing through."

Court Approval of the Final Offering Plan

After our analysis was concluded, we submitted our final offering plan to the bankruptcy trustee for the court's approval. One of the interesting aspects of the plan was that it allowed the lender to bid in accordance with the U.S. Bankruptcy Code. Arguably, the lender could buy any or all of the properties at the auctions if it thought that the price bid for any property was off the mark. Consequently, it would have to prepare to bid just like any other bidder—except if it bought something it ultimately planned to immediately list with a broker and resell in the hopes of getting a better price than it paid for the property(ies) at the auction.

United Homes's lawyer made the necessary motion and distributed it to all of the parties that were part of the proceedings. This time the hearing before the judge went a little differently—he just approved it because everyone loved the way the case was evolving. They believed our plan was going to work.

Arranging Third-Party Financing for Buyers

We followed the basic methodology that I've discussed in other chapters: We advertised and promoted the auctions through massive amounts of advertising, public and brokerage relations, and direct and e-mail marketing. We prescheduled showing dates and times for the various properties and planned seminars for bidders that would provide them an opportunity to prepare for the auctions. We also prearranged construction and mortgage lending sources through our banking connections. Unfortunately, no one bank could handle properties in all three states, so we lined up a different bank for each state. As part of this process, we interviewed a number of banks and made sure that the ones we chose had a wide repertoire of loan products and were rate competitive. In return, we promoted the lenders chosen in our solicitation materials on the theory that even if any given buyer didn't use them here, he or she might use them elsewhere; we used the auctions to help the chosen lenders get business even if it wasn't our business.

We ultimately produced three promotional brochures as shown in Figure 8.2.

Properties Are Tuned Up for Sale

We were dealing with a huge amount of properties and wanted them to sell for good prices. Our clients were prepared to let buyers make good deals provided they were fair deals. Consequently, we continued to inspect the properties and tune them up to the extent that our experience dictated that the dollars spent on property tune-up costs would be fully recovered.

FIGURE 8.2 *Brochures Describing United Homes Auction*

It was a peculiar situation. The owner, United Homes, didn't want to do anything. Its lender was hoping to get $15 million and would fund our tune-up recommendations. Who was to do the work? Our company opted to contract the tasks to a dependable contractor who had an army of subcontractors already in place. Doors were fixed, leaky roofs repaired, mounds of dirt spread, and on and on. The properties were ready within three weeks.

FIGURE 8.2 *Brochures Describing United Homes Auction, continued*

RED DOG RANCH
Cave Creek, Arizona

*R*ed Dog Ranch is a community of 72 luxurious single-family homes, all situated on huge estate-sized lots. Lots range in size from one to four acres, dimensions that allow flexibility in both structural design and landscaping.

Located in the upscale community of Cave Creek, in the foothills just north of Scottsdale, Red Dog Ranch is just a short drive from several local golf courses and country clubs, shopping, cultural activities and fine restaurants. The greater Phoenix area offers its residents outstanding services and amenities, including the Cave Creek School District, Arizona State University, and Phoenix Sky Harbor International Airport.

Seven Luxurious Residences

Suggested opening bids: $100,000 per home

Certified or cashier's check required to buy: $15,000 per home

TO BE SOLD ABSOLUTE, REGARDLESS OF PRICE!

PROPERTY INFORMATION:

Address	Lot	Acreage	1999 Taxes	PIN Numbers	Sq. Ft.
5535 Desert Winds Circle	23	2.43	$618	211-82-060	2,937
5767 Canyon Springs Drive	4	2.98	$663	211-82-041	3,560
40555 Canyon Ridge Trail	51	1.76	$618	211-82-088	2,937
5872 Red Dog Drive	63	3.45	$663	211-82-100	3,560
41497 Ironwood Bluff	69	3.33	$663	211-82-106	3,339
41401 Ironwood Bluff	71	3.76	$663	211-82-108	3,483
41399 Ironwood Bluff	72	3.63	$663	211-82-109	2,469

HOMESITE INFORMATION:

Address	Lot	1999 Taxes	PIN Numbers	Lot Size
	68	$663	211-82-105	Irregular-143,312 s/f
	8	$593	211-82-045	Irregular-89,298 s/f

5535 Desert Winds Circle

The Residences at Lot 23 and 71:
Four bedroom, three bath Territ-style homes, with master suite, three-car garage, laundry room, fireplace, kitchen, and walk-out covered porch.

The Residences at Lot 4, 51, 63, 69, and 72:
Arizona contemporary homes, with four bedrooms, three baths, master suite, three-car garage, first floor laundry room, fireplace, kitchen, and walk-out covered porch.

Two Estate Homesites of 2.05 and 3.29 Acres

Suggested opening bids: $20,000

Certified or cashier's check required to buy: $ 2,500 per site

TO BE SOLD ABSOLUTE, REGARDLESS OF PRICE!

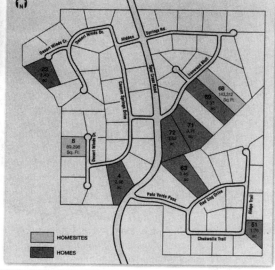

HOMESITES

HOMES

DIRECTIONS: Take Interstate Route 17 to Carefree Highway east, and proceed to Cave Creek Road. Turn northbound to Spur Cross Road, and continue two miles to Red Dog Ranch.

THE MARKET REACTS

Each auction fielded over 1,000 calls. People mobbed the properties. These were great properties being offered at great prices. Some of the properties had some "hair" on them, but the hair could be removed if the property were bought right; the effort of participating in the auction would be well rewarded.

FIGURE 8.2 *Brochures Describing United Homes Auction, continued*

The lender's view was that it had the right to buy anything it thought it could sell at a profit—just like any other buyer. The risk, of course, was that it might overpay for a given property and then have to resell it at a loss. Talk about human drama.

The auctions went off flawlessly. Over 1,000 people attended each auction. Not only did all of the properties sell, but more than half of

FIGURE 8.2 *Brochures Describing United Homes Auction, continued*

WOODSIDE GREEN

Holland, Michigan

Designed and engineered to be a community that combines old country charm and progressive ideals, Woodside Green is set amid gently winding streets and quiet neighborhoods of brand-new residences, townhomes and condominiums. Bordered by a meandering creek, the subdivision is located in the burgeoning residential area between Holland and Zeeland, just minutes from downtown Holland. Schools, shopping and employment facilities are nearby, and a host of recreational opportunities are minutes away.

The highly rated West Ottawa School District serves the community, and nearby colleges include Holland's Western Theological Seminary, Hope College, Grand Valley State University, Aquinas College and Calvin College.

The Condominium development plan at Woodside Green was to improve the site with 73 single family attached condominiums.

Two Single-Family Homes and Three Townhomes

Suggested opening bids, per parcel:
Parcel A: $45,000 • *Parcel B:* $35,000
Certified or cashier's checks required to buy, per parcel:
Parcel A: $4,500 • *Parcel B:* $4,000
TO BE SOLD ABSOLUTE, REGARDLESS OF PRICE!

10982 Thornberry Way: Two bedrooms, 2.5 baths, Colonial-style, with eight rooms, an upper level master suite, full basement, two-car garage, laundry, family room with fireplace, eat-in kitchen, front porch and rear deck.
LOT SIZE: 10,634 square feet.

10834 Thornberry Way: Contemporary home with six rooms, three bedrooms, 2.5 baths, upper level master bedroom suite, full basement, two-car garage, dining room with vaulted ceiling, family room with fireplace, eat-in kitchen, front porch and rear deck.
LOT SIZE: 10,608 square feet.

10921 Aspen Trail: Two bedroom, 2.5 bathroom Ranch-style townhouse has a full basement with bedroom and bath (1,196 additional square feet), two-car garage, fireplace, eat-in kitchen, walk-out basement and patio.

10923 Aspen Trail: Two bedroom, one bathroom Ranch-style townhouse has a full unfinished basement, two-car garage, eat-in kitchen, walk-out basement and patio.

PARCEL A: TWO SINGLE-FAMILY RESIDENCES

Address	Lot	1999 Taxes	Fees	PIN Numbers
10982 Thornberry Way	2	$3,200	$76	70-16-11-376-002
10834 Thornberry Way	16	$3,432	$76	70-16-11-398-010

PARCEL B: THREE TOWNHOMES

Address	Unit	Bldg.	1999 Taxes	Fees	PIN Numbers
10921 Aspen Trail	22	G	$2,664	$76	70-16-11-397-021
10923 Aspen Trail	23	G	unavailable	$76	70-16-11-397-023
10927 Aspen Trail	25	G	$2,732	$76	70-16-11-397-025

10925 Aspen Trail: Two bedroom, 2.5 bathroom ranch-style townhouse has a full basement with bedroom and bath (1,184 additional square feet), two-car garage, eat-in kitchen, second floor rear deck, walk-out basement and patio.

Seven Townhome Sites, Four Townhomes and Eight Single-Family Homesites

Suggested opening bids:
Parcel A: $25,000 • *Parcel B:* $80,000 • *Parcel C:* $50,000
Certified or cashier's checks required to buy:
Parcel A: $3,000 • *Parcel B:* $10,000 • *Parcel C:* $5,000
TO BE SOLD ABSOLUTE, REGARDLESS OF PRICE!

PROPERTY DESCRIPTIONS:

PARCEL A: SEVEN MULTI-FAMILY HOMESITES, SOLD IN BULK

Address	Unit	Bldg	1999 Taxes	Fees	PIN Numbers
10902 Aspen Trail	8	c	$475	$76	70-16-11-397-008
10900 Aspen Trail	9	c	$475	$76	70-16-11-397-009
10898 Aspen Trail	10	c	$475	$76	70-16-11-397-010
10896 Aspen Trail	11	c	$475	$76	70-16-11-397-011
10890 Aspen Trail	12	d	$475	$76	70-16-11-397-012
10888 Aspen Trail	13	d	$475	$76	70-16-11-397-013
10886 Aspen Trail	14	d	$475	$76	70-16-11-397-014

PARCEL B: FOUR TOWNHOUSES, SOLD IN BULK

Address	Unit	Bldg	1999 Taxes	Fees	PIN Numbers
10914 Aspen Trail	4	b	$2,600	$76	70-16-11-397-004
10910 Aspen Trail	6	b	$2,306	$76	70-16-11-397-006
10885 Aspen Trail	15	b	$1,993	$76	70-16-11-397-015
10901 Aspen Trail	21	b	$2,008	$76	70-16-11-397-021

PARCEL C: EIGHT SINGLE-FAMILY HOMESITES, SOLD IN BULK

Address	Lot	Taxes	PIN Numbers
10924 Thornberry Way	7	$693	70-16-11-398-001
10992 Thornberry Way	1	$693	70-16-11-376-001
10976 Thornberry Way	3	$693	70-16-11-375-003
10958 Thornberry Way	5	$693	70-16-11-376-005
10908 Thornberry Way	9	$693	70-16-11-398-003
10900 Thornberry Way	10	$693	70-16-11-398-004
10879 Riley Street	25	$693	70-16-11-399-016
10991 Thornberry Way	51	$693	70-16-11-344-001

SPECIAL SEALED BID AUCTION: SEPTEMBER 15

50 Homesites at Woodside Green

Certified or cashier's check required to buy: 5% of bid price
TO BE SOLD ABSOLUTE, REGARDLESS OF PRICE!
50 multi-family homesites, to be sold in bulk in a sealed bid auction format. This is an excellent opportunity for a developer to acquire immediate inventory on which to build highly profitable townhomes in an established residential community.

DIRECTIONS: From Business Route 196 exit at 112th Avenue north to Riley Road. Turn onto Riley Road heading west. You will see the main entrance on the north side of the street. Enter the development by turning north on Thornberry Way.

them closed in 10 days following their respective auctions; virtually all of the rest of the properties closed within 60 days.

All in all, the auctions garnered $4.3 million *more* than Barry Chatz, my former camper, needed to make his clients happy; the fighting for who got what part of the surplus continued long past the auctions.

FIGURE 8.2 *Brochures Describing United Homes Auction, continued*

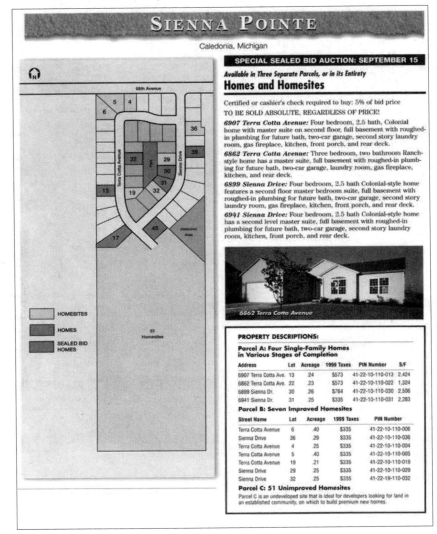

SIENNA POINTE

Caledonia, Michigan

SPECIAL SEALED BID AUCTION: SEPTEMBER 15

Available in Three Separate Parcels, or in its Entirety

Homes and Homesites

Certified or cashier's check required to buy: 5% of bid price

TO BE SOLD ABSOLUTE, REGARDLESS OF PRICE!

6907 Terra Cotta Avenue: Four bedroom, 2.5 bath, Colonial home with master suite on second floor, full basement with roughed-in plumbing for future bath, two-car garage, second story laundry room, gas fireplace, kitchen, front porch, and rear deck.

6862 Terra Cotta Avenue: Three bedroom, two bathroom Ranch-style home has a master suite, full basement with roughed-in plumbing for future bath, two-car garage, laundry room, gas fireplace, kitchen, and rear deck.

6899 Sienna Drive: Four bedroom, 2.5 bath Colonial-style home features a second floor master bedroom suite, full basement with roughed-in plumbing for future bath, two-car garage, second story laundry room, gas fireplace, kitchen, front porch, and rear deck.

6941 Sienna Drive: Four bedroom, 2.5 bath Colonial-style home has a second level master suite, full basement with roughed-in plumbing for future bath, two-car garage, second story laundry room, kitchen, front porch, and rear deck.

6862 Terra Cotta Avenue

HOMESITES
HOMES
SEALED BID HOMES

PROPERTY DESCRIPTIONS:

Parcel A: Four Single-Family Homes in Various Stages of Completion

Address	Lot	Acreage	1999 Taxes	PIN Number	S/F
6907 Terra Cotta Ave.	13	.24	$573	41-22-10-110-013	2,424
6862 Terra Cotta Ave.	22	.23	$573	41-22-10-110-022	1,324
6899 Sienna Dr.	30	.26	$764	41-22-10-110-030	2,506
6941 Sienna Dr.	31	.25	$335	41-22-10-110-031	2,283

Parcel B: Seven Improved Homesites

Street Name	Lot	Acreage	1999 Taxes	PIN Number
Terra Cotta Avenue	6	.40	$335	41-22-10-110-006
Sienna Drive	36	.29	$335	41-22-10-110-036
Terra Cotta Avenue	4	.25	$335	41-22-10-110-004
Terra Cotta Avenue	5	.40	$335	41-22-10-110-005
Terra Cotta Avenue	19	.21	$335	41-22-10-110-019
Sienna Drive	29	.25	$335	41-22-10-110-029
Sienna Drive	32	.25	$335	41-22-19-110-032

Parcel C: 51 Unimproved Homesites

Parcel C is an undeveloped site that is ideal for developers looking for land in an established community, on which to build premium new homes.

FIGURE 8.2 *Brochures Describing United Homes Auction, continued*

FIGURE 8.2 *Brochures Describing United Homes Auction, continued*

TIFFANY FARMS

Antioch, Illinois

*S*ettled in 1832, the village of Antioch is a town of traditional values, but has an eye on the future. The premier town of the Fox Chain of Lakes region, Antioch is perfectly situated midway between Chicago and Milwaukee. The entire area is a recreation mecca, with boating, fishing, golf, and water sports of all types during summer; winter brings cross-country skiing, snowmobiling, ice skating and ice fishing.

Tiffany Farms exemplifies suburban living at its finest. Generously proportioned homesites on quiet cul-de-sacs unite with the natural beauty of its surroundings; nearly one-quarter of the development has been preserved as nature intended. Antioch offers a highly-rated school district, with elementary schools in District 34; high schools are in District 117. The area is also serviced by McHenry County College.

Homesites Offered in Bulk–
A Tremendous Opportunity for Residential Developers!

21 Bulk Homesites

Opening bid: $175,000
Certified or cashier's check required to buy: $17,500
TO BE SOLD ABSOLUTE, REGARDLESS OF PRICE!

HOMESITE SUMMARY:

Address	Lot	Acreage	1999 Taxes	PIN Number
Creek Bend Lane	8	0.20	83	02-07-213-024
Creek Bend Lane	1	0.23	93	02-07-213-017
Creek Bend Lane	2	0.20	81	02-07-213-018
Creek Bend Lane	3	0.20	81	02-07-213-019
Creek Bend Lane	4	0.20	88	02-07-213-020
Creek Bend Lane	5	0.24	88	02-07-213-021
728 Creek Bend Lane	18	0.20	81	02-07-213-009
722 Creek Bend Lane	19	0.20	81	02-07-213-008
714 Creek Bend Lane	20	0.20	81	02-07-213-007
706 Creek Bend Lane	21	0.23	91	02-07-213-006
Indian Trail	99	0.34	135	02-07-102-001
Indian Trail	100	0.18	71	02-07-101-001
Indian Trail	101	0.18	71	02-07-101-002
Indian Trail	102	0.28	111	02-07-101-003
Indian Trail	103	0.26	103	02-07-101-004
Indian Trail	104	0.17	67	02-07-101-005
Indian Trail	105	0.18	71	02-07-101-006
Indian Trail	106	0.17	69	02-07-101-007
696 Creek Bend Lane	127	0.24	97	02-07-210-005
688 Creek Bend Lane	128	0.28	112	02-07-210-006
691 Creek Bend Lane	134	0.23	91	02-07-210-012

One Custom Home

757 Creek Bend Lane • Opening bid: $50,000
Certified or cashier's check required to buy: $6,000

RESIDENCE SUMMARY:
757 Creek Bend Lane (Lot 9)
• Four bedrooms, 2.5 baths, English look-out basement, two-car garage, on a 9,190 square foot site.
• Master bedroom suite.
• First floor laundry room.
• Family room with fireplace.
• Kitchen with island.
• Open rear deck.

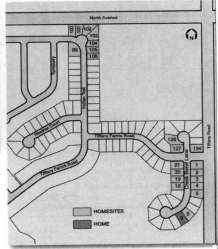

DIRECTIONS: Take I-94 to Route 173 and exit westbound.
Continue west to Tiffany Road, turn north and proceed to Tiffany Farms' entrance on the left.

Source: Reproduced with permission from Sheldon Good & Company Auctions, LLC.

B arry A . C hatz

"The UHI unsecured creditors committee was concerned that a market be generated for the benefit of its interests. In order to do this, substantial marketing funds were generated through the cooperation of the secured lender to facilitate the ability of Sheldon Good & Company to make the market for the properties at issue. At the auction sales, hundreds of potential buyers were bidding prices well in excess of anyone's anticipation.

"The Chicago auction, which I attended, had in excess of 500 people in the room bidding on single lots of partially developed, undeveloped, or fully developed real estate. The auction was extraordinary. Numerous bidders, with clear emotional desires to obtain what were premium properties in the Chicago area, paid larger than expected prices.

"This writing is not intended to be a sales pitch for Sheldon Good & Company, but from the standpoint of gathering the information required and creating sales through targeted marketing programs, Sheldon Good & Company is without competition. The members of the creditors committee who attended these events were shocked at the vigorous nature, as well as the competitive strength, of the marketplace.

"It is also very satisfying to work with people who have a history of being your friends. One never knows at initial intake whether the execution will satisfy the parties. I personally pushed strongly to ensure that Sheldon Good & Company, and not some other entity that had a lesser presence, was utilized for the potential savings of nominal monies. The ability to attract and generate demand was clearly facilitated and thus satisfied all of the parties. There were also diverse counsel for the lenders as well as numerous mechanics' liens claimants who were facilitated in the process.

"The particulars can be collected in detail in minutia, but the facts are that the properties were sold, and no one questions whether the 'market' was made. This is the key in the bankruptcy process, so no parties can

(continued)

be criticized within the process for Wild West tendencies. People don't want to be killed off by their clients in the future, so ensuring that the best results have occurred for them to their benefit is the key and necessary outcome."

9

THE JAILHOUSE ROCKED

The strangest call I ever received started with a question—"You ever sell a jail before?"—and ended with a full-blown auction in the Porter County Board of Commissioner's chambers in downtown Valparaiso, Indiana.

It was late one spring morning when I received a call from David Burrus, the president of the Porter County Board of Commissioners, which is based in Valparaiso, Indiana. Valparaiso is a small, quaint midwestern town located about a 75-minute highway drive from downtown Chicago. Although in some parts of the country a 75-minute one-way drive doesn't change the landscape much, in this case it's like Scottie from the television show *Star Trek* beaming you to a different planet. Roughly 75 minutes separates Batman's Gotham City from Andy and Opie Taylor's Mayberry; but just as in the television show, a lot of activity surrounded the goings on at the Mayberry jail.

The conversation started with Burrus explaining that he was the president of the Porter County Board of Commissioners, a three-person elected body. Everything that he and his fellow commissioners did was subject to the review and scrutiny of the public at large. At the outset of our conversation, he wanted to make it clear there was no such thing as confidentiality in the county commissioner world. He was calling me

D *a v i d* **L .** **B** *u r r u s ,* **PRESIDENT**
Porter County Board of Commissioners

David Burrus has a bachelor of architecture degree from Texas A&M University and also holds a bachelor of science in business administration degree and a master's degree in history from Valparaiso University.

David was an officer in the U.S. Navy Civil Engineers Corps and did two tours of duty in Vietnam with the Navy Seabees. After 27 years in reserve service, he retired in 1999.

David was an excavating and paving contractor for Porter County, Indiana, before serving as an engineer for the Valparaiso Water Department in 1987. In 1995, he began work as a project manager for Harza Environmental Services, an international engineering firm. With Harza, his projects included sewer and water systems rehabilitation in Georgetown, Guyana, South America.

In November 2000, David was elected to his first term as South District commissioner, an office he will hold until the end of 2004. He is currently president of the board of commissioners. In addition, he is an assistant professor of construction management at Purdue University, North Central.

because he and his fellow commissioners had done extensive research to find someone who could sell a really odd property—their four-story, 35,000-square-foot Porter County Jail, a facility that included 123 prison cells and an adjacent 51-car parking lot.

The county apparently was just completing the construction of a new and larger county jail and would be vacating the 30-year-old structure momentarily. Burrus went on to further explain that the commissioners had researched some of their selling options and were coming up goose eggs; basically, no one wanted the jail—period. As a result, they had commissioned a study to determine the cost of demolishing the jail, because the jail was located about two blocks from the center of downtown Valparaiso's shopping district. They were concerned that once the county transferred the inmates to the new jail, the old jail would become a community eyesore. Furthermore, the demolition estimates indicated that it would cost $300,000 or more for the jail to be torn down, which basically made the situation even worse. Not only would the county get stuck with a potential eyesore but it would have to reach into its pockets to make the problem go away.

By now you have probably deduced I am a good storyteller—but even I'm not good enough to make this one up. The guys in our firm still laugh at the fact that despite having sold tens of thousands of properties all over the hemisphere, we are still waiting for our first *easy* deal.

Clearly, this deal would be no exception.

Dave Burrus sounded like a really nice guy on the telephone. Having been involved in politics on a variety of levels ever since I was in college, I know that being the president of *any* county's board of commissioners meant that this guy was no slouch and was *really* powerful. I also put one and one together by gathering that he also ran the local jail, which I never previously even wanted to visit on grounds that the only reason I would be visiting it would be as a result of driving too fast on the interstate highway that passed *through* Dave's county. Nonetheless, Dave had a way about him, even on the telephone, that came across as being a down-to-earth, nice guy from hometown America.

I explained to Dave that our company had a lot of experience in selling unusual properties, although we had never actually sold a jail. A couple of years earlier we had sold a 300-bed nursing home to the state of Wisconsin, which made it into a juvenile detention center. Oddly enough, I joked that the Wisconsin property was a 75-minute interstate drive in the opposite direction but still required the same driving time from Chicago. I also highlighted that we had sold numerous unusual properties

D *a v e* **B** *u r r u s*

"With the continuing growth and urbanization of Porter County came the need to expand the capacity of the county jail. Severe overcrowding (220 inmates in a facility designed for 150) contributed to security problems and liability issues. The 'fix' took the form of a new $38 million, state-of-the-art facility with four times the floor space and a design capacity of 450 inmates."

D *a v e*   **B** *u r r u s*

"As the Porter County commissioners approached the time to vacate and dispose of the soon-to-be former jail, it was less a novelty and more a dilemma than Steve Good had realized. The building had been offered to other local government entities with negative responses. The commissioners had investigated the option of converting the 30,000-square-foot building to office space, but jails are designed and built for a specific purpose and are not easily or economically reconfigured. This same reality, along with high operating costs, prohibited numerous civic and charitable organizations from pursuing their interest in it, even if the building were donated to them at no cost.

"To establish a benchmark from which to evaluate a sale, the commissioners ordered an appraisal of the jail "as is" along with an alternative appraisal of the vacant site with the building demolished. The dilemma came home with force when the appraisal indicated a value of $150,000 for the vacant site and a value of –$275,000 (that's a negative number!) with the building standing. In addition, an estimate was procured suggesting a cost of between $300,000 to $350,000 to demolish the structure.

"While the need for, and the size of, the new jail was determined by a citizen's committee, public controversy prevailed concerning the $38 million cost. Critics were closely watching the apparent inactivity regarding the disposal of the old facility, knowing that the county would find it difficult to fund the operating costs of both the old and the new, simultaneously."

that often required a large amount of renovation; they included schools, churches, libraries, college campuses, fire stations, and a bunch of other odd stuff. Dave told me he already knew that as he and his fellow commissioners had already done their research and were calling me for a reason. I have to admit that his comment made me sit up straight in my chair; this guy didn't mess around. I liked him.

We concluded the call by making an appointment to get together at his office the following week to develop a plan for the sale of the jail. On hanging up with him, I walked down the hallway of our Chicago office and into one of our senior project manager's office. I had met the project manager when he was an officer of the Adventurer's Club of Chicago and I had attended a lecture given by one of my clients there. Our guy had retraced Marco Polo's trip through China—the point being that our project manager was a pretty adventurous guy. He enjoyed adventures, and I knew that I was about to lay one on him.

I started the conversation by asking him if he'd ever been locked up. He looked at me like I was crazy but admitted that there were times in rural China or Afghanistan when he was convinced he was going to be locked up if for nothing other than the sport of it. I then told him of my conversations with Dave Burrus, and he immediately jumped at the chance to do the deal with me. Besides, he was a great fan of Elvis Presley's and started singing a couple of bars of "Jailhouse Rock." I told him to cut it out and this was serious, but he was right—this was really going to be a riot.

FIRST WE MEET THE COMMISSIONERS

We got directions from Chicago to the commissioners' offices in downtown Valparaiso. Even though Valparaiso is only 75 minutes from downtown Chicago, both the project manager and I live about 45 minutes in the opposite direction from downtown Chicago, so we decided to check into a hotel the night before the meeting in order to beat the traffic.

We had both been *by* Valparaiso via the interstate highway system, but neither of us had ever been *in* downtown Valparaiso before. As we were driving into the town, we learned that a massive university was located there—called, of all things, Valparaiso University. After breakfast that next morning, we also found the commissioners' offices, which were part of a brand-new $20-million-looking county office complex two blocks from downtown Valparaiso and the Porter County Jail.

It was midspring but cold the day that our meeting was scheduled, and we were right on time. We had arranged to meet the commissioners and their legal counsel at 10:00 AM to be followed by our inspecting the jail. When we walked in the county building, we were impressed; it was a brand-new limestone and glass office complex that had all the bells and whistles. It was clear that no expense had been spared here. An information desk was in the main lobby, and the county person behind the desk immediately directed us to the commissioners' offices. There were a number of county offices in the building so it took a minute for us to find the right one. We opened the door to see a small Formica table with four chairs in front of a counter that had a small bell on it and a sign that said Ring Bell for Service—which we did. Before the bell went silent, an attractive middle-aged woman came out from behind the door and greeted us. After we explained who we were and who we were here to see, she offered us coffee and asked us to sit down and wait for the commissioners, as she knew they were expecting us.

"What a pleasure," I thought. "It's nice to be somewhere where they really have their act together." Two minutes later Dave Burrus came out and greeted us. He was a fit, middle-aged guy with gray hair who wore wire-framed glasses and looked like one of my favorite college professors. He shook hands with both of us and suggested that we move to the commissioners' chambers because we were going to need seating for six people and the table in the reception area held only four.

As we walked through the commissioners' offices on the way to their chamber, he introduced us to the two other commissioners and the commissioners' attorney. The attorney was an attractive sandy-blond-haired woman about my age who had a straightforward, no-nonsense way about her; she looked each of us right in the eyes when she shook hands. I liked that.

A couple of minutes later the six of us were sitting at a series of tables put together to form a rectangle with about 20 or so chairs around it. Dave Burrus started the meeting by reiterating the conversation he and I had previously had on the telephone. He also made sure to mention that whenever this group convened, it could not do so in private so that anyone walking into their chambers during the meeting was welcome to listen. "So this is life in a fishbowl," I thought.

The idea of people listening to what we said was insignificant, because on many previous occasions we had been hired to create an arm's-length transaction by owners, both public and private, who needed to avoid any appearance of impropriety or insider dealing. Besides, Dave also explained that their dilemma about the sale of the jail had been well covered by the media who reported on all of the commission's comings and goings, so there was nothing to hide here. The commission basically wanted to get rid of the jail and avoid a $300,000 price tag to do it.

WE FORMULATE A PLAN

Once the decision to make the jail go away was adopted by the commissioners, the best program to use became clear to us. We immediately recommended an open outcry auction program whereby the property would be sold absolute, on the spot, with no minimum bid or secret reserve price. The commissioners and their counsel especially liked the idea because it provided everyone who was interested in the jail, if anyone really was, the opportunity to bid publicly, with everyone bidding for the jail on the same "as is, where is" terms. We also thought that the marketing for the jail should be done on a local, regional, and limited national basis for no other reason than the unpredictability of the winning bidder's identity.

We stressed in this meeting that if the commissioners were going to go forward with us, it would be because they bought into the process. Furthermore, if done right, no one could fault them, win, loose, or draw, if the jail sold at a low price or not at all, in which case they would have no alternative but to demolish it. They saw us as an opportunity to validate whatever decision ultimately surfaced as a result of the auction.

About 20 minutes before the meeting with the commissioners concluded, the lights and the power in the building went out. Two minutes later a secretary came running in and informed us that a semitrailer had swerved off the interstate and crashed into an electrical tower severing the power lines to the city. She said that the police were setting up emergency stations, as many people relied on electricity as their heating source for their homes and businesses, and it would be hours before the power lines were repaired.

Our meeting ended about 20 minutes later with a tentative game plan in place. We would conduct a single property auction for the jail in the commissioners' chambers about 30 days after the prisoners were transferred to their new facility. We would promote the property on a local, regional, and national level and *hope* to save the county $300,000.

Because we had planned to inspect the jail right after our meeting ended, Dave had arranged for a couple of sheriff's deputies to be standing by as our tour guides. Just as the meeting broke, he asked us in his low-key way if it would be possible for us to reschedule our inspection. We couldn't understand why he was asking us this until he explained that the power outage had forced the sheriff to lock down the jail—

which meant we couldn't get in. He added that had our meeting broken half an hour earlier and we had been touring the jail, we would have been locked down too. I shivered and gladly agreed to arrange to see the jail some other time.

When we walked out of the meeting, my associate and I looked at each other in disbelief—someone up there had watched out for us. When we got in the car, I called my wife and told her the lockdown story. She said it was too bad the meeting had dragged on, because it probably would have been a cool experience to be part of a lockdown. I told her that she watched too much television and being locked down in the Porter County Jail was the last experience in the world I needed.

THE RETENTION PROCESS

Because we had already mapped out our game plan with the commissioners at our meeting, it was easy to write the proposal—we knew where we were going. My associate had seen the jail, and we had gathered all of the information about it from the commission's legal counsel. The group really had a handle on everything, which made our job that much easier.

I received a call from Dave a couple of weeks after our initial meeting. The commission had reviewed our proposal and loved it. It was just what we had discussed; in order for them to adopt it, I would have to present our proposal at a formal meeting of the Porter County Board of Commissioners so the commissioners could legally retain us. Having formal legal training is an enormous benefit, for I was going to be called as a witness. I would be asked questions relating to our company credentials, programming, costs, and time lines and why we had made the recommendations that we had. I told Dave that I had a lot of experience doing this and looked forward to seeing him and his crew at the meeting.

Dave had asked me to get to the meeting early just in case anything unexpected surfaced. This time we knew where their offices were and everyone knew us. We walked right into their offices and spent about half an hour with the commissioners, who told us they had integrated our proposal with the questions that would be asked at the meeting.

At the appointed time the commissioners took their assigned places in the commission's chambers. I took a seat, along with my associate, in the audience. It was an impressive event when the commission's meeting was formally called to order. A protocol is followed at these types of events. They are governed by statute, and the people running the meetings are aware that opponents of the substantive issues often seek to find a flaw in the procedural aspect of the process to ultimately defeat the substance of the approved items. Consequently, great care is taken to make sure that no procedural defects occur in these meetings.

After the meeting was called to order, President Burrus presented to the Porter County Board of Commissioners the proposition at hand. He reiterated the issues surrounding the Porter County Jail, the research results, and the conclusion that our company's program was the solution to their problem. Within 15 minutes of the meeting's commencement, I was officially asked to publically respond to the commissioners' questions about our proposal.

D a v e   B u r r u s

"The view held by critics became acutely accurate when two major national steel producing firms with facilities along Lake Michigan in Porter County declared bankruptcy and ceased paying taxes that amounted to 20 percent of the county's annual budget. Porter County was facing a very real possibility of halting or severely reducing public services.

"The decision to call Sheldon Good & Company was based on the fact that we knew we needed a firm with a much larger marketing reach than we had locally. In addition, Indiana law requires that government assets to be sold are to be sold through competitive bids. Our hope was that Sheldon Good & Company could successfully meet both requirements.

"The local suspense was compounded when computer software issues delayed the occupancy of the new jail by four months. The sale could not be scheduled until the old facility was vacant. The budget crisis resulting from the steel bankruptcies continued to escalate amid speculation that 'those Chicago auctioneers' with their 'up-front sales costs' were simply profiteering on our problem and adding to the dilemma."

When I was a junior in college, I was fortunate to be selected by Senator Adlai Stevenson III to serve as an intern in his Washington, D.C., office during America's bicentennial celebration in 1976. I was 19 and lucky to get this summer job. The serendipitous aspect of the experience is that I spent an entire summer listening to people testify before various U.S. Senate committees and subcommittees. Who would have believed that 25 years later I would be the guy doing the talking?

The commissioners asked me a battery of probing questions. What were our credentials? Why us? Explain the program. Explain the budget. Who's the targeted market? On and on they went. About half an hour later the questions ended and a vote was taken. We won—three to nothing.

When the meeting concluded, Dave came up to me and commented that he never thought that I could speak so well. I apologized to him by commenting that I was sorry that I was not as dumb as I looked.

WE IMPLEMENT THE PROGRAM

This was a challenging deal. Who would buy it? Every once in a while, when I have an unusual deal, I tell my wife and kids about it and ask their thoughts. I don't know why this is, but getting their attention at dinner is an impossible task. When I finally got their attention, they wanted to know what famous criminals had been in the jail and none of them wanted to visit it. I told them that John Dillinger had been in the

D *a v e* **B** *u r r u s*

"During all conversations with Steve Good, I don't believe he had any idea of the gravity of the financial crisis in Porter County and how much we desperately needed to sell a jail at a price that would not only prove our critics, but also our appraisers, wrong. Steve and his company had their work cut out for them, and not only were they in a fish bowl but they were under the spotlight."

jail in the next county but that I wasn't aware of any famous criminals having served time in the Porter County Jail.

When I pressed the kids as to who they thought might buy the place and its potential uses, their suggested alternatives were a house, condos, an office building, some other jail or prison, razing the building altogether, and a cool place to take a date.

Irrespective of my family's dinner conversation, our company had focused on a number of alternative uses for the property. They included these:

- Private prison operators
- Residential redevelopers
- Office redevelopers
- Mixed-use retail redevelopers
- Restaurant operators
- Demolition companies
- Bar and nightclub operators
- Investors looking for a good deal

We targeted these groups through a variety of solicitation media, including print and electronic advertising, direct mail and e-mails, broker solicitations, and our normal massive marketing techniques (see Figures 9.1 and 9.2). The element of this deal that particularly attracted me was the publicity of selling such an odd deal. The idea of selling a *jail* was something that I thought would be especially interesting. Even if we weren't handling the sale, I would have been interested in reading a blurb somewhere about some *other* guys selling it. For no other reason than it was a good *story* and a potentially cool experience, I wanted to be involved.

Once learning of this oddity, the media loved it. I got calls from The Associated Press, the *Wall Street Journal,* and even a couple of radio personalities in Las Vegas who urged their high-rolling listeners to buy the jail on a lark—where else could you buy a property based on the *cell* compared with a normal room or unit count?

One of the stories that ran is shown in Figure 9.3.

FIGURE 9.1 *Brochure from Sheldon Good & Company*

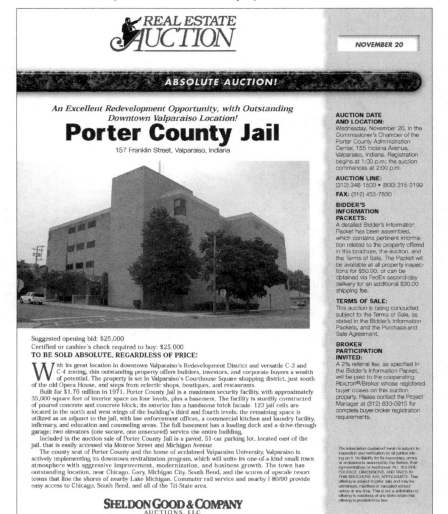

THE MARKET REACTS

We do a good job reporting to our clients reactions to our programming. The information is usually forwarded to them in confidential reports. The problem in this case was that any information we provided the commissioners was subject to immediate public review; consequently, we can show you in Figure 9.4 what we told them was the result of our efforts.

FIGURE 9.1 *Brochure from Sheldon Good & Company, continued*

Source: Reproduced with permission from Sheldon Good & Company Auctions, LLC.

THE AUCTION

We had scheduled the auction for 2:00 PM in the commissioners' chambers. Our staff got there at noon and by 1:00 PM we were signing in bidders. In order to bid, each bidder was required to bring a certified or

FIGURE 9.2   *Press Release*

RUBENSTEIN ASSOCIATES, INC.

Public Relations

FROM: **SHELDON GOOD & COMPANY AUCTIONS**
           333 W. Wacker Drive, Suite 400
           Chicago, IL 60606

FOR IMMEDIATE RELEASE

**JAIL FOR SALE!! SHELDON GOOD & COMPANY AUCTIONS TO OFFER
INDIANA JAIL NOVEMBER 20**

*   *   *

Porter County Jail, Valparaiso, To Be Sold Without Reserve Day of Auction

Valparaiso, Indiana—Sheldon Good & Company will hold a one-day, open outcry auction of the Porter County Jail in Valparaiso, Indiana on Wednesday, November 20th, beginning at 1:00 p.m. at The Porter County Building Commissioner's Chamber, 155 Indiana Avenue, Valparaiso. The Porter County Jail is a 35,272-square-foot, 123-bed maximum-security prison located at 157 Franklin Street in downtown Valparaiso. The **property will be sold "absolute, without reserve, regardless of price"** that day at auction. The suggested opening bid is $25,000. The seller, the County of Porter, Indiana, has built a brand-new state-of-the-art prison facility and all inmates will be transferred there.

"A jail is obviously a very unusual real estate offering," said Steven L. Good, CEO of Sheldon Good & Company Auctions. "Porter County has elected to sell this property at auction for two reasons: a jail is a very difficult class of asset to place value on since so few are ever on the market, so determining an asking price is problematic, and in addition, the county does not want to incur the costs associated with marketing the asset through traditional real estate brokerage and waiting until an appropriate buyer is identified. The auction format allows for an immediate sale in an open, competitive bidding environment and avoids the problem of taxpayers incurring long-term maintenance costs of an obsolete real estate asset."

"The Porter County Jail is located in the heart of downtown Valparaiso's central business district with various clothing, antique and gift shops nearby, as well as several restaurants," said Paul Galanis, senior project manager at Sheldon Good & Company Auctions. "The building itself is a four-story brick-and-concrete facility that could easily be redeveloped as an office building or medical facility, or the property could be used as a private prison."

The Porter County Jail benefits from a high-profile corner location at Franklin and Monroe Streets and features a full basement, loading dock, two elevators, operational kitchen and laundry facilities and a 51-car parking lot. The property is convenient to major highways and regional passenger rail service to Chicago and South Bend.

A bidder's packet, required for registration to bid at the auction, is available from Sheldon Good & Company Auctions by contacting the Information Office.

FIGURE 9.2 *Press Release, continued*

The property is open for inspection, by appointment only, on Wednesday, October 23, Tuesday, October 29, and Tuesday, November 6. On the inspection dates, Sheldon Good & Company staff will conduct a bidder's seminar, review the offering in its entirety and answer questions.

About Sheldon Good & Company Auctions, LLC:

Sheldon Good & Company Auctions, LLC is the nation's largest real estate auction company. Since 1965, Sheldon Good & Company has sold over 37,000 properties from coast to coast, throughout Canada and the Caribbean for a total value of over $8 billion. The company is extensively involved with auction programs in both the commercial and residential real estate sectors. In addition to its new Forestry Division, the company's growth areas include a nationally oriented "Trophy Home" Division and a Hospitality-Resort Division to auction resort properties from Canada to Mexico and from Hawaii through the Caribbean.

# # #

---

cashier's check for $25,000. We also had a cadre of spectators and news-people who wanted to personally see what happened.

As you've probably figured out by now, I have a good time being part of the auction show. As our company has grown, we have a bunch of people who are good at being the auctioneer at our events. I usually act as the master of ceremonies and in that capacity run the event, although someone else calls the bids. In this case I had been slated to do the whole show and was excited about it. I liked the entire Porter County crew, and they looked forward to my performance—anticipating something good happening on the one hand and angst that no one would show up to bid on the other. If no one showed, they would have to pick up the $300,000 bill for knocking down the jail plus our fees.

My associate and I got to the auction early and met with Commissioners Dave Burrus and John Evans. Commissioner Larry Sheets was ill and couldn't make the auction, but the commission's legal counsel was there. The two commissioners and their counsel greeted us when we got to the auction and invited us to their private offices to huddle up, as it were, before the game while waiting to take the field.

It's amazing how slow time passes when you are waiting for an auction to start. It's like being an athlete waiting in the locker room before

FIGURE 9.3 *Associated Press Article about the Sale of the Jail*

Old county jail piques interest of bidders nationwide

Valparaiso facility too expensive to operate, say commissioners, who have put it up for auction.

Associated Press
October 05, 2002

VALPARAISO, Ind.—The old Porter County Jail is drawing interest from Arizona to Massachusetts as the date for it to go on the auction block draws near.

A national auction house specializing in unusual properties will auction the four-story, 138-bed facility on Nov. 20.

Sheldon Good & Co. Auctions of Chicago was called in to conduct the sale after local buyers failed to materialize for the 31-year-old structure.

Inquiries from around the country have come in "from all walks of people," according to Paul Galanis, senior project manager with Sheldon Good.

Galanis declined to name prospective bidders, but he said most seem to have some tie to Indiana, whether they grew up here or went to school in the state.

Because of the unusual nature of the offering, several national media outlets have reported the story, Galanis said.

"It's not often you hear of a jail being sold," Porter County Commissioners

President David Burrus told The Times of Munster.

Sheriff's officers and inmates are moving from the jail to a new jail on Ind. 49.

Demolishing the 35,272-square-foot jail could cost as much as $300,000, county officials said. The minimum bid will be $25,000, though Galanis said it was difficult to determine an asking price for the jail because so few are on the market.

With a loading dock, two elevators, laundry facilities, full basement and a 51-car parking lot, the former jail is being marketed as a "unique" property.

Burrus said the commissioners set up the auction because the county was reluctant to continue paying operation costs.

"We can't afford to own it. We can't afford to operate it. We can't afford to tear it down," Burrus said.

Several charitable organizations also lost interest in the property when they heard about its $10,000-per-month utility costs, he said.

Source: Reprinted with permission of The Associated Press.

the championship game. You basically know the game plan, but the anxiety of waiting to take the field is something that I still have never quite adjusted to. To kill time while we were waiting in the commissioners' offices, Dave Burrus told me that he and their attorney teach at Purdue University and Valparaiso University, respectively. I knew there was something I really liked about them.

It was now time to start the auction. We had a packed room and were ready to go. The commissioners took their assigned seats. After

FIGURE 9.4 *Report to Client*

Sheldon Good & Company
333 West Wacker Drive
Chicago, Illnois 60606
(312) 346-1500
Fax (312) 453-7833

SHELDON GOOD & COMPANY

November 20   __Auction Day__

Porter County Attorney
Porter County Administrative Center
I 55 Indiana Avenue, Suite 205
Valparaiso, Indiana 46383

Re: Porter County Jail Auction

Dear:

This letter shall serve as a status report that will summarize our efforts, progress and results to date, in preparing for the sale of your property at public real estate auction.

A.   *DUE DILIGENCE MATERIALS*

All requested materials have been provided and incorporated into our materials.

B.   *MARKETING MATERIALS*

1.   *Direct Mail Two-Page Flyer:*
A two-page self-mailing flyer was created and mailed to approximately 2,000 prospects in the state of Indiana, with an emphasis on the five counties surrounding the property, and in the Chicago metropolitan area.

2.   *Web Site:*
The property has been added to the Sheldon Good & Company web site.

3.   *Brochure:*
A four-color, two-page brochure featuring the Porter County Jail located in Valparaiso, Indiana being offered in the open out-cry auction on November 20, 2002, has been approved and printed.

4.   *Purchase and Sale Agreement:*
The Purchase and Sale Agreement has been approved by you.

Realtors® • Auctioneers • Consultants

Strategic Offices Throughout America

FIGURE 9.4 *Report to Client, continued*

Porter County Jail
November 20,

5.   Bidder's Kit Status:
The Bidder's Kit has been approved by you.

6.   Public Relations:
Rubenstein Associates, Inc. our advertising agency has released the auction story to approximately 350 Media Outlets. National & local, correctional, and real estate: trade magazines, radio & TV news programs, daily and weekly newspapers and magazines, wire services, and appropriate editors and syndicated columnists are the primary categories within their distribution efforts. Currently, we have received articles in a variety of papers including the Indianapolis Star (three times), Boston Globe, Associated Press, Chesterton Tribune, CLTV Chicago, The Naked News and the WPVI Channel 6 (Philadelphia). The agency will continue to follow up with these papers and other outlets.

7.   Radio:
We have bought time on two local AM radio stations, 670 The Score and WBBM News Radio 78.

C.   MARKETING METHODS

1.   Advertising:
You have approved the classified advertisements for the Porter County Jail located in Valparaiso, Indiana. Display ads were created with the same copy. The advertising schedule to date is as follows.

	September	*Corrections Forum*
	November	*Correctional News*
10/2	Wednesday	*Wall Street Journal*
10/6	Sunday	*Valparaiso Times*
10/6	Sunday	*Indianapolis Star Tribune*
10/9	Wednesday	*Wall Street Journal*
10/9	Wednesday	*Chicago Tribune*
10/12	Saturday	*Realty & Building*
10/13	Sunday	*Valparaiso Times*
10/13	Sunday	*Indianapolis Star Tribune*
10/20	Sunday	*Valparaiso Times*
10/20	Sunday	*Indianapolis Star Tribune*
10/27	Sunday	*Valparaiso Times*
11/3	Sunday	*Valparaiso Times*
11/3	Wednesday	*Chicago Tribune*
11/6	Wednesday	*Wall Street Journal*
11/10	Sunday	*Valparaiso Times*

FIGURE 9.4 *Report to Client, continued*

Porter County Jail
November 20,

2. Personal Meetings:
We have talked with a number of the more important brokers in the local area, to educate these brokers on the auction process and to learn about current conditions in the local market and its attributes and negatives to buyers.

3. Direct Mail:
Our direct mail program has included mailing the two-page flyer, and personalized letters. Approximately two thousand copies of this flyer have been mailed to our custom lists including businesses in the property's area, real estate investment trusts, real estate developers, private, federal and state correctional institutions, sheriff offices, legal & accounting services, motion picture, television studios & producers, audio-visual production services, theaters, film production companies, local and regional real estate brokers, prospects from other previous school, mental health services and self storage facilities Indiana/Illinois auctions, where cross-over interest is logical. The color brochures will be distributed to prospects on targeted direct mail lists, open house attendees, and to all call-ins. We expect to see many of the call-ins at the site inspections, as they have received a mailing and have usually read the ads placed in the newspapers, visited our web site, heard our radio ad, and/or have been exposed to another form of media promoting the sale of this property at auction. This program is being supported by a targeted callback program.

4. Signage:
We have placed an auction sign at the corner of the property to capture the attention of the traffic heading in all directions on Franklin and Monroe Streets, and we have placed the correct contact information on the signs. Not only have we sold many properties as a result of the signs—but they also create validity to the offering with prospects and the community.

5. Broker Announcement:
We have announced to the broker community the upcoming auction of your property. A mailing will be sent to members of the area brokerage community, giving them details of the auction, inviting their participation and informing them on how to register their clients. We have also e-mailed the Property Information Profiles to all brokers with the CCIM (Certified Commercial Investment Member) designation. They are recognized experts in the field of commercial real estate.

6. Radio:
We have advertised with spots on both The SCORE AM 670 and WBBM AM 780 Radio in Chicago, during prime drive times. This medium is a great reinforcement for the print media. The weekly listening audience for these stations is 400,000 and 1.2 million respectively, and has the highest average, individual and family income levels in the marketplace for the 25 to 54 age group.

(continued)

FIGURE 9.4 *Report to Client, continued*

Porter County Jail
November 20,

RESPONSE TO MARKETING

1.   Call-ins:

To date we have had fifty-three (53) prospects inquiring about the property. The calls breakdown is as follows:

Newspaper	
Wall Street Journal	8
Chicago Tribune	6
Post Tribune	6
South Bend Tribune	2
Indianapolis Star	1
Hammond Times	1
Boston Globe	1
CLTV	1
Word of Mouth	11
Signs	8
Mailing	7
Radio	1

Geographically, the 53 calls came from 12 states. Almost all calls in Indiana came from the greater Valparaiso area:

Indiana	32
Illinois	9
Florida	2
Tennessee	2
Georgia	1
Kentucky	1
Massachusetts	1
Michigan	1
Ohio	1
Pennsylvania	1
West Indies	1
Washington D.C.	1

Many call-ins are currently from people in the Valparaiso area who now know they must act now if they have an interest in the property.

2.   Site Inspection Attendees:

We have held all three of the scheduled open houses and two additional showings; thus far we have had 23 different parties attend open houses. With each open house, we are better able to identify prospects and ascertain their interest or concerns. We will keep you informed.

FIGURE 9.4 *Report to Client, continued*

Porter County Jail
November 20,

3.   Broker Registrations:
To date we have received four broker registrations for your property. Since our marketing is effectively penetrating the marketplace, we feel that we are successfully casting a larger net than the local brokers can.

4.   Bidder's Kit Sales:
We have received 9 orders for a Bidder's Information Packet (BIP). The sales of the BIP usually accelerate at two points, first when they are available, second in the last ten days of a program. It is always one of the best barometers of whether or not a buyer plans to come to bid.

ISSUES & RECOMMENDATIONS

Our program is running as planned. We are capturing the attention of the marketplace. The response for the auction of your property is good. Even though we all know that this special use property is in need of significant renovation, and the cost of the renovation or demolition is extensive, still, there is still interest in the property. The market is soft for investment, development or redevelopment in the Valparaiso area. The auction process has already produced 53 people who inquired about the Jail. We are just beginning to get the temperature of the marketplace for this property.

Potential uses that are surfacing during this time include private prison operators, a restaurant, a nightclub, redevelopment into residential and/or office use, and complete demolition. Clearly there is great divergence of opinion as to how this property should be re-developed, and our progress has been effective in drawing every type of adaptive reuse viable for this situation.

The initial feedback indicates limited Chicago area interest in this property. As we discussed we are drawing the most amount of interest from Northern Indiana and the Chicago metropolitan area. As we suspected, there is a thin market for this property, and we have drawn significant interest in eight weeks. We will continue our efforts and keep you advised. We believe at this time that we will see bidding at the auction, but it is too early to predict the price level.

Please call us at your convenience to discuss this report.

Sincerely,

SHELDON GOOD & COMPANY
Auctions

Steven L. Good, AARE
Chairman and Chief Executive Officer

Enclosures: Sample Advertisement
                    Initial Marketing Materials

PAG/kd

going through the introductions, terms of the auction, and a practice round of bidding, I opened the bidding.

"Do I have an opening bid of $25,000?"

"Yes," cried one of the two auction spotters.

"How about $35,000?" I cried.

"Yes."

"How about $50,000?"

The property ultimately sold for $365,750, which was reached in increments of $5,000, $10,000, and $15,000; the commissioners had saved the taxpayers $731,500. The press immediately swarmed the winning bidders: two Greek brothers and one of the brother's sons who was their lawyer. After they signed the contract, we learned their thoughts about what they were going to do with the jail: make it a destination nightclub.

My middle son had pegged the deal right—he can't wait to grow up and take a nice girl to jail in Valparaiso on a Saturday night date.

D *a v e* **B** *u r r u s*

"The sale proceeded much as Steve has described, but I think he may have missed the nervous glances exchanged among the commissioners and our attorney as the gavel came down and the bidding began. Nor did he note the expressions of relief as the bids progressed past the break-even point" With Steve conducting the bidding and his staff working the audience, bids continued to climb toward the ultimate sale figure and our relief turned to euphoria. Even though the jail was a sound building and worth the price paid for it, the challenge was to bring a buyer and seller together. Steve Good was able to accomplish this even if a jail is not a particularly hot commodity. We are especially grateful to Steve and his company for their professionalism in marketing and selling a unique property. We are convinced that any other approach to our sale would have been much less successful."

10

SCHOOLYARD
FOR SALE

Serendipity: the faculty or phenomenon of finding valuable or agreeable things not sought for (*Merriam Webster's Collegiate Dictionary,* 10th ed.).

It is amazing how serendipitous life can be—especially when you don't expect it to be.

When I was nine, my parents decided to move our family to the older, well-established Chicago suburban community of Evanston. Evanston at the time was famous for four things. First, it was the home of Northwestern University. Second, it had some of the biggest, oldest, and best-preserved houses in the Chicagoland area. Third, it was dry—that is, liquor sales of any kind were prohibited. Finally, it was known for having one of the best completely racially integrated public school systems in America. I am proud to say that I am a product of the Evanston/ Skokie School District 65 system and graduated from Evanston Township High School, which at the time had some 5,400 students in 1974.

A CALL FROM THE BUSINESS MANAGER

One afternoon in late fall, I received a note from our director of sales indicating that the company had received a blind call from the business

H *a r d y* **M** *u r p h y* **, PH.D., SUPERINTENDENT OF SCHOOLS**

Evanston/Skokie District 65

Dr. Hardy Murphy attended New Mexico State University on an athletic scholarship, served in the U.S. military, and then pursued a master's degree in education from Southwest Texas State University and a doctorate in educational psychology from the University of Texas at Austin.

After working in the Fort Worth Independent School District for most of his professional career, Hardy was appointed superintendent of schools for Evanston/Skokie District 65 in June 1999. As superintendent for the Evanston elementary district, he serves the families of approximately 7,000 students.

A number-one priority for Hardy and the entire District 65 School Board is academic achievement. The programs and services available to District 65 families are designed to accomplish that number-one priority.

Hardy also brings with him a commitment to community. While living in the Fort Worth area, he served as chairman of the board of directors for the Tarrant County Hospital District, gaining extensive experience with the funding and development of public service facilities. During his tenure on the hospital board of managers, the hospital district undertook an extensive building initiative that resulted in the construction of several full-service community and neighborhood clinics. In 1991, Hardy earned recognition as Fort Worth Man of the Year. Since joining the Evanston community, he has been appointed to the McGaw YMCA Board and the Evanston Hospital Board, demonstrating his continued commitment to community support.

manager of Evanston/Skokie School District 65. I was given the form, which had been filled out by the director of sales' assistant; the assistant was directed to give the call to me because one of the areas of our practice on which I concentrate is the sale of surplus school properties. I have personally been involved in the sale of many, many surplus elementary, middle, and high school properties as well as surplus college campuses, administration buildings, libraries, and other similar properties that are owned by school, library, or municipal boards. Everyone in our office knows that I have a strong affection for these properties and the boards that control them. As I mentioned in an earlier chapter, these groups are mostly volunteer driven by people who are trying to give back to their communities. My experience in the arena of school board property is extensive with the realization of income of more than nine figures, and these boards have a unique element to them: Their members are usually elected or politically appointed and often serve as a flashpoint for their community. Anyone who has a child going to public school is the school board's constituent, and parents won't hesitate to speak up publicly where they perceive that their kid's education is concerned.

Most public school boards employ an army of administrators who are professionally trained educators. They are led by the superintendent of schools, who is charged with the responsibility of running several or more schools, in the district in which the schools are located. Issues like curriculum selection, teacher retention, strategic planning, and a zillion different issues relating to the running of the school district fall squarely on the superintendent's shoulders. Many larger school districts hire a business manager who reports to the superintendent and is responsible for, as the title suggests, managing the business affairs of the school district. The business manager's role often includes negotiating purchase contracts for goods and services required by the district, negotiating leases (either as a tenant or a landlord), and many other similar tasks. Although both the superintendent and the business manager play vital roles in running a school district, the district's school board members, as elected officials, ultimately hear the praise or criticism of the community in virtually every area the school district touches.

Understanding the nature of this situation was important when I called the school board's business manager. I was concerned about a number of things. He might be only in the information-gathering stage. Was he the person in charge of our potential retention? What was his relationship with the superintendent? The school board? A number of other questions popped into my mind because I had been in this spot before, and this part of our practice was fraught with great amounts of nuance.

I called the business manager back but couldn't reach him. After several return calls, my assistant arranged a time for us to talk; and when we finally connected, I was excited. He had called to tell me that the Evanston/Skokie School District Board had decided to sell its headquarters' administration building, which was located in the best area of Evanston. Having grown up there, I had only driven by the property a million times and had to do everything I could for him not to see that I was leaping out of my seat. He went on to explain that the school board had appointed a building committee, and he was calling on the committee's behalf. The committee had decided to interview four real estate companies and would be sending our firm a formal Request for Qualification (RFQ) to which he wanted to make sure that we responded.

The business manager seemed like a nice guy, and as the conversation progressed he told me that the school board strongly favored doing business with Evanston-based companies as a way of keeping business in their own community. I responded that we had sold many properties in his town and although we weren't based there, we had a special expertise and experience level that set us apart from our competitors. I also asked him, point blank, if the school board already had someone else in mind, because it took anywhere between 10 and 20 man-hours to respond to RFQs and if we were being played as a staulking horse for someone already favored by the board, I would really appreciate knowing it. He was diplomatic in his answer, almost cryptic in fact, and told me that he wouldn't have gone through the effort of reaching me *personally* if he and his board didn't want to consider us for the job. He was merely trying to tip me off that we had a couple of biases working against us; not being located in Evanston was one of them.

When the call concluded, I wasn't quite sure what to think. I was excited and perplexed all at the same time. Here was an opportunity to come back and represent my alma mater and yet, because I worked in the town next door, someone less qualified might get the call. I felt I was back in high school running for student council again.

THE FIRST MEETING

As promised, about a week later the Request for Qualification (RFQ) came in the mail. It was so nondescript that I was glad the business manager called to tip me off that it was coming. The way in which it was prepared gave the impression that 50 companies were being solicited to vie for the assignment but, because I knew they were only sending it to four companies, I took it seriously. This was a piece of business I really, really wanted. We had great credentials, and I was going to give it a college try. One of the things I have learned through the years is that effort and sincerity go far in life, and I was going to let these folks know that we meant to get and do their business.

After reading the RFQ, I immediately called the business manager and arranged to physically inspect the property. I also asked him to have all of the substantive, descriptive, legal, and financial information available so that we could do a complete workup of the property. The facility was located about halfway between my house and my office and was easy to get to. Consequently, I made the date early in the morning on my way downtown.

I had been by the building countless times, but had never actually been in it. It was eight blocks from my former elementary school and ten blocks from the post where I was the crossing guard patrol captain when I was in fifth grade. My best friend in grammar school had been bar mitzvahed at the synagogue next door. It was like childhood déjà vu.

The building was a stately 18,000-square-foot mansion that the school district had bought from Northwestern University 40 years earlier. The district had converted the building to offices and was bursting out of it. As I walked in the front door, I passed an archway with a sign reading Superintendent's Office. It's funny, but as I walked by the sign I felt a nervous twitch in the pit of my stomach as if I had done something wrong—shades of being sent to the principal's office I guess.

On the second floor I was shown to the business manager's office by a school-administrator-type secretary. The business manager came out immediately and greeted me warmly. As it turned out, he was originally from the greater New York area and had only recently taken a job in Evanston. We exchanged New York geography stories as we toured the main building, which was when I learned that two other buildings were involved in the sale too. After we visited all of the buildings, the business manager suggested that I meet the superintendent before I left. I was thrilled.

Every once in a while you just catch a break, and that day was my lucky one. One of the major Chicago newspapers had published an article about one of the other deals that I was working on (for the Marshall

Field family), and the business manager had read it while drinking his morning coffee before I arrived. As he escorted me into the superintendent's office, he brought the newspaper with him and showed it to the superintendent simultaneously with introducing me.

The superintendent was a tall, stately man who looked like Danny Glover with the style of Clint Eastwood. At the moment I shook his hand and said, "It's a pleasure to meet you, Dr. Murphy," he looked down at me and replied, "It's Hardy, not Doctor Murphy." What a great guy. It's amazing what a handshake and a kind word can do.

THE PRESENTATION BEFORE THE BUILDING COMMITTEE

A lot of legal details surround selling school and municipally owned properties. Having handled many of these types of situations, I'm very conversant with the technicalities that can make a difference between having a great success or a bust. When I was reviewing the RFQ, I had noticed that although it had been prepared with great care, I thought that I could demonstrate our sophistication by embellishing some of the more complicated nuances that would arise because of the property's nature as a historic landmark and the statutory framework that the board probably didn't fully understand. Most boards of their type don't often sell surplus properties.

After the business manager called to tell me that he had received the 15 copies of our proposal in response to their RFQ, he told me I had been scheduled to give a 45-minute initial presentation to the school district's building committee. What he didn't tell me was what I learned when I arrived at the administration building on the appointed evening. All four companies had been lined up to make their presentations the same evening; I was a gladiator waiting to be led into the coliseum.

I've mentioned earlier that most civic and charitable groups meet at night because their members are volunteers, almost all of whom have day jobs. When I got to the meeting I was greeted, escorted to an empty office, and asked to stay there with the door closed until the business manager came to get me. I was scheduled to go on at 8:00 PM and spent about 15 minutes by myself waiting in the empty office.

Anyway, the business manager came to get me, and as I was walking up the stairs, a group of guys in suits and ties were walking down the stairs. It didn't take a rocket scientist to figure out that I wasn't the only gladiator being led into the business equivalent of matched-pair battle. I had purposely come by myself and had a ton of materials under both arms, including videotapes, slides, brochures, and anything else I thought I could use to demonstrate that we could—and had—outperformed our competitors in selling surplus school property.

The meeting room was on the third floor of the mansion and used to be a private ballroom. It was large and opulent—I imagined what great parties must have been held there in the property's heyday. Now it was being used as a public meeting room for a school board.

There were about ten people sitting behind a couple of six-foot-long card tables, and theater-style seating occupied the rest of the room. There were maybe four or five spectators already seated to watch my presentation as these meetings are always open to the public. As I walked over to put all of my stuff down, I immediately recognized the superintendent, Dr. Hardy Murphy. Seeing him brought an immediate smile to my face and I relaxed. As I started to set things up, the group just started talking. I had slides for case studies. I had videotapes of auctions. I had everything. About midway through my unpacking ritual, I asked a question of the chairperson of the committee that had just dawned on me: "Would you like to see Hollywood or would you just like to talk?" The answer was unanimous—"Let's talk."

The committee members started asking questions and I answered them. I explained the selling process as mandated by a number of statutes, including the state's school code. Two of the three buildings were designated as historical landmarks, which meant they had to be treated in a special way. The entire property fell inside a landmark district, which would require close interactions with the city of Evanston and the Evanston Landmark Commission because some of the most prominent city residents lived in the neighborhood. There were also well-funded community watchdog groups closely scrutinizing this transaction. Finally, it was also clear that the school district had to clear between a million and a million and a half dollars from the sale of the property to meet its budget projections.

This was a really cool deal. Would they hire the expert from afar (i.e., the next town over) or a local broker? The 45-minute meeting went by in a flash. The chairperson and Hardy thanked me for coming, and as I was walking down the stairs, the next group of real estate guys passed me going up. It was clear that the battle of the real estate gladiators was continuing.

THE NEXT STEP

The business manager called me a couple of days later to tell me that the building committee had enjoyed my presentation and wanted me to come back. Considering that I hadn't actually made a presentation, I felt good because of their positive feedback. I asked if I had won, and in his diplomatic way he told me not yet but we were in the finals. He scheduled another meeting, and told me this time to forget bringing Hollywood with me.

This meeting couldn't have gone better. The committee had checked out everything I had told them, and everything that I had told them had checked out. We all knew this would be a challenging deal. At the end of the meeting, they told me the good news: merit had prevailed over politics.

Hardy asked me to meet with him in his office a couple of days later along with the chairperson of the building committee and the local alderman in whose district the property was located. It's funny how a once formidable place—Hardy's office—was becoming our strategic headquarters. This meeting was important because we needed to develop a time line for the auction, which would coincide with the completion of the district's new administration building, which was already under construction. As with all real estate construction projects, a *projected* move-in date is just that—a projection. It was also important that we create a vehicle whereby the community could provide input about the potential redevelopment of the property, which is why we enlisted the aid of the local alderman.

The meeting started as a reintroduction of all of us on a more intimate basis. Hardy had a wonderful way of making everyone feel comfortable with one another in an otherwise pressured situation. After all, a lot of money was at stake, the deal would be scrutinized through a microscope by community leaders, the property was designated a landmark, and the school board didn't quite know when it would be ready to move. Within an hour we had mapped out our game plan. First, the school board would retain us. Then we would call a meeting of community residents and city officials to get their input on the redevelopment of the property. Next, we would set the terms of the auction and auction date, which would allow the school district to lease back the buildings after the deals closed in case it needed more time.

It was a good plan. We broke from our huddle, and I was put on the formal agenda of the next school board meeting.

THE FORMAL SCHOOL BOARD CONVENES

The next meeting was set for us to appear before the formal school board and was slated several weeks later in the library of the middle school, where my college roommate had gone to school (now, middle school déjà vu strikes again). Hardy had called to ask that I attend a premeeting session with the entire school board present. The premeeting session occurred in the faculty lounge, and I brought a project manager with me to introduce him to the board. He would be gathering a lot of data once we were retained, and I wanted to be sure that the board was comfortable with him.

The project manager and I got to the premeeting a little early and were greeted by the district's business manager, who had been waiting for us. He showed us to the faculty lounge but told us to wait outside the room until we were called in. He pulled two plastic chairs out of one of the schoolrooms and put them in the hallway outside the lounge to provide us with somewhere to sit. About 15 minutes later we were shown into the lounge. The room was packed with board members and School District 65 staff. We took the only two open seats. It was at this point I learned two things that almost knocked me out of my chair. The first was that the building committee was composed of the majority of the school board's members. Because the committee members had unanimously agreed to our retention, we already had a majority vote of the board. The second corker was that the president of the school board was one of my best friend's older brothers but whom I hadn't seen in 25 years. After shaking hands and exclaiming what a small world it was, I advised the board of our previous relationship, which made everyone laugh.

The premeeting lasted 20 minutes. We were third on the agenda when the formal meeting began. We went upstairs and took an open seat at the board meeting in the school's library. The meeting convened shortly thereafter. About half an hour into the meeting, the school board president called on the chairperson of the building committee to give her report. Within ten minutes she had summarized four days of meetings and my telephone conversations. At the conclusion of her presentation, the president of the school board asked if any of the board members had further questions. A flurry of questions followed, all of which were building a record of the cogency of the board's ultimate decision, which would be determined by a final board vote.

Once the internal public questioning subsided, the president called me to a podium set up for speakers to address the board. He asked me to briefly describe our auction program. I described our firm's background, track record, and planned methodology for their property. When my formal presentation ended, the president asked if any board members had further questions. Several members followed up on his invitation, and I answered their questions. As often happens in these types of meetings, a pause ensued and prompted the president to ask me if there was anything else that I wanted to add. I paused and a funny thought

D r . H a r d y M u r p h y

"In a geographically small community where land is at a premium and real estate transactions have to complement a fiercely guarded community vision founded on taste and tradition, he was the ticket. After a presentation before our board's building committee, which had the responsibility of sheparding this effort for the full board, and then a public presentation before the board, we selected him as our agent . . . and then the fun began.

"State code required us to sell by auction. His description of the entire process, the fine nuances of the process, and details of getting it done made us all feel that we were on the inside of a grand production community theater where everyone had a starring role. We all felt important. We all felt necessary. We all felt that what we and our district's community wanted was what mattered most. All the while, he was delivering turnkey services of the highest quality."

Dr. Hardy Murphy

"Our community was informed and included in a series of community meetings that he handled with style and grace. Our local government officials felt respected and were treated with consideration. The residents of the immediate neighborhood were consulted. They felt reassured. Our school board, which had made the decision to sell the old mansion with so much history and meaning in its veneer of tradition under intense public scrutiny, knew that it was in the capable hands of an experienced professional who knew that the entire city was his client."

entered my head, which I spontaneously shared with the board. I told them that I was a product of the Evanston/Skokie School District 65, and in 1966 when I was in fifth grade I was elected captain of the Crossing Guard Patrol, my post being the corner of Forest and Dempster Streets; if someone had told me that 34 years later I would be called on by the school board to sell the corner of Ridge and Dempster, I never would have believed it.

Everybody laughed. The motion to retain us passed with a unanimous vote.

IMPLEMENTING THE PROGRAM

We had structured a two-stage program. First, we would be formally employed and then we would design the property-specific program. Immediately on our retention, the announcement advertisement was released (see Figure 10.1). The announcement of the auction was followed by the equivalent of a town hall meeting led by the local alderman. We had coordinated a planning effort between the city of Evanston, the mayor, local aldermen, and a number of Evanston community groups. The meeting was attended by over 50 people, many of whom were concerned neighbors who wanted to share their thoughts as to how the property should be redeveloped and incorporated into our program. The meeting concluded in about 90 minutes.

FIGURE 10.1 *School Auction Is Advertised*

SHELDON GOOD & COMPANY
AUCTIONS
is pleased to announce its retention by

EVANSTON/SKOKIE SCHOOL DISTRICT #65

to design a Spring 2002
Real Estate Auction program for:

The Joseph E. Hill Administrative Building	District Warehouse Building	Food & E.S.C.C.A. Building
1314 Ridge Ave.	**1311 Asbury Ave.**	**1321 Asbury Ave.**
EVANSTON, IL	EVANSTON, IL	EVANSTON, IL
14,880 sq. ft. building	7,285 sq. ft. building	5,500 sq. ft. building

All located on a 94,560 + / - sq. ft. site

For brochure, inspection date & Terms of Sale, call:
(312) 630-0915

©2001 Sheldon Good & Company **www.sheldongood.com**

Source: Reproduced with permission from Sheldon Good & Company Auctions, LLC.

We designed a marketing program that was both local and regional in scope (see Figure 10.2). Limited national promotions also overlaid our marketing program. We slated the property to be sold on a stand-alone basis in an open outcry auction that was to be held in downtown Evanston. The district's property was on a prime site that had a limitation on the way that it could be redeveloped because of the property's historical background. We structured a deal that also made sense for the buyer in that the school district wanted to stay pending the completion

FIGURE 10.2 *Brochure Announcing School Auction*

REAL ESTATE AUCTION

MAY 8

THE LARGEST LAND PARCEL TO BE OFFERED IN EVANSTON IN DECADES!

Three Historic Buildings on 2.1 Acres

Dempster Street at Ridge Avenue, Evanston, Illinois

Suggested opening bid: $750,000 • Certified or cashier's check required to buy: $75,000

This Incredible Offering Includes:

- The Joseph E. Hill Administration Building 1314 Ridge Avenue
- The District Warehouse 1311 Asbury Avenue
- The Food Service & E.S.C.C.A. Building 1321 Asbury Avenue
- All located on 2.1 acres of super-premium land, in the heart of Evanston

Few buying opportunities in Chicago's real estate market compare to this premium residential/development property, perfectly located on 2.1 acres, in the heart of historic Evanston. Sizable land parcels in Evanston have been non-existent for decades, making this auction offering a true once-in-a-lifetime opportunity for developers and investors alike. Zoned R-1, the property is easily divisible, ideal for a variety of lucrative residential development projects.

For an individual buyer who seeks to own a historic residence, along with auxiliary buildings of untold character and lineage, there is simply no better choice than the elegant Joseph E. Hill Administration Building, which was once known as the Dryden Mansion.

The Joseph E. Hill Administration Building

1314 Ridge Avenue

Currently used by District 65 as its administrative headquarters, the building is an outstanding example of the Georgian Revival architectural genre. Completed in 1917 at a cost of $150,000, the residence was designed by renowned Chicago architect George Washington Maher, who was known for creating bold, individualistic residences.

The three-story residence totals 14,880 square feet, including a finished 5,440 square foot basement. Artisan flourishes are found throughout, and include hardwood and tile floors, custom woodwork, fine built-ins, and high ceilings. Heat is supplied via underground pipes from the service building located at 1311 Asbury, and the building is centrally air conditioned.

BUILDING SUMMARY:
- *First Floor:* Offices and restrooms
- *Second Floor:* Offices, storage, and restrooms
- *Third Floor:* Ballroom, kitchen, and storage areas
- *Basement:* Lounge, storage rooms, conference room, and restrooms

SHELDON GOOD & COMPANY
AUCTIONS, LLC

of its new facility, which was only semipredictable. The benefit to the buyer was that it could buy the property but the school district would pay the carrying costs during the redevelopment planning stage. From the school district's point of view, the investment income from the proceeds of the sale would pay the rent.

I love being in the middle of a deal that is good for both sides.

FIGURE 10.2 *Brochure Announcing School Auction, continued*

Source: Reproduced with permission from Sheldon Good & Company Auctions, LLC.

THE MARKET REACTION

Hundreds of interested parties flocked to the opportunity to acquire this surplus school property. High-net-worth individuals contemplated converting the mansion to its original splendor. Adaptive reuse residential developers evaluated how they could convert the historic building to multiunit condominiums and then build either houses or townhouses on the remaining site. Corporate buyers also loved the property for a potential corporate headquarters office building complex, similar to the way the property had been used by the school district. Even nonprofit religious organizations seriously evaluated the site, although the school board required the site to be put back on the tax rolls in spite of a given organization's tax-exempt status.

During the course of the preauction showing program, armies of contractors, architects, and the like put on their creative thinking caps— all striving to take advantage of this unusual situation.

THE AUCTION

We had a premeeting session with the school board prior to the auction. It wanted to make the right decisions and relied heavily on our experience and recommendation. The board was in unfamiliar territory, and we were its trusted guides.

We had a stellar response and were confident that the competitive bidding process would yield a fair price. The question of course was: What *is* a fair price? The school board had determined its expectation for the property long before our retention as part of its budgeting process when it opted to build a new administration building. The board had set a selling range of between a million and a million and a half dollars. As far as we were concerned, any additional monies garnered were a bonus earned as a result of the auction. Consequently, our recommendation was for the board to empower the president to accept the highest bid *during the bidding* if the bidding surpassed $1.5 million. After a great amount of discussion and consideration, a vote was taken. The result? Go for it.

At the auction an excited audience packed the ballroom. Everyone was there: all the school board members, their staff and interested teachers, the Evanston City Council and its supporters *and* detractors, the council's zoning staff, and even the who's who of the local citizenry. As part of their ongoing civic coverage, Northwestern University local student newspaper reporters were also there. No one was going to miss the conclusion of this piece of local history.

Unknown to the audience, we had a packed crowd of registered bidders as well; every category of bidder we had anticipated came to bid. We had a great horse race in the making, but for confidentiality reasons I can't share the details. All I can say is that we were going to hit the ball out of the park and I was thrilled. It's fun knowing that something good is going to happen for your alma mater, let alone people with whom you've really grown to respect and like.

D r. H a r d y M u r p h y

"The day of the auction dawned. It was sunny. This is not always the case in the lakeshore area around Chicago. I wondered if Steve had anything to do with that. I arrived at the hotel that had been chosen as the site for the auction amidst an air of subdued excitement. The place was packed as he said it would be. I recognized many of the faces as dignitaries from our business community and local government. Some attendees were curiosity seekers there for the history of it all. Steve was there with his team. I couldn't help but smile. The man was a stranger to no one, even people that I knew he was meeting for the first time.

"After a graceful period of meeting and greeting for the crowd to be put at ease through the setup of refreshments, finger food, and music, Steve approached me and my board president and simply stated, 'OK guys, it's time.' The three of us took seats to the left of the podium where Steve's 'barker' would conduct the auction. The crowd took seats if they could find them. Those that couldn't lined the walls. This was reassuring, as some had wondered if there would really be much interest considering the zoning restrictions associated with the building.

"I scanned the crowd while wondering who would make the winning bid. I saw mainly suits, sport coats, some shirtsleeves, and a pair of work boots with jeans. Steve's spotters took strategic positions around the room to offer counsel to prospective buyers and make sure that bids were registered. Smoothly the barker took the podium and with fanfare struck the gavel to get the crowd's attention, announcing that the auction would commence after a brief description of the property.

"And the magic began, opening at a price that all of us wondered was too low. 'What if it stayed low? What if starting low would cause the bidding to taper off too quickly?' we asked. 'Not to worry,' Steve explained, 'until we reach a critical moment of announcing that we accept the bid on the spot and are selling without reserve. We could fold our tents and try again,' but he indicated that we wouldn't have to do this. It was reassuring to know that we wouldn't be committed to letting our prized property go for a song and dance.

"Steve had talked about a pace and rhythm to this type of auction that he had a feel for: sometimes it moved fast from beginning to end and sometimes it ebbed and flowed. He had also indicated that in measuring this ebb and flow in the pace of the bidding, there were strategic moments, the most important of which came when there was a lull and bidders reached a moment of indecision that required motivation. At this moment he had indicated the opportune thing to do was to halt the auction temporarily and announce that we as the owners were deciding to sell on the spot without reserve.

"Such a change signaled to the bidders that we were serious about selling, that a price range had been reached at which someone was going to walk away with an acquisition, and that if they really wanted to stay in the hunt, they would have to ante up. By prearrangement with our board, we had decided when that moment would be for us. My board president and I had the responsibility of signaling to Steve when that moment was. When the time came, we signaled to Steve with an imperceptible nod. He rose, took the podium, and made the announcement that the property would, in fact, be sold at the drop of the gavel. The bidding took off again.

"I felt like I was at the races. There was another surge of bidding that rolled through the crowd and then began to taper off. I looked around the room at the faces in the crowd. My board was pleased. My staff was excited. My board president and I, sitting and facing the crowd, put on our best poker faces but could hardly contain ourselves. Two buyers remained in the hunt for the prize.

(continued)

"I was surprised. One of the two was a suit. I had expected that. The other remaining bidder was the work boots and jeans. And when the gavel fell, the work boots and jeans had carried the day. It just goes to show that looks can be deceiving.

"The final bid was well north of what we were asking and of what the property was appraised for. I sat back and beamed at my board president. We both agreed that the deal had been done right. Rising to extend my congratulations and appreciation to Steve for what he had done for us, I noted the time on my watch. This had taken a matter of minutes. It had been one heck of a ride. It had gone as planned and it had not taken long to do it.

"I looked around the room as the crowd began to disperse and filter out into the lobby. Everyone was in good spirits; I decided that in the world of business, sometimes everyone could come away a winner. I believe that day everyone there did. The buyer had a profitable investment to develop. Our community had a revenue-generating property that would appreciate in value. More important, it would enable us to build a new administration building and education center to house our prekindergarten programs and serve the youngest of our students."

After the introductions, the bidding opened at $750,000. At $1.5 million, as planned, the president of the school board, *during the bidding*, had us announce that the board would accept the bid. If you have ever been in a lightning storm, the sky of bidders lit up the room.

The property sold for $2.96 million. We were all geniuses.

The article in Figure 10.3 appeared in a local medium following the auction.

EPILOGUE

We scheduled a dinner to enjoy the success of our program with Hardy (the superintendent of School District 65), the mayor of Evanston, the president of the school board, the president's mother and father, and my wife and me. The night of the dinner I was grounded in New

FIGURE 10.3 *Local Newspaper's Review of Auction*

Chicago firm bids $2.8 million for District 65 property

District 65's historic headquarters complex at Ridge Avenue and Dempster Street drew a top bid of $2.8 million during a competitive auction May 8, selling to Terra Nova Properties, a small Chicago firm specializing in the rehabilitation of vintage properties.

Realtor Vladimir Novakovic, of Terra Nova Properties, at 1136 Pratt Ave., is tentatively planning to rehabilitate the main mansion and rear coach house into an undetermined number of condominiums while preserving the exterior facades in keeping with preservation requirements.

Interviewed minutes after he had posted the winning bid, Novakovic said he planned to add townhomes or single-family residences on the perimeter. The property is currently zoned R-1 for single-family homes.

Novakovic said last week that he planned to preserve the expansive yard to the east of the former Dryden mansion, keeping the Ridge Avenue view of the estate intact. He predicted that the residences would be priced between $600,000 and $900,000.

Twelve registered bidders came with $75,000 cashier's checks in hand to compete for the property, which auctioneer Steven Good called "arguably one of the most prominent sites on the North Shore."

Novakovic, who is working with Evanston resident Mike Niazmand on the project, emerged as the successful buyer when another unidentified investment group dropped out after bidding $2.75 million. The open outcry auction was held at the Hilton Garden Inn, at 1818 Maple Ave.

The addition of a 5 percent buyer's premium brought the total purchase price to $2.94 million. Of that amount, Shel-

don Good and Co. will receive a 7 percent commission, or about $205,800. Under the firm's agreement with the District 65 School Board, the district paid an up-front fee of $25,000 for marketing costs.

Terra Nova Properties posted a 10 percent down payment on the property this week and must come up with the remainder of the purchase price by the closing date, which must occur within 60 days.

Once the transfer of ownership has occurred, the School Board can continue to occupy the premises for a period of up to six months, but must pay $24,000 a month in rent to the new owner.

District 65 is scheduled to move its administrative offices into the new Joseph E. Hill Education Center, at 1500 McDaniel Ave., later this year. The center also will house the district's early childhood programs.

Once the auction bidding passed the $1.5 million mark, the School Board waived the right to reject the final bid and announced that the property would be sold at the auction.

Elated over results

School officials were visibly pleased by the results of the auction and the price.

"The district did all the right things, following process, and it came to a good conclusion," said Larry Shanock, chief financial officer for District 65.

The School Board had conservatively projected that $1.5 million in proceeds from the administrative complex would be available to supplement the $27.5 million that was borrowed with voter approval to finance $36 million in projects, including the construction of the $14.3 million Joseph E. Hill Education Center.

(continued)

A one-page information sheet provided by Terra Nova Properties after the purchase said that Novakovic has "developed, managed and sold over 25 other properties at a total cost of over $50 million."

He owns and manages several large income-producing properties and is currently working on several large condominium conversion projects.

Laura Atwood, also of Terra Nova, vowed that the firm's redevelopment of the site would preserve the historic integrity of the complex.

Niazmand, a financial partner on some of Novakovic's projects, brought the upcoming auction sale to the attention of Novakovic and Terra Nova Properties. The ownership structure for the proposed development has not yet been determined.

"Obviously, the mansion itself is unique in Evanston," said Niazmand, who was not at the auction, but was reached by telephone Tuesday.

"I'd like to preserve it and beautify it, and bring it back to its old glory," said Niazmand, a financial consultant with offices in Evanston and Schaumburg.

Niazmand said he has known Novakovic and his father, a geologist who founded a soil testing firm, for nearly two decades—first as clients and later as business partners on certain ventures.

Brief look at property

Niazmand said neither he nor his partners spent a lot of time inspecting the property or conducting any in-depth research as to the zoning or preservation requirements.

"We had very limited viewing of the property before the auction because we didn't know we were going to be the purchasers," Niazmand said.

Niazmand said he did not know whether the stucco building at 1321 Asbury Ave., which houses District 65's food services and the Evanston School

Children's Clothing Association, will be rehabilitated as part of the project.

While the entire complex is located within the Ridge Historic District, the district's preservation ordinance allows demolition under certain circumstances.

"Our understanding is that the stucco has to be evaluated for its soundness to see if it is past rehabilitation or not," he said. "I don't know what the structural integrity is right now."

Niazmand said they will meet with their architect, bankers, city representatives, the alderman and neighbors "to get a consensus of what works for everyone.

"We really are kind of open to a lot of things and inputs," Niazmand said.

The financial partner said his three-fold interest was to preserve the integrity of the main mansion so it is not "drowned out" by other components of the development; to develop a project "economically viable for us and the city" and create something that makes neighbors happy so they are not overwhelmed.

"We don't want to cause congestion," he said. "I would like to have it a low density. That is really our blueprint. What we do within that blueprint is being examined at the moment."

Binding review

Because the complex is part of an Evanston historic district, plans are subject to binding review by the Evanston Preservation Commission.

One investment group led by Jerry Stover and Doug Hood had formed the Dryden Estates LLC, a limited liability corporation, with the intent of creating a low-density development of no more than 14 units. The group dropped out of the competitive bidding after offering $2 million.

"We think the people who bid ($2.8) million are going to have to build maybe 18 or 20 units so they may have a big fight with the neighbors," Stover said.

D r. H a r d y M u r p h y

"As I walked away, I realized that I had one more thing to do. Steve indicated that as a student of Evanston, he was formerly captain of the crossing guard patrol when he was a 5th grade student in our district. He had asked me for a crossing guard belt as a remembrance of our work together. I made good on the promise gladly. It was a small thing. But it was the kind of thing that made me realize why we chose Steve for the job. He's a winner too."

York because of bad weather and my wife, Jami, entertained our guests. She knew how thrilled—and disappointed—I was as I sat in the airplane waiting on the tarmack at LaGuardia for it to take off on time. It didn't.

The school district and the city of Evanston had something nice in store for me too. It is shown in Figure 10.4.

FIGURE 10.4 *Acknowledgment by School District 65 of Steven Good's Contribution*

On behalf of the Evanston/Skokie
School District 65
the Superintendent of Schools and
School Board President
hereby formally acknowledge the
care and concern of
a former District 65
patrol guard in his continuing
pursuits for the protection
and welfare of the Evanston/Skokie
District 65 Community

Presented to Steve Good this 29th day of July

11

THE MAN BEHIND
THE CURTAIN

When I came back from lunch one summer afternoon, a note was in my message box that read "Donald Trump" with a 212 area code telephone number written on it. I thought to myself, "What joker left a message like this for *me*?" As odd as it sounds, I didn't even return the call. As a result of going to Syracuse University, I have some old college friends living in New York City who wouldn't hesitate to do something like sending me phony telephone messages. I had been sitting in my office for a couple of hours when my assistant came in and asked me if I had called Donald Trump yet. I told her that I hadn't called him because I thought someone was playing a practical joke on me. She stopped dead in her tracks and told me she had fielded the call, and it was legitimate—Donald Trump had really called to talk with me.

I was stunned. What could Donald Trump possibly want with me? I was impressed. I asked my assistant to place the call to the Manhattan number, and I waited for her to transfer the call into my office. A moment later, sure enough, I was talking to Donald Trump. He sounded just the way I had heard him on television except lower key. He explained that he had heard of our firm through a variety of his New York friends and had seen our advertisements promoting properties that we were selling in greater New York.

Trump asked if I was familiar with the Palm Beach, Florida, area and I told him that not only was I familiar with that area but I had grown up frequenting Palm Beach during various Christmas and spring vacations. The Breakers was where we hung out. In fact, I was admitted to the Florida bar after passing the bar exam when I graduated from DePaul University College of Law years earlier. He told me he wanted to see me and asked if I would be in New York City soon. I responded that I was frequently there and we had an office in Manhattan about ten minutes away from Trump Tower. We concluded the phone call by making a date to get together the following week.

I was excited and immediately had my assistant book an airplane ticket for me and one of our senior officers. Apparently "the Donald" had some friends that thought we could help him, and the telephone call had made my day.

FIRST MEETING

I like going to New York City and particularly to conduct business. There is a reason the place is nicknamed "The Big Apple"—because it is! The vibrancy and bustle of New York City is like nowhere else I've ever been, especially in the United States. I had a date to see Donald Trump at his offices in Trump Tower, which is in the heart of the Upper East Side's Fifth Avenue shopping district. I still get excited when I think about the first time we met.

We had set the appointment for midmorning; I walked into Trump Tower a couple of minutes early. A guard standing by the elevator banks asked my name before allowing my associate and me to get on the elevator. He called someone upstairs and within a minute we were on the elevator. When the doors opened, we saw a sign on the exterior glass doors that read The Trump Organization.

As we entered the office, an attractive receptionist greeted us and showed us to an area further inside the office, outside Donald's private office, where we took a seat and waited. Within a couple of minutes Donald's assistant, who had finalized the appointment with my assistant, showed us into his office. She warmly welcomed me and asked how my assistant was and how things were in Chicago. As I walked into Donald's office, I was overwhelmed by all the cool stuff on his walls. Awards, magazine covers, pictures—you name it, it was up there. There was no question whose office we were in. The coolest thing I noticed was a model jet passenger airplane that had the word *Trump* written on it; the airline was then being operated as Trump Airlines. In fact, I had flown on the Trump Shuttle between New York and Washington a couple of weeks earlier.

Donald was seated behind his desk and stood up when we were within handshaking distance. He greeted us warmly and we shook hands. I had read somewhere that he didn't like shaking hands with people, but that wasn't the case here. I was also impressed by his size. He is almost a full head taller than I am, which I noticed immediately—it's funny how you can't judge people's size by what they look like on television.

Donald got right down to business. He had bought a twin-tower condominium building that faced Palm Beach and renamed it Trump Plaza of the Palm Beaches. Condominium sales there had been going at a rate slightly less than he would have liked. He was concerned that come the end of the season, which ends around Easter, he might have to carry a goodly portion of unsold condos until the next selling season, which wouldn't start until the following November. Donald wasn't exactly sure how many units remained, but he had heard that we had a good track record selling these types of properties and wanted our take on the viability of our programming to his situation.

I explained that our block condominium retail auction program took about ten weeks to implement from start to finish. We had sold thousands of properties like his and had the drill down. As we spoke further, each of us became more excited at the prospect of doing business together. Our initial meeting lasted about half an hour and concluded with Donald's arranging for us to view the property in West Palm Beach later that week.

We shook hands over a tentative plan to continue our dialogue after investigating the property.

THE PROPERTY INSPECTION

The property was located on a main drag across the Intercoastal Waterway with a fabulous view of Palm Beach. I already knew the buildings because you have to drive by them to get to the entrance of Palm

Beach, a drive that I had made many times before. As I said earlier, Trump Plaza of the Palm Beaches consists of twin condominium towers with midrise townhouses in the front as you drive up to the building.

The inspection of the property took about half the day; we were shown the property by an attractive middle-aged woman who had flown down from New York City and was living at the property as one of the on-site salespeople. The property had basically three aspects. The first was four floor plans that accounted for most of the unsold units. They were interspersed between four tiers and were virtually identical except for the floor they were on. The second inventory type was expensive unfinished penthouses that were at least twice as expensive as their standard unit counterparts. The third inventory type was unfinished townhouses, which accounted for 17 of approximately 100 unsold properties.

Having sold thousands of units like these, by the end of the day I knew the plan that we would propose: The townhouses could be sold in bulk as they needed one central developer to finish them; then after they were finished, the developer would, in turn, sell them via a retail sales program. The main concern I had here was making sure that we didn't flood the market for this property. Retail sales were going on but just not at an acceptable volume. Our task was to accelerate the rate of sales, which we would do through a national promotion of the property culminating with an auction.

THE PROPOSAL

After doing the research, we thought the market for the property should be broken out with about 50 percent of prior buyers coming from southern Florida, 30 percent from the Northeast, and 20 percent from the Midwest. Consequently, one of the keys to generating enough demand to make the auction successful would be to generate buyers from these areas. I proposed, therefore, that the auction be conducted in *three cities* via an audio simulcast, which would allow buyers to attend the auction in any of the three places.

The main site would be the PGA National Resort Complex in Palm Beach Gardens, Florida, which is located 15 minutes driving time north of the property. By having one of the auction sites there, a buyer could arguably fly in from wherever, view the property, and then bid at the auction. The two other sites were the Waldorf Astoria Hotel in New York City and the Swissotel in downtown Chicago. We selected these two places for their centrality to potential buyers, thereby allowing these buyers to view the property prior to the auction and at the same time bid closer to home. Without the two satellite sites, bidders would be forced to make multiple trips to Palm Beach, which we thought might effectively disfranchise them from participating in the auction. Fewer bidders would mean fewer sales. The three-city simulcast was the way to go.

We also designed prescheduled off-site open houses in the hotels in the satellite cities so that buyers could learn about the property directly from a knowledgeable salesperson *before* deciding whether to physically view the property. This required shuttling on-site salespeople between Florida and the satellite cities and developing temporary sales offices that were open for three hours each Saturday before the auction in each city where our salespeople could distribute pictures, floor plans, and other information about the property as well.

We planned a major public relations effort and asked that Donald make *personal* appearances in Palm Beach, New York City, and Chicago as a way of kicking off the announcement of the auction. We sought to take advantage of his broad appeal as a business celebrity to direct attention to our auction. The fact that the auction would actually occur in each city also made covering the story appealing, as it brought a local angle into the mix.

We put together a massive national advertising campaign, which included advertising in the *Wall Street Journal, Miami Herald, New York Times,* and *Chicago Tribune.* In fact, a giant picture of Donald and me together appeared on the front cover of *Palm Beach Society* magazine heralding the event.

We decided that arranging financing was important as many buyers might need it to close their purchases. Because we were looking to move a goodly volume of units, we had learned that offering attractive financing was a good way to broaden the market. We also wanted the units to close as quickly as possible, but because of Florida's rights of recession laws, the earliest that we could close the sales were 16 days *after* the auction. By having our own financing source in place, we could close our sales in the desired time frame.

The proposal was good and Donald loved it. We met in his office and discussed it about two weeks later. He arranged for me to meet his lawyers so that our retention could be finalized.

THE RETENTION PROCESS

The day following the meeting, I received a call from a lawyer representing Donald and made a date to see him after having sent him our normal retention contract. He enlisted several colleagues to review the agreement and asked that we meet in New York a couple of days later to go through it together personally.

The meeting was held in a conference room in a temporary sales office that had been set up as a preconstruction sales center for a condominium building that Donald was building on the Upper East Side of Manhattan. It was attended by me and three of Donald's lawyers, who had studied our retention agreement and had numerous comments. The meeting had gone on for over an hour when we hit a serious snag: The lead lawyer wanted to negotiate our fees and payments that were business terms I had already agreed to with Donald a couple of days earlier. The lawyer insisted that he could make a better deal with one of our competitors and would if I didn't give in to his requests. The meeting ended abruptly with my wishing him good luck, thanking him and his associates for their time, and catching a cab back to our offices.

A Competitor Intervenes

The lawyer had meant what he said. A competitor was hired and actually conducted an auction eight weeks later right before Christmas. It was held at The Breakers in Palm Beach.

There was a serious problem—Donald was very unhappy with the result and sued the auction company, claiming it had done an unsatisfactory job. It was reported in the newspaper that fewer than 15 units actually sold.

INTEREST IS REKINDLED

Donald called me right before the first auction to tell me that he had a bad feeling about it. I told him we had been disappointed by his decision to hire someone else and he should see how the auction went. If it went poorly, we would be glad to revisit our original program.

I got a call from him almost immediately after the first auction, and within four weeks we were retained to do a *second* auction. It was important to get it off before the season ended, so there was no time to lose.

A different set of attorneys was engaged this time out. These attorneys had worked with us before in selling properties we had handled for a mutual financial institution client and the client's customers. These guys were good. Really good. We had structured a complex real estate deal, and they made sure there were no loopholes that would cause us grief. We needed their expertise on four levels. First was making sure we had a clear understanding—in writing—of our plan; this came in the form of our retention agreement. Second, we had to make sure that the offering of these properties was done in such a way as to not violate any federal or state laws. Third, we had to generate binding contracts that would be used by a national audience and were fair because they were nonnegotiable; unfair contracts would alienate buyers. Finally, we had to make sure that the financing monies we had arranged were prepared in such a way that our lender could ultimately sell the newly made mortgages on the units that we were being engaged to sell without giving a discount.

It is fun playing in a championship, and this was a game that we were playing to win. If the deal went well, we would have the greatest promoter of our time saying that we were terrific; if it went poorly, as it most recently had, I didn't want to think about it.

THE LAWYERS TAKE THE FIELD

Within two weeks the legal side of the deal was done. Our in-house general counsel, along with the senior partners of the New York–based law firm, had papered the deal well. I caught a break by being a licensed Florida and Illinois attorney, because Florida, New York, and Illinois had some peculiar state laws that necessitated our being sure we addressed them to stay clear of trouble. For example, we had to make sure that the property was registered in New York in compliance with the Martin Act, which governed the rules by which properties with condominium associations can be sold in that state. We had also found a law passed in the mid-1940s in Illinois requiring us to address in our Illinois advertising such obscure issues as where schools are located relative to the property. Our review of the Florida law uncovered the fact that if we *closed* any transaction *prior* to the expiration of the buyer's right of rescission, which was then 15 days, the seller would have to refund the buyer's monies even though the deal had closed.

During this time I saw Donald infrequently. He had good people and so did we. His people worked with our people. Together we structured a world-class deal.

LIGHTS, CAMERA, ACTION: THE CURTAIN RISES

We were ready to go. Stories about the second auction hit. Donald and I were on the cover of *Palm Beach Society* magazine. The scheduled press conferences took place. Everybody wanted to know what Donald Trump was doing, and he was glad to have their interest.

It was during this time that I got to know Donald. Having read about and watched his career, like millions of other business spectators, Donald already came highly recommended. True, he was involved in a number of other troubled deals at the time, but I was convinced this one was a winner. Our predecessors, in my view, had just missed the market in their pursuit of pre-empting us and landing Donald's business. He was by far the most charismatic guy I had ever met, and he's the kind of guy who makes your life great if he likes you. If he doesn't—you're cooked. For me, life was great.

I can't speak for him, but in hindsight I think he respected our work ethic and unusual expertise. We were hardworking, straightforward guys who intended to do a job. Having had a bad experience just two months earlier, Donald wanted to be supportive of our efforts but didn't want to get burned—again. Everywhere we went together, people fell over each other to meet him. He was a stellar promoter and got behind our program in a way that no one else could have. We were on television. We were covered on the radio. The newspapers covered every angle of this deal they could think of. When Donald wasn't available, I was the guy; between the two of us we just went to town drumming up interest for Trump Plaza of the Palm Beaches.

Shortly after the public relations activities, our advertisements rolled out locally, regionally, nationally, and internationally. Donald Trump was sponsoring an auction in Palm Beach—be there or be square! Even Fuji television in Japan covered the story. We produced the brochure shown in Figure 11.1 that described the property, and everyone who called received one.

FIGURE 11.1 *Brochure Describing Trump Plaza of the Palm Beaches Auction*

FIGURE 11.1 *Brochure Describing Trump Plaza of the Palm Beaches Auction, continued*

One of life's experiences is the opportunity missed. Who among us has not expressed regret at the property we should have bought when prices were advantageous. We are now offering just such an opportunity.

The remaining residences at Trump Plaza of the Palm Beaches are a triumph of design and location. For those who have contemplated the purchase of a primary or additional residence in an outstanding resort area, this is the time to take advantage of a home purchase that will enrich your life now and long into the future.

AUCTION DATE
Sunday, April 28
1:00 P.M. E.S.T.

AUCTION LOCATION
P.G.A. National Resort
400 Avenue of the Champions
Palm Beach Gardens, Florida

and via simultaneous transmission

The Waldorf Astoria
50th & Park Avenue
New York, New York

Swissôtel Chicago
323 East Wacker Drive
Chicago, Illinois

AUCTION LINE
(In Florida) (407) 655-1200
(Outside of Florida)
(800) 888-1620

Source: Reproduced with permission from Sheldon Good & Company Auctions, LLC.

THE MARKET GOES CRAZY

We were selling some nice properties and interested buyers knew it. We were going to sell the units individually, but our articulated goal was to sell as many units in bulk as the market could absorb. If you were in a position to act and liked the property, you *had* to come play in our game.

The first thing that happened was a Miami-based developer stepping up and buying the entire townhouse piece within a month of our announcing the auction. He didn't want to risk being outbid; mission accomplished: These units sold and closed prior to the auction.

We had set up an on-site office at Trump Plaza of the Palm Beaches to deal with walk-in buyer traffic. We were also fielding telephone inquiries and had set prescheduled viewing dates during which all of the units would be made available to interested buyers. However, because we were seeing buyers on vacation seeming to magically appear at the property, we decided to have a representative sample of units available for viewing on a daily basis to accommodate these unscheduled visitors.

Within six weeks of announcing our auction program, over 2,000 *parties* had been through the property. We had committed to sell no fewer than 15 units on the spot, regardless of the price, and had advertised 45 units from which buyers could choose. The mob scene that ensued prompted us to increase the choice to 77 available units; we were there to sell if the buyers were there to buy.

THE AUCTION

This auction was really three auctions all linked with each other through the use of simulcast technology. Consequently, whatever was needed was needed in triplicate. The main staff was made up of about 75 people, including me, and was located at the PGA National Hotel in Palm Beach Gardens. The two other staffs numbered about 25 people each and were dispersed in New York City and Chicago. The tasks for the auction were identical and included the following:

- An auctioneer(s)
- Four to ten spotters (people who help the auctioneer spot bids)
- Five to ten runners (people who escort winning bidders to the contract signing area)
- Five to 20 contract signers
- Five to 20 mortgage representatives to make and complete mortgage applications for winning bidders—and included underwriters as well
- Closing scheduling people to schedule closings

- Fifteen to 40 registration people
- Three to ten question answerers: people who, having been at the property, could answer detailed questions that might come up at the last minute.
- Techies: the people who linked the three locations together with their sound boards and other technical wizardry

An unbelievable amount of planning went into this event; after all, millions and millions of dollars were on the line. Furthermore, if anything went seriously wrong, we would have to deal with either an angry Donald Trump (no thanks) or angry buyer(s) (double, no thanks). The nice thing here is that we were experienced in having done events like this before and had a large experienced staff. The staff at each location was well trained to run their own show should something unexpectedly go wrong. The biggest area of vulnerability was our technology. The success of the program relied heavily on bidders feeling comfortable in being able to bid outside of the main auction site in Florida. We had set up the auction site so that a potential buyer had to visit the property only once and then could elect to bid from a site nearer to where he or she lived. If only one of the three auction sites failed, all three of the sites would fail because of the unpredictability of where the winning bidders would be physically located at the auction.

We had thought out this problem and had two backups. First, all of the rooms were linked by a conference call telephone line, and we all had cell phones as well. If the main audio system failed, our plan would be to assign a staff person to convey bids via the telephone to the auctioneer, who would in turn convey the bids to the audience, who in turn could participate in the bidding process.

We also had great concern about the size of the crowd; thousands of parties visited the property during our preauction viewing program. The demographics of the buyers' backgrounds were pretty close to what we had originally thought. About half the group had been southern Florida residents with another 30 percent coming from the Northeast and 20 percent from the Midwest. We had arranged ballrooms that could accommodate a crowd of about 1,750 people split in the proportions we had forecast.

One thing we did that in hindsight I regret is letting a couple of local auctioneers work for us as spotters and runners to ensure a positive relationship with them. One of our senior officers was involved in their trade association, the National Auctioneer's Association (NAA), and to be a nice guy invited some of his NAA member friends to help. We paid each of them something like $500 for the day and were pleased with the limited work they did for us. The mistake was not realizing that these guys were in business for themselves; and immediately following the event, they developed promotional material heralding that they had been involved in the sale of Trump Plaza of the Palm Beaches.

Bidders started registering about an hour before the scheduled start times. I say "start times" because we had to be mindful that the locations of the auction sites transcended two different time zones. The auction rooms were set long before we opened the doors, so when the doors opened, we were ready for our customers. After the bidders were registered, they were shown into an appropriate-sized luxury ballroom with seats arranged theater-style and an auctioneer's podium in the front of the room. A three-man band was playing background music with a point-of-purchase display area manned by experienced salespeople, who stood ready to distribute materials and answer any bidder's last-minute questions.

We were keeping statistics at the registration desks in each city to see where the buyers were coming from. The New York location drew bidders from greater New York, which included all of Manhattan, the boroughs, Westchester County, and Long Island. Additional bidders there came from all over: New Jersey, Connecticut, Boston, and even Philadelphia. The Chicago location had a similar experience, drawing bidders from greater Chicago but also from Milwaukee, Detroit, Kansas City, St. Louis, and Toronto. The Florida site drew a mishmash of bidders from southern Florida in addition to a number from everywhere, as many of the Florida-site bidders had no problem making a second trip to Florida to be at the main auction site just in case.

Donald Trump came into the Palm Beach ballroom about half an hour before the auction. The crowd went wild! Oz was here and the excitement generated from his persona was magical. He was as pleased as he could be. The room was filling to capacity, so we flipped the switch: the auctioneers from the two other cities started talking to us and each other through the public address system, which further excited the audience. Palm Beach, New York, Chicago—everyone was checking in and it was almost time to launch.

The media all the while were swarming Donald, taking countless pictures of him. I had assured him that the auction would be a winner, and with great confidence he let the media know it. In fact, right before the event started, he pulled me to the side and told me that he was impressed with the job we had done, and he could particularly appreciate it in light of the problems he had had with his first auctioneer. He also told me that his plan was to leave right after the auction started and asked if I would get him the results later. At that moment I realized that I had made friends with the great and powerful Wizard of Oz (or at least I thought so).

Five minutes later the show began. Our auctioneer in Florida started:

"Do I have an opening bid of $75,000?"

"Yes," a spotter cried out in Palm Beach as bidders' hands shot up to bid.

"How about $100,000?" the auctioneer continued.

"New York bids $150,000," the auctioneer from New York's Waldorf Astoria cut in on the public address system,

"And Chicago bids $175,000," the Chicago Swissotel auctioneer joined in.

"Palm Beach bids $200,000"

"Chicago $225,000"

"New York $235,000"

On and on all afternoon it went until all of the properties were sold. Most of the buyers opted to finance their purchases through our lending source and scheduled closing of their sales 17 days later.

Donald called me the next day to thank us for a terrific job. He also asked if I thought we could sell a number of units that he hadn't given us for the auction because they were rented out for the season. I told him I was sure we could sell them because we still had people calling to find out if any more units were available.

When the dust settled, we had sold 88 units for more that $19 million. This chapter had a truly happy ending.

12

THE MORAL OF
THE STORIES

I attend a lot of professional and business events. Consequently, I listen to a lot of speakers talk about a lot of different topics. Like many people, my time is very valuable, and unless I think I'm going to learn something or hear something with "take-home" value, I prefer to spend my time doing something else. The first thing that I think to myself when someone starts to talk to me, with no disrespect intended, is, "What am I going to learn from what you are telling me?" As far as I'm concerned, the rest is either preamble or postscript.

I've had a good time writing this book, and I'd like to specifically address why what we did worked out and what lessons can be learned from each story other than its interesting details.

"So you say you want to sell a *thousand houses*" had a lot to it. Here was a case where our client, a bank, was overloaded with properties, which was affecting its financial performance greatly. The nature and scope of the problem gave rise to one of its senior people trying to find a creative solution through our programming. The important element here was that the client and its leadership had *no previous experience* in the area of real estate auctions. Our main task was educating the client and doing so on a massive scale. Thousands of people participated in this program as it unfolded, but the most important part was that it all started with *one* guy, Jim DePalma, who had a light bulb go off in his head after being educated by us. Once the concept gained momentum within his organization, our joint task was to expand the education platform within the various areas of the bank that needed our guidance and experience. This was done through our people, who we are constantly teaching and who, in turn, are teaching our clients. It is hoped happy clients beget other happy clients, and, as a result, everybody makes money.

Another challenging aspect of this deal was the sheer number of buyers involved—more than 20,000. That's a huge number of people to deal with in selling a limited number of houses and condos. Think about it. How many people normally call a real estate agent to buy any given house? Ten? Twenty? Most houses don't field more than a couple of bona fide offers, and those that do are an exception. Not only did we set up a system to respond to their calls, but we also arranged showings of the real estate, financing, bidders' seminars to answer the buyers' questions, and, of course, the auctions themselves.

In a nutshell we created a flexible template that traveled well and set the standard of practice used even today.

The *Art Deco hotel* chain deal was a different animal. In this case we were dealing with a highly specialized and very narrow market. Think about it. How many organizations are qualified to buy and run, let alone completely renovate, five historically significant hotels? These were *not* run-of-the-mill $50-per-night room propositions. They were jewels waiting to be polished in an area of Miami that was ready to explode onto the real estate development scene. The challenge here was defining the market and then reaching it in a timely and effective fashion. Part of the skill required here was for us to articulate and communicate the positive attributes of the properties. In particular, our ability to project the *future* viability of the real estate and the South Beach community was the key.

Another important challenge was communicating with the decision makers of the properties, who were spread all over the country. Personal relationships are important on deals this size. I have found that an in-person meeting has a dimension not amenable to duplication on the telephone. One of the hurdles was the impossibility of all of us meeting together. Consequently, the flow of information that developed during the unfolding of this deal was very hard to manage. You always hear on television that "my people will call your people," and then the deal gets done. *Not so in real life.* The guy driving this deal was me; dealing through our proxies and the client's proxies was anything but easy.

Probably the most difficult part of this deal was actually presenting the bids. Because we had a zillion of them, which bids to present in which order was a confounding proposition. Should we present the highest bid on each individual property? What about combination bids for some but not all of the properties? If we had been able to have everyone in one room together, it would have been infinitely easier to manage the process.

As it turned out, the prevailing bidder for the portfolio of the Art Deco hotels more than validated the process. At the time this bidder paid a fair price, and the bidder's qualifications to do the deal were unquestionable.

Mission accomplished.

The *Montana mineral rights* deal presented a completely different set of challenges. The sheer geography of where everything was located presented a challenge in and of itself. Most of the mineral rights parcels weren't accessible by land, and we had grave concerns that we might unknowingly sell some parcel that our client didn't even own. Mapping the property into digestible parcels became a huge priority and drove many of our decisions regarding how and to whom the property would be sold.

The 2,000 or so acres of surface parcels that we sold were likewise unusually challenging. Did you ever sell a gold mine? How about a patented mining claim? Hell, before this deal most of us didn't even know what a patented mining claim was. Having a formal legal education was absolutely essential here because we were dealing with land rights outside the mainstream of most real estate disposition practices. Because we could *learn* what the nature of these rights were and then interpolate how the market would react meant the difference between success or failure. Our ability to articulate the benefits of these unusual rights to their relevant marketplaces is what turned the corner here. Obviously, no one wanted these properties to mine gold. Our job was to find the equivalent of an adaptive reuse developer or user who would see value in these properties for some use other than mining gold.

Another problematic aspect of this deal was the acrimony between our client, a gold mining company, and environmentalists, the latter endowed with great power through their ability to articulate and execute a defined political agenda. I often had to remind reporters and others:

"Please don't shoot me, I'm only the piano player," meaning that we were merely hired to sell off the properties and weren't involved in the litigation that was occurring between Canyon Resources, the State of Montana, and various private landowners. Ultimately, one of the private landowners persuaded a local judge to lock up a portion of the auction proceeds *without a judgment*. The State of Montana, through a referendum that carried by only 21,000 votes, shut our clients out of a billion-dollar profit on their discovering the largest proven gold reserve in the United States. I remember talking to the geologist who found the claim and hearing first his elation and then his despair at what had gone on in his life since he had struck gold.

Consequently, everything the gold mining company did was closely scrutinized and criticized regardless of the company's intentions. This was a hard place to be, and considering the amount of adversity it involved, I thought we all did OK.

Michael Jordan's Restaurant building shifted the focus of merely selling real estate to getting behind the scenes in a debtor-creditor dialogue. As is the case regularly in life, procedure often drives substance, which was what was going on here. Every party involved in this transaction was ultimately at odds with every other party and everyone was paying some pretty expensive lawyers to wipe the other guy out. There was no such thing as fair, and without our participation in the deal, everybody involved would have been worse off.

What we were able to do was offer a solution, a way out so that everyone could get what each wanted *without* a protracted legal battle. The debtors got a fair price for the building. The secured lender, Northern Trust Bank, was paid off in full. The restaurant operator settled his dispute with the landlords-owners.

The challenge in this deal was having the foresight to formulate a vision that would work for everyone and steer clear of the conflicts that would ultimately knock us off track if we allowed them to distract us. It was also important to explain the vision so that each of the parties fully understood why it was in his or her own *self-interest* to support our program. Mutuality is always a powerful tool to help make a deal. It carried the day here.

One of the more peculiar aspects of this transaction was that we had to work almost exclusively through lawyers who were *litigators*—that is, lawyers who argue cases before judges. This makes litigators the most argumentative type of lawyer, because they are used to judges making decisions as opposed to business lawyers who are used to resolving their differences through negotiation. This case was actively being litigated before a judge, and every time someone had an issue, that party threatened to litigate it. An irony existed in that every time someone threatened litigation I, being the court's appointed agent, actually did bring it before the judge so that we could settle the issue(s) involved and move on.

Another interesting lesson here was the attention the building garnered in the media because of its namesake, Michael Jordan. Had this place been called something like Joe Smith's or Good Restaurant, we would never have gotten the attention that we did. It's no wonder that my kids wear sneakers with a logo of a guy with a basketball flying through the air.

The *Lutheran Church* portfolio deal was one of my favorites. To get this deal done, four things had to happen. First, we had to have access to a strong leader within the organization who would validate our programming and then articulate it internally through the group. Without this dynamic, it would have been virtually impossible for us to succeed because we were advocating a program that was completely unfamiliar to a group that was relatively unsophisticated in the area of real estate. Second, the group had to have an open mind to an idea that was unfamiliar to them. They had to be willing to buy into a new idea; one strong naysayer in the group would probably have been enough to torpedo our program. Third, the merits of the program that we advocated unfolded the way we told them it would. Our ability to predict what would happen and how it would happen inspired the already growing enthusiasm for our program to gain momentum and ultimately succeed. Finally, the willingness of the broader congregation to delegate *with great trust* decision-making authority, which required considerable integrity, to designated members of its leadership allowed decisions to be made that had a moral as well as a business aspect.

One of the lessons I learned here was that this deal was a renewal of my faith in volunteer organizations. Here was a case where virtually everyone was a neighborhood volunteer. No one was a sophisticated real estate or legal type. In spite of this seeming drawback, this group pulled off one of the most sophisticated real estate transactions of which I'm aware by a religious organization. The group sold eight churches in one fell swoop, leased one back, and then used the proceeds to build a new church, all within two years, and had a million-dollar surplus left over. Kudos to the congregation.

The *National Association of Realtors® and Urban Land Institute's International Real Estate Auction* program was one of the most exciting and dynamic events that has ever been done. The fact that these two trade association powerhouses decided to come together by pooling their collective resources was an awesome thing. That we were tapped and asked to develop an international auction forum where one had never previously existed was an unparalleled compliment.

The international auction program required a great amount of vision and planning. More than 40 organizations participated, and the *Wall Street Journal*'s sponsorship brought the credibility of the forum to a new level. The challenges here were numerous. First, garnering unified support for the program was paramount, for jealous competitors served as constant reminders of the potential for failure. Neither trade association leaders nor our company was afraid to take a risk by trying something new. Leaders who truly lead are rare these days, and the fact that we all lined up together was terrific. The breadth of the geography from where we received properties spanned the entire Northern and Southern Hemispheres. It took one of our guys 16 hours by plane *one way* to see one of the properties included in the auction. The logistics of marketing properties located in different countries owned by different parties was a marvel in and of itself.

I learned a lot in these transactions, which is why I am called on regularly by the media to comment on a variety of real estate issues. We have been innovators in our area of real estate auctions my entire career, and we see great opportunities presenting themselves as the real estate markets further organize themselves to react to a globalized economy. Overlay the power of the Internet and its evolving role and it is easy to see why being a perpetual student is so important. The ability to question, learn from questioning, and question again is the key to creative thought, let alone creative programming. We are continuing our efforts to expand our programming for properties with worldwide markets and will continue to search for appropriate trade association and strategic private sector partners. I like the math where one plus one equals ten.

The *United Homes* series of auctions combined a number of elements of our programming in one place. There were the debtor/creditor conflict issues. The U.S. Bankruptcy Court was involved. Some 320 properties in 14 subdivisions in 3 states were sold in two weekends. The proceeds cleared the target by almost $5 million. The litigants are still fighting about who gets what. The players involved are world class and continue to do business together in spite of their experience with United Homes.

The challenges in this deal were numerous with our main enemy being time. The longer the properties languished on the market, the worse off everybody was. Our ability to review the portfolio, formulate a disposition plan, articulate the plan to a huge cast of stakeholders, get a court order in place, and then execute the plan was the key to making this deal work. We also caught a break in that the three leading players in this transaction (i.e., the debtor's lawyer, the chairman of the unsecured creditors committee, and the main representative of the secured lender) were extremely competent guys. Not only were they competent but they were open-minded and believed we were competent too. Without their allowing us to do our job, there is no way we would have succeeded here. Once they bought into our plan, they left us alone *trusting* that we knew what we were doing and would act in a way worthy of their trust. I know this sounds corny, but it's *true*. A lot of peoples' integrity goes right out the window where large amounts of money (like $19 million) are concerned. The parties here were in a bad situation and had an enormous amount to lose. Our integrity and our ability to articulate and then demonstrate the cogency of our plan are what ultimately carried the day.

Another important aspect of this transaction was the show at the auctions. I understated what actually happened at each event in Chapter 8. Imagine at least a thousand people lined up outside our hotel ballrooms registering to bid. Do you have any idea what a thousand people looks like? Let me ask another question. A thousand people physically come to a place to bid on a hundred properties. Then they bid. Do you want to argue that we missed someone who would have paid $3 more than the amount that was bid? No one in their right mind would argue with us as the visual impact of the show did our arguing for us. That old saying that sometimes "one look is worth a thousand words" summed it all up. The market came, bid what they thought the properties were worth, and that was that. It is amazing to me that even now, when I meet new clients, I have to persuade them that an auction draws the real market. It is too bad that I can't just take the microchip out of my head and put it in theirs. It would save all of us a lot of brain damage.

I included the *Porter County Jail* story in the book for its oddity. I also wanted to encourage those of you in business to share what you are doing with your kids. The best part of the jail story was the pride it brought to my middle son when he learned that I gave him credit in this book for guessing who would win the bid.

In our house, as you probably have guessed by now, we talk about cool deals and odd properties all the time. I try to take my kids with me, alone—one at a time—as often as possible when I go out of town to look at some interesting job. My mission is *not* to seduce them into my business, although many times people think that is why I take them. The real reason is so they can *share* with me the experience that I am involved in. At a minimum, they (1) get up early in the morning; (2) put on a buttoned-down shirt and a (sometimes clip-on) tie; (3) get on the airplane and take a taxi to the hotel; (4) attend a business dinner; and (5) if we're lucky, spend a day or two tooling around while hooking in a ski trip, fishing expedition, or something else fun.

The ironic part of the Porter County Jail story was the reason I personally opted to do the deal in the first place. You have probably figured out that it was a small deal in comparison with the deals that I normally do. When I originally talked with Dave Burrus, I thought he was a nice guy that I could help. I did have an ulterior motive: I meant to have each of my three sons come with our project manager and visit the jail while it was occupied as a way of teaching them firsthand that jail is a bad place. I had hoped by having this experience in a business context, each of my boys would think twice about what went on at teenage and college parties without my having to lecture them about it.

The ironic thing here was that I was the one who almost learned the lesson. Had my initial meeting with the commissioners concluded 45 minutes earlier than it did, I would have been the guy locked down in the jail and learned the lesson that I meant for my kids to learn.

In the meantime I was glad that we took the assignment and could help the Board of Commissioners of Porter County, Indiana. Who knows, someday maybe I'll get the opportunity to be a guest speaker at Purdue or Valparaiso University. I'm sure that stranger things have happened there.

The story about the *Evanston/School District 65 administration building* was a trip down memory lane. I was nine years old when I first rode my bicycle past the old Dryden mansion. My whole elementary, middle, and high school existence was focused on staying *out of* the superintendent's office. Only problem kids knew the principal or superintendent in our neighborhood, and I sure did everything I could to stay off that radar screen.

It was ironic that 34 years later, my alma mater reenlisted me. I was thrilled to get the call and even more thrilled at the result of the deal. The key to that deal was understanding that the community *needed* to have a say in the structuring of the deal, and the ultimate buyer couldn't develop the property without the approval of the community. A longer lead time was necessary here to make sure that all of the community leaders as well as the potential buyers could map out a plan that would work for everyone.

Good dealmakers do that—make deals that work for everyone involved.

Another important aspect of this transaction was understanding and then articulating the development limitations of the historic nature of the property. This property could not be demolished; rather, it had to be redeveloped *and* put back on the tax rolls. The school board knew that it would have to live with this deal long after it closed and wanted to make sure that it sold the property to a qualified party who understood and could comply with the rules. Getting my old crossing guard belt was just the icing on the cake.

Trump Plaza of the Palm Beaches was a triumph in and of itself. Donald Trump reached out for help and got it despite the false start to the deal. He had judged the deal right; it was just that the velocity of his retail sales program fell a little behind. A crucial mistake was made here: determining that all auction programs were the same and thus fees should be negotiated as they would for any other commodity. This judgment proved fatal in the first auction and was corrected by the time we got involved. Our edge in the deal was our company's size, the sophistication of our staff, and our experience in penetrating local, regional, national, and international markets. Anyone can *tell* you how to do a job, but there's a big difference between talking about it and doing it. The big regret here on my part was that my underlings invited competitors as day help, and then the competitors took credit for what they hadn't earned.

The good news was that Donald Trump ultimately learned the difference between talking and doing, which frankly makes all the difference in the world to me. Last year our company was doing an auction at the Intercontinental Hotel in New York City when I bumped into Donald and a friend in the lobby. Apparently he was speaking to the University of Pennsylvania's Wharton Graduate School and our meeting was entirely by chance. We were both surprised to see each other, although we talk to each other fairly regularly about other real estate and business matters. He introduced me to his tall, attractive female friend as the greatest real estate auctioneer in the world. I can't tell you how that made me feel except to say he liked his chapter in this book so much that he wrote the afterword. There is a lot to be said about coming through in the clutch for someone who has a long memory and knows how to tell a good story.

HAPPY TRAILS TO YOU

It is rewarding to be in a place where you regularly are able to conceive an idea, implement it, execute it, make money, become prominent, and have a lifetime of relationships and memories. The important thing to remember is that relationships based on integrity, intellectual honesty, hard work in the execution of each task, and a sense of humor go far in life—particularly one's business life.

Building a solid brand, as we've done, is about having a vision, sharing it, expanding it, and having consistent executions time after time. Building a good reputation or brand is a lot like building a good house—it's built a brick at a time by people who care and know that the house is going to be around for more than a lifetime—several lifetimes if it's a really good house.

If you have a good business story, tell it. The media will listen. They will scrutinize you but, then again, they should. Their opinions matter, and over time, given a good product and execution, they'll give you a fair shake and spread your word.

If you're lucky, you and your company will become synonymous with the best in the business and become the industry standard.

It's kind of like the old slogan that was coined by the *Wall Street Journal* some years ago: "It works for me."

~ The Power of Journal Advertising for Real Estate ~

****

IT WORKS FOR
–STEVEN GOOD–

OVER THREE DECADES OF SUCCESS.

"We selected The Wall Street Journal as our international marketing partner in 1965. And since then, The Journal has helped us sell some 40,000 properties valued in excess of $8 billion at auction and conventionally across America.

* * *

"Over the years, buyers and sellers have found some of our best deals in The Journal. Whether it's a trophy home in the Hamptons, hotels in South Beach, condos in Chicago, development deals in Denver, or any of the better than 70 different types of real estate that we handle from coast to coast, the regional, national and international exposure we've gotten from The Journal has helped turn our company into a household brand name.

"Advertising in The Journal works for us. And it will work for you too."

Steven L. Good
Chairman and Chief Executive Officer

SHELDON GOOD & COMPANY
www.sheldongood.com

What The Journal does for Steven Good it can do for your business.
Contact your Journal representative today at 1-800-366-3975 or log on to advertising.wsj.com.

THE WALL STREET JOURNAL.
USA ◆ EUROPE ◆ ASIA

DOWJONES

40 WALL STREET
BY DONALD J. TRUMP

I *called Donald after I finished writing the chapter on Trump Plaza of the Palm Beaches to tell him I was writing this book and invited him to be a contributing author. He not only volunteered enthusiastically to be a contributing author but wanted to provide a story that he thought was terrific too. Here is one of his favorite deals.*

40 Wall Street, in addition to being the tallest building in Lower Manhattan, is a 1.3-million-square-foot landmark. I got it for $1 million.

Even people who know very little about real estate can be duly impressed with that price. How did this happen? I'll tell you.

In the 1960s and 1970s, 40 Wall Street was a fully occupied building; it was indeed a hot property. However, in the early 1980s, it was bought by Ferdinand Marcos. Regretfully, the revolution in the Philippines required his full attention, and the skyscraper at 40 Wall Street fell into decline. Dealings became chaotic, and long story short, the whole thing was a mess. Marcos was out.

Then the Resnicks, a great real estate family, descended on 40 Wall Street, but after a long period of negotiation it became clear that Resnick and Citibank weren't going to make it, and 40 Wall would once again be back on the block. I wanted very much at this time to make my move, but this was the early nineties, and I was in no position to do so.

D o n a l d J . T r u m p , PRESIDENT AND CEO
The Trump Organization

In New York City, the Trump signature is synonymous with the most prestigious of addresses. Among them are the world-renowned Fifth Avenue skyscraper, Trump Tower, and the luxury residential buildings, Trump Parc, Trump Palace, Trump Plaza, 610 Park Avenue, Trump World Tower, and the soon-to-be converted Delmonico Hotel at Park Avenue and 59th Street (Trump Park Avenue). Trump International Hotel and Tower is a 52-story mixed-use superluxury hotel and residential building located at the crossroads of Manhattan's West Side on Central Park West at Columbine Circle. It was designed by the world-famous architect Philip Johnson and has gotten the highest sales prices and rentals in the United States. The General Motors Building, a 2-million-square-foot tower located on Fifth Avenue and 59th Street, is directly across from Central Park. This prestigious asset is widely regarded as the most valuable office building in the United States.

Trump is also the owner of the largest parcel of land in New York City, the former West Side Rail Yards. On this 100-acre property, fronting along the Hudson River from 59th Street to 72nd Street, the biggest development ever approved by the New York City Planning Commission is being built. When completed, this $5 billion project, known as Trump Place, will have 5,700 residential units and more than five million square feet of commercial space. Thus far, four towers have been completed and are occupied, and two additional buildings are under construction. There will be a total of 18 buildings on the site.

Other acquisitions in New York City include The Trump Building at 40 Wall Street, the landmark 1.3-million-square-foot, 72-story building located in Manhattan's Financial District directly across from the New York Stock Exchange and the tallest building in downtown Manhattan. In addition, Trump built 610 Park Avenue (at 64th Street), formerly known as the Mayfair Regent Hotel, which was very successfully converted into superluxury condominium apartments. Further east, adjacent to the United Nations, construction has been completed on The Trump World Tower, a 90-story luxury residential building, the tallest residential tower in the world.

More recently, Trump announced plans for his first foray into Illinois, where he entered into a joint venture with the Chicago Sun-Times to build a 3-million-square-foot signature skyscraper, one of the biggest in Chicago, on the banks of the Chicago River directly west of Michigan Avenue (the most prominent site in Chicago). In 2002, he purchased the fabled Delmonico Hotel, located at 59th Street and Park Avenue. It is now being developed in partnership with General Electric into a state-of-the-art luxury high-rise condominium to be named Trump Park Avenue. It's Trump's desire to make this the most luxurious building ever built in New York City. Trump's new partnership ventures in 2002 included the $600 million Trump Grande Ocean Resort and Residences in Miami Beach, Florida, and a superluxury 60-story condominium tower on the Las Vegas strip.

An accomplished author, Trump's first autobiography, *The Art of the Deal,* has become one of the most successful business best-sellers of all time, having sold in excess of 3 million copies, and being a *New York Times* number-one best-seller for 32 weeks. The sequel, *Surviving at the Top,* was on the *New York Times* best-seller list and was also a number-one best-seller, as was his third book, *The Art of the Comeback.* His fourth and most recent book, *The America We Deserve,* is a departure from his past literary efforts. This book deals with issues most important to the American people today and focuses on his views regarding American political, economic, and social problems.

A native of New York City, Trump is a graduate of The Wharton School of Finance and is involved in numerous civic and charitable organizations, including the board of directors of the Police Athletic League and United Cerebral Palsy. He also serves as a chairman of the Donald J. Trump Foundation as well as cochairman and builder of the New York Vietnam Memorial Fund.

Trump is a founding member of both the committee to complete construction of the Cathedral of St. John the Divine and The Wharton School Real Estate Center. He was also a committee member of the Celebration of Nations commemorating the 50th anniversary of the United Nations and UNICEF. More recently, he was designated Developer of the Year by the Construction Management Association of America. In June 2000, he received his greatest honor of all, the Hotel and Real Estate Visionary of the Century, given by the UJA Federation.

The market was terrible, and, in addition, my own financial woes were exactly that—woeful.

It was then announced that the Kinson Company, a group from Hong Kong, was buying 40 Wall Street. They made a great deal. After their purchase was complete, I called them and said I'd like to meet them about a possible partnership. As it turns out, they weren't interested in a partnership but in making 40 Wall Street the downtown equivalent of Trump Tower—with an atrium. What they would do with the steel columns that held up a 72-story building never seemed to enter their minds. I was truly dumbfounded.

Unfortunately, as you can probably guess by now, the Kinson Group proved to be relatively clueless about renovating, running, and leasing a NYC skyscraper. They weren't in the real estate business to begin with; they were in the apparel business. They were also in way over their heads. I thought this might prove to be the end of 40 Wall Street.

As it turns out, Kinson had been pouring tens of millions of dollars into the building and getting absolutely nowhere. They had problems with tenants, contractors, suppliers, architects, and even the owners of the land, the Hinneberg family. Eventually, they wanted out, and they called me. I was thrilled.

Three years of dealing with a situation out of their bailiwick had taken a toll on Kinson. It was now 1995, and the market still wasn't so good. Kinson had every reason to want to get out, and they wanted to do so quickly and quietly. So the negotiations began, with my offering them $1 million in addition to assuming and negotiating their liens. I also made the deal subject to a restructured ground lease with the Hinneberg family.

They accepted my terms without question—they obviously just wanted out and fast. Sad as their story is, it's true in New York real estate—if you don't know what you're doing, you simply won't make it.

The next thing I do is call Walter Hinneberg himself in Germany, and we worked out a new lease, extending the term to over 200 years. The agreement was also modernized, which served everyone's best purpose. The rest is history.

Very soon after acquiring 40 Wall Street, the markets turned for the better, and the downtown area experienced a Renaissance in both commercial and residential properties and developments. The timing could not possibly have been better. I'm not one for miracles, but this comes close.

I make approximately $20 million a year in rentals from 40 Wall Street. So aside from owning the most beautiful building in Lower Manhattan, I have the added attraction of making a profit. Have you been to The Trump Building at 40 Wall Street? If you have, you'll know why I'm so proud. There is nothing like Wall Street, and there is nothing as beautiful as this building.

Share the message!

Bulk discounts
Discounts start at only 10 copies. Save up to 55% off retail price.

Custom publishing
Private label a cover with your organization's name and logo. Or, tailor information to your needs with a custom pamphlet that highlights specific chapters.

Ancillaries
Workshop outlines, videos, and other products are available on select titles.

Dynamic speakers
Engaging authors are available to share their expertise and insight at your event.

**Call Dearborn Trade Special Sales at 1-800-245-BOOK (2665)
or e-mail trade@dearborn.com**

Dearborn™
Trade Publishing
A **Kaplan Professional** Company